Microsoft® PowerPoint® 97
One Step at a Time

Microsoft® PowerPoint® 97
One Step at a Time

Marilyn Gratton Kyd

IDG Books Worldwide, Inc.

An International Data Group Company

FOSTER CITY, CA · CHICAGO, IL · INDIANAPOLIS, IN · NEW YORK, NY

Microsoft® PowerPoint® 97 One Step at a Time

Published by
IDG Books Worldwide, Inc.
An International Data Group Company
919 E. Hillsdale Blvd., Suite 400
Foster City, CA 94404
www.idgbooks.com (IDG Books Worldwide Web site)

Library of Congress Catalog Card Number: 98-75158

ISBN: 0-7645-3277-4

Printed in the United States of America

10 9 8 7 6 5 4 3 2 1

1P/SU/QT/ZZ/FC

Distributed in the United States by IDG Books Worldwide, Inc.

Distributed by CDG Books Canada Inc. for Canada; by Transworld Publishers Limited in the United Kingdom; by IDG Norge Books for Norway; by IDG Sweden Books for Sweden; by Woodslane Pty. Ltd. for Australia; by Woodslane (NZ) Ltd. for New Zealand; by TransQuest Publishers Pte Ltd. for Singapore, Malaysia, Thailand, Indonesia, and Hong Kong; by ICG Muse, Inc. for Japan; by Norma Comunicaciones S.A. for Colombia; by Intersoft for South Africa; by Le Monde en Tique for France; by International Thomson Publishing for Germany, Austria and Switzerland; by Distribuidora Cuspide for Argentina; by Livraria Cultura for Brazil; by Ediciones ZETA S.C.R. Ltda. for Peru; by WS Computer Publishing Corporation, Inc., for the Philippines; by Contemporanea de Ediciones for Venezuela; by Express Computer Distributors for the Caribbean and West Indies; by Micronesia Media Distributor, Inc. for Micronesia; by Grupo Editorial Norma S.A. for Guatemala; by Chips Computadoras S.A. de C.V. for Mexico; by Editorial Norma de Panama S.A. for Panama; by American Bookshops for Finland. Authorized Sales Agent: Anthony Rudkin Associates for the Middle East and North Africa.

For general information on IDG Books Worldwide's books in the U.S., please call our Consumer Customer Service department at 800-762-2974. For reseller information, including discounts and premium sales, please call our Reseller Customer Service department at 800-434-3422.

For information on where to purchase IDG Books Worldwide's books outside the U.S., please contact our International Sales department at 650-655-3200 or fax 650-655-3297.

For information on foreign language translations, please contact our Foreign & Subsidiary Rights department at 650-655-3021 or fax 650-655-3281.

For sales inquiries and special prices for bulk quantities, please contact our Sales department at 650-655-3200 or write to the address above.

For information on using IDG Books Worldwide's books in the classroom or for ordering examination copies, please contact our Educational Sales department at 800-434-2086 or fax 317-596-5499.

For press review copies, author interviews, or other publicity information, please contact our Public Relations department at 650-655-3000 or fax 650-655-3299.

For authorization to photocopy items for corporate, personal, or educational use, please contact Copyright Clearance Center, 222 Rosewood Drive, Danvers, MA 01923, or fax 978-750-4470.

IDG is the world's leading IT media, research and exposition company. Founded in 1964, IDG had 1997 revenues of $2.05 billion and has more than 9,000 employees worldwide. IDG offers the widest range of media options that reach IT buyers in 75 countries representing 95% of worldwide IT spending. IDG's diverse product and services portfolio spans six key areas including print publishing, online publishing, expositions and conferences, market research, education and training, and global marketing services. More than 90 million people read one or more of IDG's 290 magazines and newspapers, including IDG's leading global brands — Computerworld, PC World, Network World, Macworld and the Channel World family of publications. IDG Books Worldwide is one of the fastest-growing computer book publishers in the world, with more than 700 titles in 36 languages. The "...For Dummies®" series alone has more than 50 million copies in print. IDG offers online users the largest network of technology-specific Web sites around the world through IDG.net (http://www.idg.net), which comprises more than 225 targeted Web sites in 55 countries worldwide. International Data Corporation (IDC) is the world's largest provider of information technology data, analysis and consulting, with research centers in over 41 countries and more than 400 research analysts worldwide. IDG World Expo is a leading producer of more than 168 globally branded conferences and expositions in 35 countries including E3 (Electronic Entertainment Expo), Macworld Expo, ComNet, Windows World Expo, ICE (Internet Commerce Expo), Agenda, DEMO, and Spotlight. IDG's training subsidiary, ExecuTrain, is the world's largest computer training company, with more than 230 locations worldwide and 785 training courses. IDG Marketing Services helps industry-leading IT companies build international brand recognition by developing global integrated marketing programs via IDG's print, online and exposition products worldwide. Further information about the company can be found at www.idg.com.   1/24/99

Eighth Annual Computer Press Awards ≥ 1992

Ninth Annual Computer Press Awards ≥ 1993

Tenth Annual Computer Press Awards ≥ 1994

Eleventh Annual Computer Press Awards ≥ 1995

ABOUT IDG BOOKS WORLDWIDE

Welcome to the world of IDG Books Worldwide.

IDG Books Worldwide, Inc., is a subsidiary of International Data Group, the world's largest publisher of computer-related information and the leading global provider of information services on information technology. IDG was founded more than 30 years ago by Patrick J. McGovern and now employs more than 9,000 people worldwide. IDG publishes more than 290 computer publications in over 75 countries. More than 90 million people read one or more IDG publications each month.

Launched in 1990, IDG Books Worldwide is today the #1 publisher of best-selling computer books in the United States. We are proud to have received eight awards from the Computer Press Association in recognition of editorial excellence and three from Computer Currents' First Annual Readers' Choice Awards. Our best-selling ...For Dummies® series has more than 50 million copies in print with translations in 31 languages. IDG Books Worldwide, through a joint venture with IDG's Hi-Tech Beijing, became the first U.S. publisher to publish a computer book in the People's Republic of China. In record time, IDG Books Worldwide has become the first choice for millions of readers around the world who want to learn how to better manage their businesses.

Our mission is simple: Every one of our books is designed to bring extra value and skill-building instructions to the reader. Our books are written by experts who understand and care about our readers. The knowledge base of our editorial staff comes from years of experience in publishing, education, and journalism — experience we use to produce books to carry us into the new millennium. In short, we care about books, so we attract the best people. We devote special attention to details such as audience, interior design, use of icons, and illustrations. And because we use an efficient process of authoring, editing, and desktop publishing our books electronically, we can spend more time ensuring superior content and less time on the technicalities of making books.

You can count on our commitment to deliver high-quality books at competitive prices on topics you want to read about. At IDG Books Worldwide, we continue in the IDG tradition of delivering quality for more than 30 years. You'll find no better book on a subject than one from IDG Books Worldwide.

John Kilcullen
Chairman and CEO
IDG Books Worldwide, Inc.

Steven Berkowitz
President and Publisher
IDG Books Worldwide, Inc.

CREDITS

Acquisitions Editor
David Mayhew

Development Editors
Carolyn Welch
Stefan Grünwedel

Technical Editor
Kristin Tod

Copy Editors
Robert Campbell
Timothy J. Borek

Project Coordinator
Susan Parini

Book Designer
Seventeenth Street Studios

Graphics and Production Specialists
Sarah C. Barnes
Linda Marousek
Hector Mendoza
E. A. Pauw
Dina F Quan

Quality Control Specialists
Mick Arellano
Mark Schumann

Proofreader
York Production Services

Indexer
York Production Services

ABOUT THE AUTHOR

Marilyn Gratton Kyd has worked as a technical writer for nearly 20 years. She has created (readable) user manuals for both hardware and software products and has written for numerous trade and general-interest publications.

WELCOME TO ONE STEP AT A TIME!

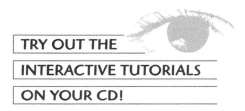

TRY OUT THE

INTERACTIVE TUTORIALS

ON YOUR CD!

The book you are holding is very special. It's just the tool you need for learning software quickly and easily. More than a book, it offers a *unique learning experience*. Along with our text, the dynamic *One Step at a Time On-Demand* software included on the bonus CD-ROM in this book coaches you through the tutorials *at your own pace*. You'll never feel lost!

See examples of how to accomplish specific tasks. Listen to clear explanations of how to solve your problems. Use the *One Step at a Time On-Demand* software in three ways:

- **Demo mode** shows you how to perform a task in movie-style fashion — in sound and color! Just sit back and watch the *One Step* software demonstrate the correct sequence of steps onscreen. Seeing is understanding!

- **Teacher mode** simulates the software environment so you can practice completing a task without worrying about making a mistake. The *One Step* software guides you every step of the way. Trying is learning!

- **Concurrent mode** enables you to work in the actual software environment while still getting assistance from the friendly *One Step* helper. Doing is succeeding!

Our goal is for you to learn the features of a software application by guiding you painlessly through valuable and helpful tutorials. Our *One Step at a Time On-Demand* software — combined with the step-by-step tutorials in our *One Step at a Time* series — makes your learning experience fast-paced and fun.

See it. Try it. Do it.

The MOUS Advantage

This book and companion CD-ROM are approved as courseware for the Microsoft Office User Specialist (MOUS) designation. The MOUS designation helps you prove your Office application skills by preparing you to take an exam. By working through the exercises in this book, you'll be prepared to answer any question that may surface in the exam. The MOUS designation offers these benefits:

- **To the reader:** The Specialist designation distinguishes you from your peers as a knowledgeable user of Office products. It can also make you more competitive in today's job market.

- **To corporations, organizations, and staffing agencies:** The Specialist designation demonstrates staff competency and helps with job placement and advancement. Having specialists on your staff can also reduce calls to your Help desk.

By using this book, you're already on your way to gaining the MOUS designation. Just follow these four easy steps:

1 Choose an application to master.

2 Use approved courseware like *One Step at a Time* to prepare for the exam.

3 Choose a testing center. Call **(800) 933-4493** for testing centers in your area and exam schedule dates. (In the United Kingdom, call **0800 973 031** or **0345 002 000**.)

4 Take the test. Good luck!

To find out more about the program, call the number above or visit the MOUS Web site at:

http://www.mous.net

To Charles. Why? Because you're my son,
for Pete's sake.

PREFACE

Welcome to *Microsoft PowerPoint 97 One Step at a Time*. This book is part of a unique series from IDG Books Worldwide, Inc. Our goal with this series is to give you quick, hands-on training, with help at every step as you're learning the features of PowerPoint 97.

Microsoft PowerPoint 97 One Step at a Time has been designed to facilitate learning in the following ways:

- Your lessons are paced to present small, manageable chunks of information, so you never feel you're in over your head.

- You learn PowerPoint 97 by doing. Each lesson is divided into a number of short exercises, presented in easy-to-follow steps, and with plenty of illustrations to help.

- Many figures accompanying the steps contain corresponding numbered callouts, so you can see the results of your actions.

- At the start of each lesson, you learn which files you need to do the lesson and how much time to set aside to complete it.

- A CD-ROM with sample files accompanies this book. It includes all the exercises you'll need to complete the lessons, and completed projects that you can compare your results against. This CD-ROM also features our exclusive *One Step at a Time On-Demand* interactive tutorial, which coaches you through the exercises in the book while you work on your computer at your own pace.

WHO SHOULD READ THIS BOOK

Microsoft PowerPoint 97 One Step at a Time is designed to get you in shape to put on professional slide presentations without falling flat on your face in the process. You will also find this book useful if you have already started using PowerPoint but want to learn more about it. This book assumes that you know how to turn on your computer and use the mouse and keyboard to interact with Windows 95. The easy-to-do exercises firm up a special skill in presentation design or construction and include completely detailed procedures so you'll feel comfortable working through these lessons.

HOW THIS BOOK IS ORGANIZED

Microsoft PowerPoint 97 One Step at a Time has a very simple structure. The Jump Start takes you through a step-by-step tour of essential PowerPoint techniques and typical features. Don't try to memorize the techniques that you're experimenting with — just follow the steps to get a sense of how PowerPoint works. You'll get more information about the techniques and features in the lessons to come.

Part I: Building Presentations introduces you to PowerPoint 97, a computerized presentation program. You can install PowerPoint 97 as a standalone program or as part of the Office 97 suite of programs.

Part II: Dressing Up Presentations demonstrates how to use the special effects that come with PowerPoint 97.

Part III: Beefing Up Presentations shows you how to use PowerPoint 97 with other Microsoft products and applications.

Part IV: Giving Presentations gives you an opportunity to present your own slide show, using all the presentation-building skills you've learned.

Finally, three appendixes cover answers to the bonus questions in the Skills Challenge exercises, practice projects, and a sample narration for a diabetes presentation.

ABOUT THE PRACTICE PRESENTATIONS

This book includes several practice presentations. As you progress through the chapters and exercises, you'll use them to learn various skills. When you're finished, feel free to adapt them to your own presentation needs.

The practice presentations are for the pretend company, The SnapTracker Corporation (which later changes its name to FotoFriendly, Inc.), which is (for the time being) a one-product company. They manufacture a little booklet that attaches to a camera strap so you can record information about pictures as you take them. The product is called SnapTracker.

There is a product overview presentation; an annual employee meeting presentation, which includes an organization chart; and an educational presentation on Diabetes.

HOW TO USE THIS BOOK

This series is designed for the way people in the real world learn. Every lesson has a consistent structure, so you can quickly become comfortable using all the following elements:

- **Stopwatch:** It is best if you can complete each lesson without interruption, so look for the stopwatch symbol at the beginning of each lesson. This stopwatch tells you approximately how much time to set aside to work through the lesson.

- **Goals:** The goals of each lesson are clearly identified, so you can anticipate what skills you will acquire.

- **Get Ready:** Here you find out which files you need to complete the steps in the lessons.

- **Visual Bonus:** This is a one- or two-page collection of illustrations with labels that help you understand a special procedure or element of PowerPoint 97 more clearly.

- **Skills Challenge:** Every lesson ends with a comprehensive Skills Challenge exercise incorporating the skills you've learned in the individual exercises. The steps in the Skills Challenge section are less explicit than those in the exercises, so you have a chance to practice and reinforce your PowerPoint skills.

- **Bonus Questions:** Sprinkled throughout the Skills Challenge exercise are bonus questions. Check Appendix A for the answers to these questions to see if you got them right.

- **Troubleshooting:** Near the end of each lesson is a list of useful tips and tricks to avoid the traps and pitfalls that many PowerPoint users experience. Look over the troubleshooting tips even if you don't have the problems, so you can avoid potential problems in the future.

- **Wrap Up:** This section provides you with an overview of the skills you learned, as well as a brief preview of the next lesson.

THE ONE STEP AT A TIME CD-ROM

The CD-ROM that accompanies this book includes the exclusive *One Step at a Time On-Demand* interactive tutorial. This software coaches you through the exercises in the book while you work on your computer at your own pace. You can use the software on its own, or concurrently with the book.

CONVENTIONS USED IN THIS BOOK

The following terms and conventions are used throughout the book to make your lessons easy to read:

Term or Convention	Definition
Click	Using the mouse, point to the specified item and click the left mouse button one time.
Double-click	Using the mouse, point to the specified item and click the left mouse button two times in rapid succession.
Right-click	Using the mouse, point to the specified item and click the right mouse button one time.
Drag	Position the mouse pointer over the specified item. Press and hold the left mouse button while dragging the item to its new location. Release the mouse button.
Enter	Type the specified text, and then press Enter on the keyboard.
Press	Press the specified key on your keyboard.
Select	Highlight the text or object by dragging the cursor over it *or* highlight an item in a list by clicking it.
File ➤ Open	On the File menu, select the Open command (all menu commands follow this format).
Enter, Tab, Shift, Ctrl	Refers to the Enter, Tab, Shift, and Control keys on your keyboard.

Several features will also help you read this book. For example:

The text that follows this icon contains a special tip intended to give you some inside information that can save you time or frustration.

The text that follows this icon explains a special note about the subject. Notes tend to be more technically oriented than the rest of the text, but the information they contain is important if you want to know "why" rather than simply "what."

Most skills and exercises let you start a project with a file from the CD-ROM that accompanies this book. Before working on these exercises, you should first copy the exercise files to your hard drive (see the CD-ROM installation instructions at the end of the book), and open the files from there. If you attempt to work on the files without first copying them from the CD-ROM, you will not be able to save changes to those files.

FEEDBACK

Please feel free to let us know what you think about this book and whether you have any suggestions for improvements. You can send your questions and comments to me and the rest of the *Microsoft PowerPoint 97 One Step at a Time* team on the IDG Books Worldwide Web site at http://www.idgbooks.com.

You're now ready to begin. Start with the Jump Start for an interesting look at PowerPoint 97, and then learn PowerPoint on your own and in your own time, in the lessons that follow.

ACKNOWLEDGMENTS

First, I want to thank the cast of thousands at IDG Books Worldwide. At one time or another it seemed as if every editor on staff (and many freelancers) contributed to making this project actually happen. I especially want to thank them for taking a chance on me and for being so helpful and supportive. Special thanks go to Stephen Noetzel and Joe Kiempisty of the CPG Media Development Group for creating the On Demand software at the back of the book, and to Stefan Grünwedel, Melanie Feinberg, and Nancy DelFavero for their editorial assistance with the software.

Second, I want to thank Chris Van Buren of Waterside Productions for offering me a chance to do this project in the first place.

I also want to thank my husband who wrote three books a long time ago, thus providing me with the incentive to write at least four books. One down, three to go. Oh yeah, and I want to publicly acknowledge and thank him for doing all the "mom" stuff when I was chained to my computer trying to meet deadlines.

Finally, I want to thank my son, who told me what to say in the dedication.

The publisher wishes to thank Tom McCaffrey, Marilyn Russell, and everyone at Real Help Communications, Inc. (www.realhelpcom.com) for creating the several thousand sound files required for the CD-ROMs in the One Step at a Time series.

CONTENTS AT A GLANCE

CONTENTS

INTRODUCTION

Congratulations on choosing Microsoft PowerPoint 97 as your presentation software package. Now, working side by side with this book, you'll be able to use PowerPoint 97 to create slide presentations to dazzle your customers, mesmerize your prospects, and impress your boss without devoting half your life to learning a new product. While PowerPoint 97 will amaze you with its capabilities, this book will help you over the hurdles and have you producing a professional slide show in no time at all.

UNDERSTANDING PRESENTATIONS

When you create a presentation using Microsoft PowerPoint 97, you are creating and organizing a collection of slides to make whatever your point is — promoting a new product, reporting on company financials, hoping for a bigger bank loan, or whatever. It's also a nice idea to include handouts so your audience cannot only follow along with the presentation but, in effect, take it home with them.

Your presentation can consist of the any combination (or all) of the following elements:

- Slides
- Speaker notes
- Organization charts
- Media clips
- Graphs
- Clip art
- Web pages

The *slides* are the overhead "pictures" you present using an overhead projector or the pictures that appear on the demonstration computer screen.

Speaker notes are your cheat sheets. You can create a special set of notes to remind yourself of what you want to say when each slide is displayed. You can also use these notes as handouts.

If your presentation is talking about the organization of your company, you may want to include an *organization chart*, which shows who's who and what's what.

To jazz up your presentation, you can include *media clips*, which may be movies or other action sequences; *graphs* and *charts* that you can create from scratch or import from Microsoft Excel; and *clip art* to illustrate features, benefits, points, or even just to entertain.

Microsoft PowerPoint 97 One Step at a Time will help you through all of these exciting possibilities.

UNDERSTANDING VIEWS IN POWERPOINT

To make moving around within PowerPoint 97 easier, there are five views available and a couple of ways to move between them. Throughout this book, I will consistently suggest opening the View menu and then choosing whatever view you want. However, there are five buttons at the bottom of the Presentation window (just above the Draw toolbar) that you can click to move among views even faster.

The *Slide view* lets you look at each slide as it will appear in the presentation. In this view, you can edit or modify each slide as you wish

The *Outline view* lets you create your entire presentation in outline form rather than dealing with it slide by slide. In Outline view, you can see the entire presentation all at once (depending on its size, of course) and simultaneously see miniature versions of each slide.

The *Slide Sorter view* allows you to organize (or reorganize) your slides after you have created them. This is especially handy when you are customizing a show for various audiences even though the basic presentation remains the same.

The *Notes Page view* allows you to create a script for each slide. Before you give a show, you can print a set of slides that includes these notes so you'll never be at a loss for words.

The *Slide Show view* allows you to preview the actual presentation, complete with sound and transition effects. What you see and hear in this view is what your audience will see and hear.

Before you actually start creating slides and building presentations, you should take into consideration a few tips about design. There are literally tons of books available on presentation design and you could spend thousands of dollars on courses teaching you everything from the fundamentals to the psychology of presentation design.

I am not going to immerse you in these theories, so don't worry. Your computer is probably armed with dozens (if not hundreds) of cool fonts, clip art images, media clips, and other neat stuff—and PowerPoint 97 comes with some really fun tools, too.

Just keep in mind a few commonsense rules and don't get carried away:

- Choose fonts carefully. Make sure your audience can read them no matter where they're sitting, and no matter how big or small the fonts may be when projected on a screen or displayed on a monitor.

- If you must use fancy fonts, do so sparingly and only to make your point. They get old fast.

- Remember always to KISS (Keep It Simple and Short). Don't use big words or long sentences on a slide.

- Pick complementary colors that are easy on the eyes and don't make the words hard to read or the images hard to see.

- Make sure your contrast is sufficient so that your screens can be read even in low or glaring light conditions.

- Remember that some people are color blind and cannot distinguish between colors. While PowerPoint 97 has taken that into consideration in creating the various master formats, you should keep it in mind, too, when you customize your color schemes.

- Don't go crazy with illustrations (clip art, symbols, graphs and charts, or sound effects). Don't use them just because you can. Make sure that using them helps make your point.

- As with any presentation, don't bore your audience. Just because you *can* make hundreds of slides doesn't mean you should. If you can make your point in ten slides, then just use ten slides!

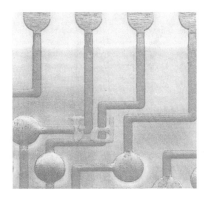

Jump Start

20 MINUTES

GOALS

In the Jump Start, you'll become conversationally acquainted with PowerPoint 97. You'll learn a few basic skills to prepare you for becoming a Master PowerPointer. For example, you'll learn these skills:

- Starting PowerPoint 97

- Opening an existing presentation

- Closing unwanted toolbars

- Moving from slide to slide

- Changing views

- Rearranging slides in Slide Sorter view

- Previewing a presentation in Slide Show view

- Saving a presentation

- Closing a presentation

- Creating a very basic one–slide presentation

1

Opening the practice presentation

GET READY

In order to successfully work through this lesson's exercises, you'll need to have PowerPoint 97 installed and working on your computer. In addition, you should make sure you've loaded the practice presentations that come on the CD-ROM.

When you're done with these exercises, you'll know how to open an existing presentation, move around in it, look at it from different views, rearrange it, save it, and get out of PowerPoint 97.

STARTING UP

Windows 95 makes it easy to start up just about any program, especially PowerPoint 97. Here's one easy way:

❶ Click the Start button on the Windows taskbar (it should be in the lower-left corner of the screen).

❷ Choose Programs (when you move the cursor to "Programs," the Programs submenu automatically opens).

❸ Click Microsoft PowerPoint.

❹ If you prefer and if you have Office 97 installed, you can skip steps 1–3 and start PowerPoint by clicking its icon on the Office toolbar.

PowerPoint 97 opens by displaying the PowerPoint dialog box, as shown to the right.

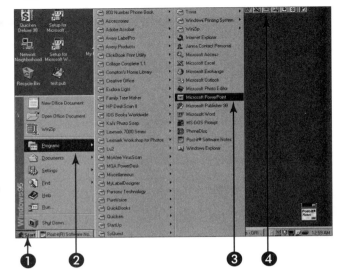

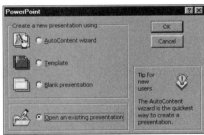

OPENING AN EXISTING PRESENTATION

You are now ready to open a presentation and look around. PowerPoint should still be open with the introductory PowerPoint dialog box displayed.

▶ Opening the practice presentation

In this exercise, you'll learn two different ways to open an existing presentation.

Opening the practice presentation

1 Double-click Open an Existing Presentation. The Open dialog box appears as shown in the illustration to the right.

2 Navigate to the folder where you installed the practice presentations.

3 Double-click SnapTracker.ppt. The SnapTracker presentation opens to the Title Master, as shown.

TIP

If you already had PowerPoint open and were working in or even just looking at another presentation, you need to use another method to open the practice presentation. You have two choices. You can click File ➤ Open and navigate to the file, or you can click the Open button on the PowerPoint toolbar and navigate to the file.

Jump Start

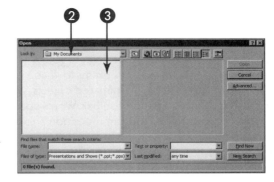

VISUAL BONUS

Anatomy of a Slide

A typical PowerPoint 97 slide has a lot of useful toolbars, icons, and buttons. Here's a basic map to help you find your way around.

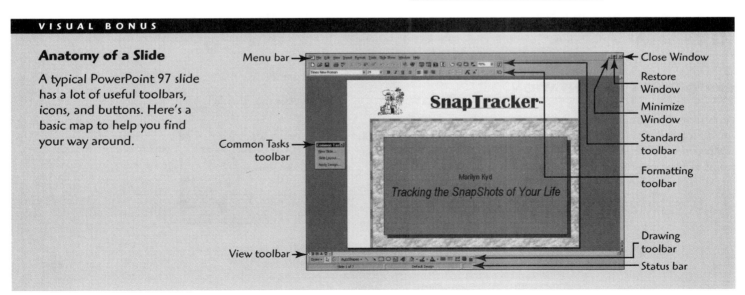

Menu bar → Close Window

Restore Window

Minimize Window

Common Tasks toolbar

Standard toolbar

Formatting toolbar

Drawing toolbar

View toolbar → Status bar

Opening and closing toolbars

TOOLBARS

Toolbars contain commands. PowerPoint 97 includes eleven
predefined toolbars and even an option to create your own. Toolbars
are designed to streamline your work. For example, if you expect to
be doing a lot of work with pictures or animated objects, you may
want to open the Picture or Animation toolbar. When open, a toolbar
"floats" somewhere on the screen. You can reposition a toolbar by
clicking in its name line and dragging it wherever you want it.

Opening and closing toolbars

When you're working in PowerPoint on your own, you may want
the Common Tasks or Master or even other toolbars open. For these
exercises, you should only have the Standard, Format, and Drawing
toolbars open. Here's how to open and close toolbars:

1 Click View.

2 Choose Toolbars. The Toolbars drop-down menu automatically
opens as shown in the illustration to the right.

3 If any toolbars other than Standard, Format, and Drawing are
selected, click to deselect them.

4 If one of those toolbars is not selected, click to select it.

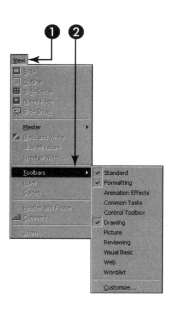

EXPLORING A PRESENTATION

A presentation consists of several slides arranged in an order that
moves logically forward to some conclusion. The SnapTracker.ppt file
is a presentation introducing a new product to potential buyers. The
point of the presentation is to provide the audience with a brief

overview or definition of the product, demonstrate the features and benefits of the product, suggest possible applications of the product, state its physical dimensions and pricing, and let buyers know where they can obtain it.

Moving from slide to slide

To begin your journey through the presentation, start with the first SnapTracker slide and simply move forward through it to the last slide. In this exercise, you'll learn to do that.

❶ Open the View menu.

❷ Choose Slide to switch to Slide view. The slide now looks like the one in the illustration to the right.

❸ Click Next Slide to advance to the next slide.

Repeat step 3 until you come to the last slide, which should look like the illustration at the bottom.

If you look in the status bar at the bottom of the screen, you'll see which slide you're looking at and how many slides there are in the whole presentation. The status bar also tells you the name of the presentation template, in this case "Default Design."

Changing views

From time to time you may want to change the view you're using to look at a slide so that you can make changes. If you've just finished the previous exercise, then you should be looking at the last slide of the SnapTracker.ppt presentation in Slide view. Hang on to your hat, you're about to change views!

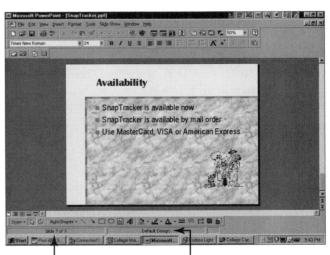

Slide Number and Total Slider   Design Name

Changing views

❶ Open the View menu.

❷ Choose Outline to switch to Outline view.

❸ Simultaneously press Ctrl+Home to move to the top of the outline. Your slide should look like the one in the illustration to the right.

TIP *You can click the slide icon next to any number in Outline view to switch instantly to Slide view.*

❹ Open the View menu.

❺ Choose Slide Sorter to switch to Slide Sorter view. Now your screen should look like the other illustration to the right.

TIP *You can double-click any slide in Slide Sorter view to switch instantly to that slide in Slide view.*

❻ With the first slide selected, click View.

❼ Choose Notes Page to switch to the Notes Page view (see the top illustration on the next page).

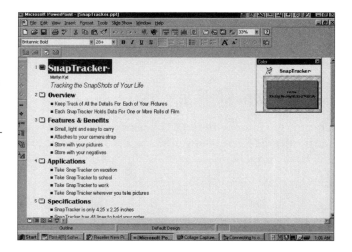

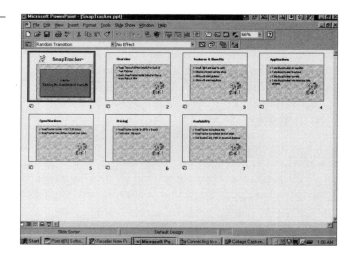

8 Select View ➤ Slide Show to see a preview of the show.

9 When you get tired of looking at a slide, click the left mouse button to move to the next slide

Rearranging slides in Slide Sorter view

It's not unusual to want to rearrange slides after you've created them. You'll learn how to do that in this exercise.

1 Choose View ➤ Slide Sorter to switch to Slide Sorter view.

2 Click and drag Slide #3 to the right of Slide #4. When you release the left mouse button, the slide will move into its new location as shown at the bottom.

TIP   *Be sure you drag the slide all the way past Slide #4 until you see a vertical line appear to the right of Slide #4. That's the indicator telling you where the dragged slide will be positioned.*

Previewing the slide show

Now that you've rearranged the slides, it might be a good idea to take another look at the presentation as it would run for an audience.

1 Choose View ➤ Slide Show to start the show.

2 Click to advance the slides until you reach the end of the show.

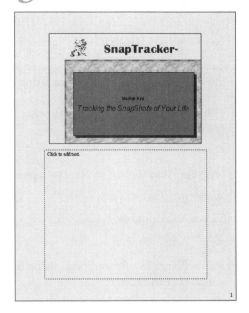

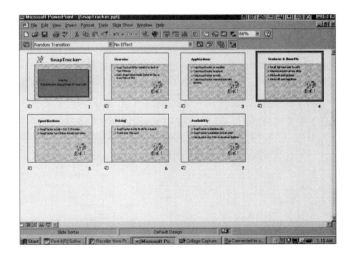

Jump Start

Creating a one-slide presentation

Creating a one-slide presentation

It's one thing to look at presentations, but I know you're just itching to *do* something. In this exercise you'll get to create a one-slide presentation. No big deal, but it's a start!

If you still have PowerPoint open to the SnapTracker presentation, perform these steps:

❶ Open the File menu.

❷ Choose New. The New Presentation dialog box opens.

If you closed PowerPoint, start this way:

❸ Click Start on the Windows taskbar.

❹ Choose Programs.

❺ Click Microsoft PowerPoint. The PowerPoint dialog box opens automatically, as shown at the top.

❻ Choose Template and click OK. The New Presentation dialog box opens as shown in the illustration to the right.

Regardless of how you go to the New Presentation dialog box, here's what you do next:

❼ On the Presentation Designs tab of the New Presentation dialog box, double-click Dads Tie.pot. The New Slide dialog box opens as shown at the bottom.

❽ On the New Slide dialog box, double-click the first AutoLayout (top row, far left). Your screen should look like the top illustration on the next page.

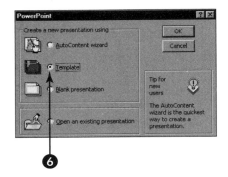

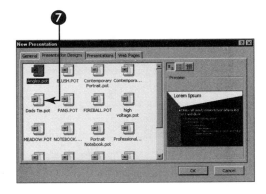

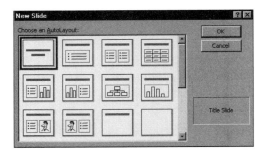

9 In the "Click to add title" area, type the following: **My First Presentation**.

10 In the "Click to add sub-title" area type the word **By** and then your own name.

11 Click Save File.

12 Navigate to wherever you installed the files that came with this book.

13 In the File Name box, type the following: **My First**.

Congratulations! You just created your first presentation.

SHUTTING DOWN

Now that you've exhausted yourself romping through the SnapTracker practice presentation, you're probably ready for a nice cool drink and a rest. Well, not so fast.

Saving a presentation

Before you can go, you need to save the changes you made to the practice presentation. (This exercise assumes that you still have the SnapTracker practice presentation open.)

1 Open the File menu.

2 Choose Save As to open the Save As dialog box.

3 Navigate to the folder where you installed the practice presentations.

4 In the File Name box, type **SnapTracker2**, as shown in the illustration to the right.

5 Click Save (or press Enter).

When you press Enter or click Save, PowerPoint 97 automatically adds the .ppt extension to the filename. All you have to type is the actual filename.

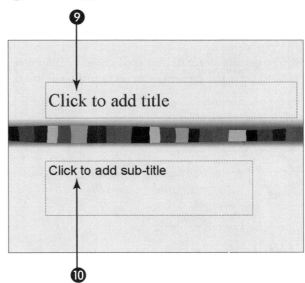

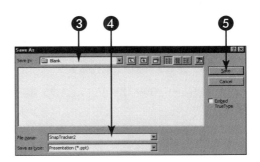

Closing a presentation

Closing a presentation

Now you're getting closer to that cool drink. In this exercise, you'll learn how to close the presentation and exit PowerPoint.

1 Open the File menu.

2 Choose Close to close the file.

NOTE *If you had not first saved the file, PowerPoint would ask if you wanted to save the file before automatically closing it.*

3 Open the File menu again.

4 Choose Exit to close PowerPoint.

TIP *You can also skip step 1 and just select File ➤ Exit. If you had previously saved the file, then PowerPoint would close it and exit the program. If you had not previously saved the file, PowerPoint would first ask if you wanted to save the file and then close.*

WRAP UP

Before you drown yourself in that richly deserved cool drink, how about a review. So far, you've learned how to

- Start PowerPoint 97 from either the Windows 95 Start button or the Office 97 toolbar

- Open an existing PowerPoint presentation

- Turn individual toolbars on and off

- Select any of the five different views

- Move from slide to slide

- Rearrange slides

- Preview a presentation

- Save a presentation

- Close a presentation

- Exit PowerPoint

Feel free to cruise around the SnapTracker.ppt practice presentation at your leisure to experiment and learn more.

In the next lesson, you'll learn how to actually create a presentation from scratch, how to create master slides and speaker notes, and how to use the AutoContent Wizard.

Now, go get that drink. You've earned it.

PART I

Building Presentations

This part introduces you to PowerPoint 97, a computerized presentation program that can be installed as a standalone program or as part of the Office 97 suite of programs. It includes the following lessons:

Lesson 1: Creating a Slide Presentation

Lesson 2: Working with a Presentation

Creating a Slide Presentation

30 MINUTES

GOALS

In Lesson 1 you get to create a slide presentation from scratch; well, sort of from scratch. You're going to start with the AutoContent Wizard and you'll be mastering these skills:

- Using the AutoContent Wizard to create a new presentation
- Creating presentation text in Outline view
- Inserting a new slide and entering text on it
- Adding a name and a logo
- Inserting slides from other presentations
- Creating Masters (Title, Slide, Handout, and Notes)
- Adding speaker notes

Starting a new presentation

GET READY

To complete this lesson, you'll need to start PowerPoint 97 (refer to the Jump Start if you forgot how to do that). You'll also need to copy the following files from the Lesson 1 folder on the CD-ROM to your own hard disk: Logo.bmp, SnapTracker.ppt, and Camera.wmf. When you're finished, your presentation should look like the one in the file AEM–EOL1.ppt.

CREATING THE PRESENTATION

You already know how to open an existing presentation. Now you're going to learn how to create a new presentation. There are two ways to start a new presentation. You can select a presentation template from the list of those that come with PowerPoint 97, or you can let the AutoContent Wizard set you up in seconds. You'll be starting with the AutoContent Wizard.

Starting a new presentation

Pretend you work as the Assistant to the President at the SnapTracker Corporation. Your boss is scurrying around trying to get ready for the first Annual Employee Meeting. At this meeting people will learn about promotions, how the company did over the past year, what the company's goals are for the coming year, and so on. Your boss asks you to prepare the slide show he'll use at the Welcoming Gathering. You say *Yes* with all the enthusiasm of someone who wants at least a raise and maybe even a promotion. Then you run to grab your *PowerPoint 97 One Step at a Time* book.

In this exercise you will start the Annual Employee Meeting presentation using AutoContent Wizard.

1 If you haven't already done so, open PowerPoint 97 so that the opening PowerPoint dialog box is displayed, as shown on the right.

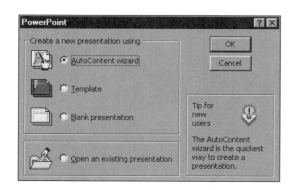

TIP

If PowerPoint 97 is already open but the PowerPoint opening dialog box is gone, do not despair. You can still use the AutoContent Wizard. Just select File ➤ New and on the Presentations tab, click the first item, AutoContent Wizard.prz.

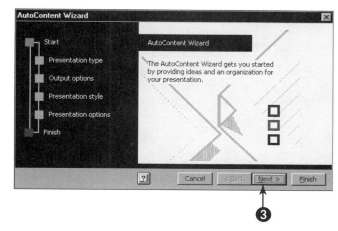

❷ Double-click AutoContent Wizard. The AutoContent Wizard Start box appears. Be patient, as it may take several seconds to appear.

❸ Click Next. The AutoContent Wizard Presentation Type dialog box appears, showing all the available predefined templates, as shown in the illustration to the right.

❹ Click Company Meeting.

❺ Click Next. The AutoContent Wizard Output Options dialog box appears.

❻ The Presentations, Informal Meetings, Handouts button should be selected by default, but if it isn't, then click to select it.

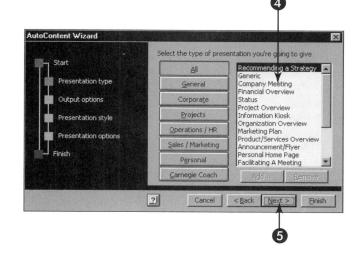

❼ Click Next. The AutoContent Wizard-Presentation Style dialog box appears.

❽ Under What Type Of Output Will You Use, the On-Screen Presentation button should be selected. If it is not, then click the button to select it.

❾ Under Will You Print Handouts, the Yes button should be selected. If it is not, then click the button to select it.

❿ Click Next to bring up the AutoContent Wizard Presentation Options dialog box.

Creating a Slide Presentation

1

⑪ Replace the default text ("Title goes here") in the Presentation Title text box by typing the following: **SnapTracker Corporation**.

⑫ Press Tab to move to the Your Name text box. Your name will probably already be displayed there, but since this is your pretend boss's presentation, you should replace your name with his, **Nosmo King**.

⑬ Press Tab to move to the Additional Information text box.

⑭ Replace the default text (it will probably be your company name or "Put any additional information here") with the following: **Annual Employee Meeting**.

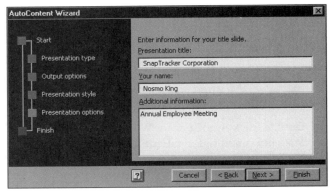

VISUAL BONUS

A Map to Outline View

Personally, I like to create presentations in Outline view because I can see the effects of my work immediately. Here, you can see where the various controls, icons, and buttons are located in Outline view. This visual map should help you get through the following exercises.

Slide number · Standard toolbar · Formatting toolbar

Slide Miniature's "X" box

Slide Miniature

View buttons →

Show Formatting

Summary Slide

Status bar · Promote · Move Up · Collapse · Collapse All

Demote · Move Down · Expand · Expand All

⑮ Click Next. The AutoContent Wizard Finish dialog box appears.

⑯ Click Finish. A 13-slide sample presentation appears in Outline view with the first slide selected, as shown in the illustration to the right. You may have to scroll down to see all 13 slides.

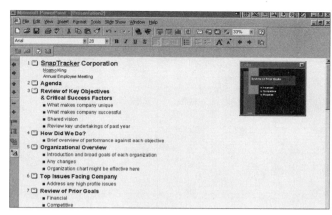

Creating a presentation in Outline view

When you can see the presentation in Outline view, it is very easy to create the text you want. All of the AutoContent Wizard templates include hints on what information to include on slides. In this exercise, you're going to use the basic design template as a starting point, but you'll use very few of the actual slides.

❶ With the new presentation open in Outline view to the default outline, position the cursor to the left of the first word on the third slide (that is, "Review").

❷ Simultaneously press Control+Shift+End to select the rest of the slides.

❸ Press Delete to remove slides 3–13.

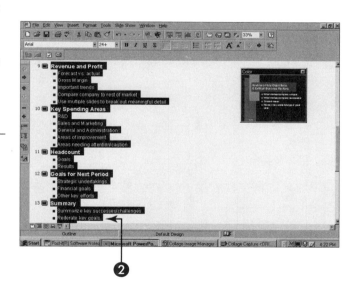

TIP

You may have to press Page Up or scroll up to see the first slide in the outline.

❹ Press Enter.

5 Click Demote (or press Tab) to create a bullet for the Agenda slide.

6 Type the following: **Welcome & Introduction.**

7 Press Enter.

8 Type the following: **Where We Are**.

9 Press Enter.

10 Type the following: **Where We're Going**.

11 Press Enter.

12 Type the following: **Summary & Closing Ceremonies**.

13 Press Enter. Your Outline should look like the one in the illustration to the right.

14 Click Promote to convert the extra bullet to the next slide.

15 At the new slide, type the following: **Where We Are**. Press Enter.

16 Click Demote.

17 At the bullet, type the following: **Financial Results.** Press Enter.

18 Click Demote.

19 At the bullet, type the following: **Balance Sheet.** Press Enter.

20 Click Promote.

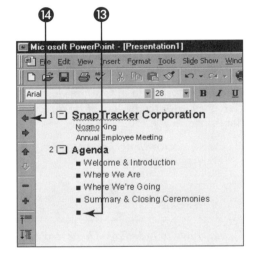

㉑ At the dash, type the following: **Our Markets.** Press Enter.

㉒ At the bullet, type the following: **Headcount.** Press Enter.

㉓ Click Promote.

㉔ Type the following: **Where We're Going.** Press Enter.

㉕ Click Demote.

㉖ At the bullet, type the following: **Increase sales by 40%.** Press Enter.

㉗ Type the following: **Maintain at least 15% profit margin.** Press Enter.

㉘ Type the following: **Establish European market.** Press Enter.

㉙ Type the following: **Have Fun!** Your Outline should now look like the one in the illustration to the right.

㉚ Open the File menu.

㉛ Select Save. The Save dialog box appears, as shown at the bottom.

㉜ Navigate to where you store these practice presentations.

㉝ In the File Name box on the Save dialog box, type the following: **Annual Employee Meeting**.

NOTE *You don't have to include the dot–ppt (.ppt) because PowerPoint will add that automatically.*

㉞ Click Save. Do *not* close the file.

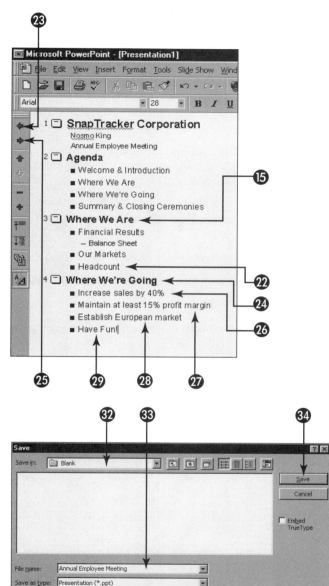

1

Creating a Slide Presentation

Inserting a new slide and entering text

Inserting a new slide and entering text

It's easy to add a slide in Outline view. You get to see where it goes, and, if the Slide Miniature feature is turned on (as it should be for this exercise), you also get to see exactly what it's going to look like. In this exercise, you'll insert a new slide mid-presentation and add text to it.

1 With the Annual Employee Meeting presentation still open in Outline view, position the cursor at the beginning of the third slide (that is, Where We Are).

2 Press Enter to insert a new slide. The Where We Are slide moves down and becomes Slide #4, and a new, empty third slide is inserted in its place.

3 Move the cursor to the newly inserted third slide.

4 Type the following: **Promotions & Reassignments.**

5 Press Enter.

6 Click Demote to add a bullet under the Promotions & Reassignments slide.

7 Type the following at the new bullet: **Company Organization Chart.** When you're done, your slide should look like the illustration to the right.

8 Click File ➢ Save, but do not close the file.

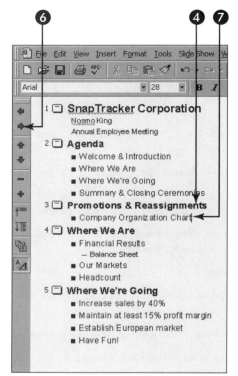

Adding a name and logo

You already have the SnapTracker name on the Title slide, but it would be nice to have it in a footer appearing on all slides. You don't want the employees to forget who they work for, after all. And since you've just selected a new company logo, this is a good time to present it to the employees. In this exercise, you'll add the company name in a footer and the company logo to the Slide Master.

❶ Open the View menu.

❷ Select Master.

❸ Choose Slide Master.

❹ Right-click anywhere in the Slide Master Footer Area to open a pop-up menu.

NOTE *If you click anywhere other than in the Slide Master Footer Area, you will see a different pop-up menu.*

❺ Select Edit Text. The pop-up menu will go away and you can type in the footer.

❻ Replace "<footer>" with the following: **SnapTracker Corporation**, as shown in the illustration to the right.

❼ Move the cursor anywhere within the Footer Area until the cursor turns into a four-way arrow.

8 Double-click anywhere while the cursor is a four-way arrow. The Format AutoShape dialog box appears, as shown in the illustration to the right.

9 Click the Text Box tab.

10 Click the down arrow for the Text Anchor Point text box.

11 Select Bottom Centered to position the footer text closer to the bottom of the Footer Area, as shown in the illustration to the right.

12 Click OK.

13 Open the Insert menu.

14 Select Picture.

15 Choose From File.

16 Navigate to the folder where you installed the practice presentations.

17 Double-click Logo.bmp (or select it and then click Insert). The logo will probably appear in the center of the slide and be too big.

18 Grab the lower right-hand handle and drag diagonally to your left to make the graphic smaller.

19 Drag the logo to the lower left-hand corner of the slide.

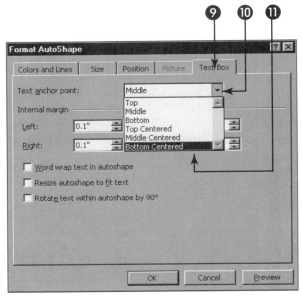

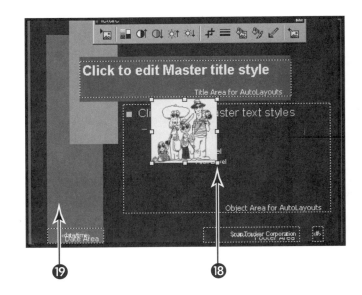

20 Select View ➤ Slide and scroll through the presentation to see how each slide looks with the name in the footer and the logo added.

> **NOTE**
>
> *The logo should now be on all but the title slide.*

21 Save, but do not close, the presentation.

Inserting slides

Sometimes you'll want to make the same point in one presentation already made by a slide in another presentation. Rather than spending the time to recreate that slide, you can simply insert a copy of it into your new presentation. In this exercise, you'll insert a slide from a different presentation into the Annual Employee Meeting presentation.

1 Switch to Outline view.

2 Position the cursor at the beginning of the third slide.

3 Open the Insert menu.

4 Click Slides from Files. The Slide Finder dialog box appears.

5 Click Browse. The Insert Slides from Files dialog box appears, as shown in the illustration to the right.

6 If you're not already there, navigate to where you installed the practice presentation files.

7 Double-click SnapTracker.ppt. The Slide Finder dialog box reappears.

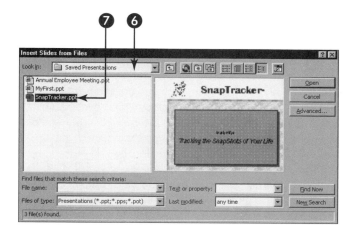

Inserting slides

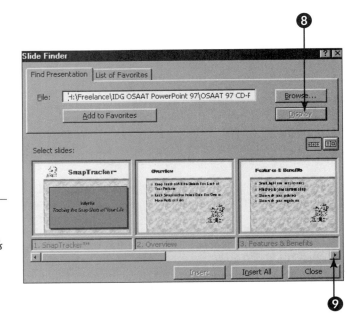

8 Click Display. The entire SnapTracker.ppt presentation appears, in slide groups of three, as shown in the illustration to the right.

9 Click the right-hand Slide Advance arrow to scroll through the presentation until the Applications slide is visible.

10 Double-click the Applications slide. It automatically drops into your open presentation to follow the Promotions & Reassignments slide, as shown at the bottom. The Slide Finder dialog box remains open, just in case you want to insert any other slides. You don't.

If you've kept the Slide Miniature visible, notice that the SnapTracker Application slide came into this presentation reconfigured to match this presentation's slide format.

11 Click Close on the Slide Finder dialog box.

12 Save, but do not close, the presentation.

MASTERING THE MASTERS

PowerPoint 97 realizes that you have more important things to do than keep creating the same thing over and over again. That's why PowerPoint 97 includes several Master formats that you can define so your slides maintain a consistent appearance without any effort on our part. There are four Masters: Title, Slide, Handout, and Notes. The Title Master defines the appearance of your title slides. Your presentation may have only one title slide (usually the first one), or it may have a title slide to introduce each segment of your presentation. Regardless, the Title Master ensures that each title slide follows the same format.

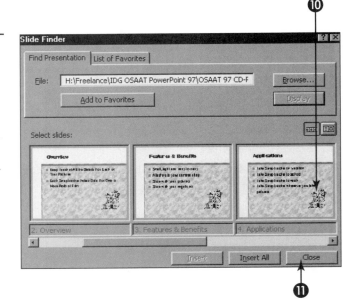

The same is true for the Slide Master. No matter how many slides you have following your title slides, you want them all to be consistent in appearance. You certainly don't want the header to move around at the top of the slide, and you don't want page numbers floating around, and so on. The Slide Master lets you define fonts, styles, font sizes, and text/object placement. You can also use the Slide Master to place a logo or other graphic that you want to appear in the same place on all slides.

The Handout Master lets you format the printed sheets that you'll hand out to your audience. You can choose a two-, three-, or six-slide presentation format and, as with the other Masters, dictate the font, font style and size, and other parameters.

The Notes Master allows you to format the manner of presentation of the notes that you will use either as speakers' notes or as handouts.

All the Masters allow you to introduce headers and footers, dates, and page numbers so those things appear the same on all slides or pages. Each of the areas that will accept text or graphics is clearly marked along with instructions to click in those areas to format them. You can also resize or reposition those areas.

▶ Moving formatting boxes

To change the location of a header, footer, or other text box, perform the following steps:

❶ Select View ➢ Master ➢ Title Master.

❷ Position the cursor anywhere in the Footer box (in the lower right-hand corner). The cursor turns into a four-way arrow.

❸ Click to display the box's handles, as shown in the illustration to the right.

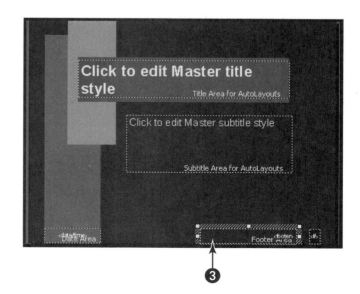

Resizing formatting boxes

4 With the handles visible and the four-way-arrow cursor inside the box, click and drag the box until it is in the bottom center of the slide.

TIP *If you're not sure you can "eyeball" the centering, you can turn on the ruler (by selecting View ➤ Ruler). When you turn on the ruler, you'll see both horizontal and vertical rulers that you can use to ensure your repositioning is exactly where you want it. Turn off the ruler by clicking View ➤ Ruler again.*

Resizing formatting boxes

To resize or reshape a formatting box, perform the following steps:

1 If you're still in Title Master view, skip to step 3.

2 Click View ➤ Master ➤ Title Master.

3 Position the cursor anywhere in the page number box (in the lower right-hand corner).

4 Click to show the box's handles, as shown in the illustration to the right.

5 Position the cursor over the right-middle handle. The cursor changes to a left-right pointing arrow, as shown in the illustration to the right.

6 Click the left-right pointing arrow and drag the box's right side to the right about a quarter of an inch.

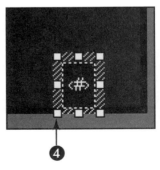

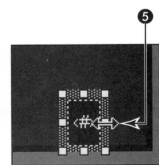

When you click to move the side, the left–right pointing arrow changes to a large plus sign. After you move the line and release the mouse button, it reverts to the left–right pointing arrow. You can make all text and formatting boxes larger or smaller, as your needs dictate. When you use one of the corner handles, then you can move, enlarge, or reduce the size of the box without affecting its proportions.

❼ Save, but do not close, the presentation.

▶ Creating a Title Master

A Title Master is a slide that defines the appearance of all other title slides. For example, Slide #1 in the Annual Employee Meeting presentation is a title slide. You may have as many title slides as you care to create in a presentation. PowerPoint 97 figures you have enough other things to remember; you shouldn't have to remember what font or font size you used to create a title slide each time you want to create a new one. In this exercise, you'll format the Title Master.

❶ With the Annual Employee Meeting presentation still open in Title Master view, right-click anywhere in the text line in the Title Area for AutoLayouts. A pop-up menu appears, as shown in the illustration to the right.

❷ Click Font. The Font dialog box opens.

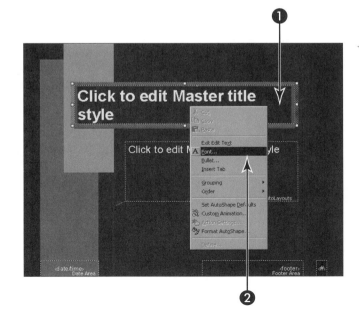

3 Scroll through the fonts to find and select Times New Roman.

4 Select Bold Italic from the Font Style window.

5 Choose 40 from the Font Size window.

6 Click Preview to see how this looks.

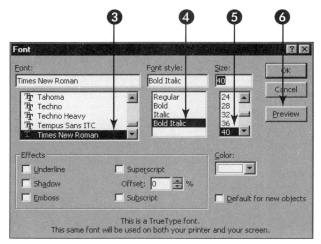

NOTE *If the Font dialog box is in your way, drag it out of the way so that you can see the preview.*

7 Click OK to apply those font changes.

8 Click View ➤ Outline.

9 Save, but do not close, the presentation.

TIP *If you right-click in an area that contains no text, the editing menu will be slightly different, but you can still use it. Click Edit Text to select all the text in the Title Area for AutoLayouts. If you do this, you can modify all the text at once by selecting Format ➤ Font and proceeding as described previously. Another option would be to press Delete to get rid of all the selected text. The key point is, by selecting Edit Text, you're editing all the text at once. You could also click Font from the menu and just work with the font styles and sizes.*

By the way, these procedures work in the Subtitle Area for AutoLayouts, too. There are a lot of other things you can do in the Title Master, and you'll get to do some of them in later chapters.

Creating a Slide Master

In the same way that you created a Title Master, you can also create a Slide Master. By defining fonts, layout, font size, and so on in the Slide Master, you ensure that all of the slides in your presentation will present a uniform and professional appearance. In this exercise, you'll format the Slide Master.

❶ With the Annual Employee Meeting presentation still open in Outline view, click View ➤ Master ➤ Slide Master. The Slide Master appears.

❷ Right-click anywhere in the Title Area for AutoLayouts. A pop-up menu appears, just like the one you saw on the Title Master.

❸ Click Font. The Font dialog box opens, as shown in the illustration to the right.

❹ Scroll through the fonts to find and select Times New Roman.

TIP

*If you're like me, you tend to be impatient with computers sometimes. You can speed your search for Times New Roman by typing the letter **t** in the Font Text box (or **ti**, which is even faster, depending on how many fonts you have beginning with the letter T).*

❺ Select Bold from the Font Style window.

❻ Choose 36 from the Size window.

❼ In the Effects area, click Underline to put a check mark in the box.

❽ Click OK.

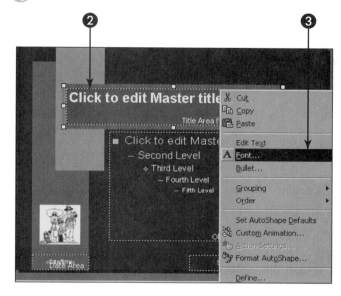

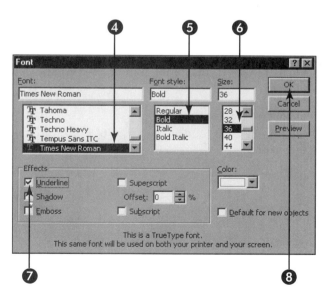

9 Click in the Object Area for AutoLayouts.

In the next few steps, you're going to format the individual levels separately. If you want to change the font uniformly for all levels (but keep other individual characteristics), follow the steps described previously for the Slide Master Title Area for AutoLayouts.

10 Highlight the main bullet text ("Click to edit Master text styles") to select it, as shown in the illustration to the right.

11 Select Format menu ➤ Font. The Font Dialog box appears as shown in the illustration at the bottom.

12 Select Times New Roman from the Font box.

13 Choose Bold from the Font Style box.

14 Select 32 from the Size box.

15 Click OK. Those font parameters should be applied to only the highlighted text ("Click to edit Master text styles").

16 In the Object Area for AutoLayouts, select "Second Level."

17 Click the down arrow of the font box on the Standard toolbar.

18 Scroll down to find and select Times New Roman.

19 Click the down arrow of the font size box on the Standard toolbar.

20 Select 28.

21 On the Standard toolbar, click the "B" button (this makes the text **bold**).

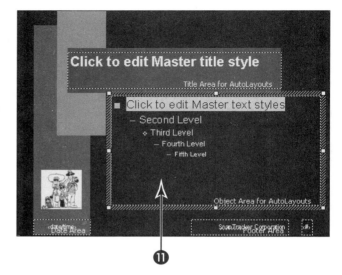

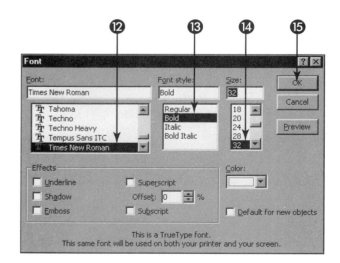

㉒ On the standard toolbar, click the "I" button (this makes the text *italic*).

㉓ Return to Outline view, and save, but do not close, the file.

NOTE *When you return to Outline view, some text may already be selected. Click anywhere outside the outline to deselect it.*

Creating a Handout Master

It's usually a good idea to print a set of handouts for your audience. That way they can follow along with your presentation slide for slide. Another advantage to doing this is that your audience can take your presentation with them so they can think about your points at their leisure or share it with their coworkers, bosses and underlings, spouses, significant others, children, shirt-sleeve relatives, the plumber, and whomever else they may encounter over the next few days.

Printing handouts also serves as a kind of insurance for you. Say you planned for a one-hour presentation, and at the last minute you're informed that your time has been cut to 30 minutes. You don't have time to redo your presentation, and you know you can't possibly cover all your important points in 30 minutes. Not to worry—while they won't have the benefit of your scintillating delivery, your audience will still be able to see all of your message.

Three formats are available for handouts: two, three, or six slides per page. You can even present the handouts in Outline form. In this exercise you will choose the six slides per page format for the Handout Master. The Handout Master even helps you by inserting your name (or, in this case, your boss's name) into the header.

Creating a Handout Master

1 Select View ➤ Master ➤ Handout Master. The Handout Master appears, as shown in the illustration to the right.

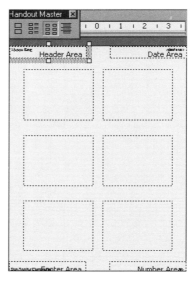

NOTE *The Handout Master toolbar automatically shows up when you select the Handout Master. It may appear just about anywhere on the screen. You can move it by clicking anywhere in the title bar ("Handout Master") and dragging it wherever you want.*

2 If the Handout Master isn't already set up for six slides per page, click the Show Positioning of Six per Page Handouts button on the Handout Master toolbar.

TIP *If the Handout Master toolbar does not automatically appear, click View ➤ Toolbars ➤ Handout Master. Then drag the toolbar wherever you want it.*

3 Position the cursor anywhere in the Header Area until it turns into the four-way arrow.

4 Click to select the Header Area box.

5 Press the Delete key to get rid of it.

6 Position the cursor anywhere in the Footer Area until it turns into the four-way arrow, and click to select the Footer Area box.

7 Press Delete to get rid of it, too.

8 Position the cursor anywhere in the Date Area until it turns into the four-way arrow, and click the select the Date Area box.

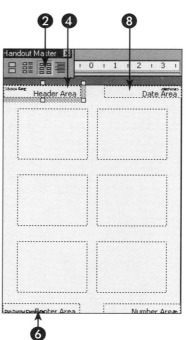

Creating a Notes Master

9 Press Delete to get rid of it. Your Handout Master should look like the one to the right (only the Number should remain).

10 Save, but do not close, the presentation.

Creating a Notes Master

While the Notes Master is most commonly used as a "cheat sheet" for the presenter, you can also use it as your handout for the audience. The format of the Notes Master allows you to create notes for each slide in the presentation so that your audience would see the slide and the text all on one page. In this exercise, you will create a Notes Master intended only for the presenter.

1 Select View ➢ Master ➢ Notes Master. The Notes Master appears.

2 Position the cursor anywhere in the Date Area until it turns into the four-way arrow, and click to select the Date Area.

3 Press Delete to get rid of it.

4 Position the cursor anywhere in the Footer Area until it turns into the four-way arrow, and click to select the Footer Area.

5 Press Delete to get rid of it. Your Notes Master should now include only the Header and Number Areas.

6 In the Notes Body Area, select "Click to edit Master text style."

7 Using the formatting method of your choice, format the selected text as follows: Arial, Bold, and 16.

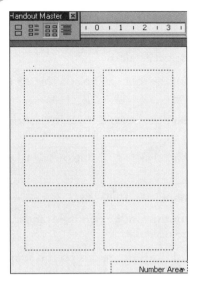

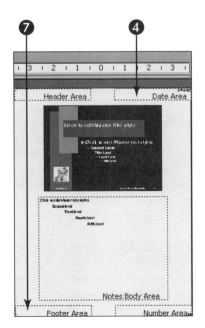

Creating a Notes Master

8 In the Notes Body Area, select "Second level."

9 Click the down arrow of the font box on the Standard toolbar, and scroll to find and select Arial.

10 Click the down arrow of the font size box on the Standard toolbar, select 12.

11 On the Standard toolbar, click the "B" button to make the font **bold**.

12 On the Standard toolbar, click the "I" button to make the font *italic*.

13 In the Notes Body Area, select "Third Level."

14 Click the down arrow of the font box on the Standard toolbar, and scroll to find and select Arial.

15 Click the down arrow of the font size box on the Standard toolbar, and select 10. Your Notes Master should now look like the one in the illustration to the right.

16 Save, but do not close, the presentation.

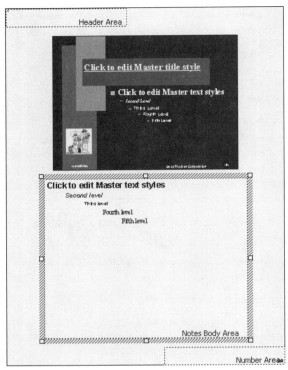

SPEAKER NOTES

Unless you're a trained actor, you'd probably rather walk naked over hot coals while carrying your mother-in-law (or some other beloved member of your family) on your shoulders than memorize lines and speak in front of an audience. PowerPoint 97 assumes that while you may be able to create a whiz-bang presentation, you'd probably be a lot more comfortable if you had some notes to guide you through it instead of having to rely on your memory. Remember those old 3 × 5 cards you used in school? PowerPoint 97's Speaker Notes are high-tech 3 × 5 cards.

You can create your notes with either (or both) of two things in mind. You can create notes that only your eyes will see. These will be truly "Speaker's Notes" you can use to record anything that will help you get through your presentation. Or you can use these notes instead of the traditional handouts. If you choose this second option, your audience will get a copy of the slide *and* the text you write to go with it. Obviously, this means you will have to be more explicit in your writing and avoid cryptic abbreviations or messages to yourself, but this can be a very effective tool if you're trying to make a critical point and want your audience to be able to see both the slide and text at the same time.

▶ Adding speaker notes

Although your boss is not a trained actor, you know he's going to be nervous making his first presentation at the Annual Employee Meeting. In this exercise, you'll create some speaker notes for him.

1 Select View ➢ Notes Page. The Notes Page view appears showing whatever slide was last selected.

2 If you're not there already, scroll to the second slide (that is, Agenda).

3 Click anywhere in the "Click to Add Text" area.

4 Type the following so it looks like the illustration to the right: **Welcome, Ladies and Gentlemen, to the first annual SnapTracker Employee's Meeting. Today we're going to let you know the long-awaited results of the recent promotions and position re-assignments. We're also going to talk about what's been happening over the past year and what to expect in the coming year. I hope you're all as excited about SnapTracker's future as I am. Click.**

5 Select all the text you just typed, including "Click."

6 Click the down arrow of the font size box and choose 18 (your boss's eyes just ain't what they used to be).

7 Select View ➢ Outline.

8 Select File ➢ Save.

9 Select File ➢ Close.

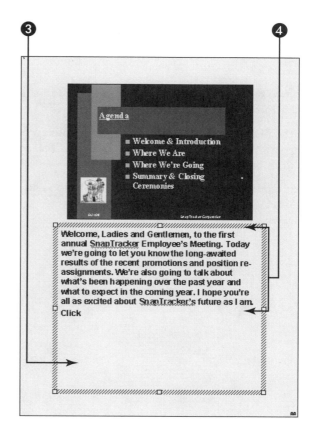

Skills challenge

SKILLS CHALLENGE

You've covered a lot of ground in this chapter. Even if this book were to spontaneously burst into flames, you've learned enough to put together a presentable presentation. This Skills Challenge should prove to you just how much you have learned.

You'll open the Annual Employee Meeting presentation, add bullets to some slides, insert new slides, place a company logo and other clip art, change text appearance uniformly on slides, add a date and time indicator, reposition text boxes to uniformly alter slide appearance, switch the Handout Master from six slides per page to three slides per page, and add text to the Speaker Notes.

1 Open the Annual Employee Meeting presentation.

 Do you remember how to start the AutoContent Wizard when PowerPoint is already open and the opening dialog box is gone?

2 Add two bullets to the Agenda slide so that it looks like the illustration to the right.

3 On the fifth slide (that is, "Where We Are") insert a bullet "Monthly Sales" with the same indentation as "Balance Sheet," as shown on the illustration to the right.

4 Insert a new slide at the end of the presentation and call it **Summary & Closing Ceremonies**.

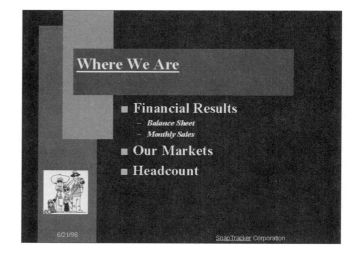

⑤ Insert the company logo so that it will appear in the same place on all title slides.

> **★2** *Do you remember how to indent a bullet on a slide and then return to the original indentation?*

⑥ On the Slide Master, make the Third Level text Times New Roman, the Font Style Bold Italic, and the Font Size 20.

> **★3** *Do you remember how to insert a slide into a presentation?*

⑦ Add the Pricing slide from SnapTracker.ppt so that it falls right after Slide #6 (Where We're Going). Your outline should now look like the one in the illustration to the right.

⑧ Insert the date and month (hint: select the default format, then use Insert ➢ Date and Time ➢ month, year) in the Date/Time area of the Title Master.

⑨ Remove the comma separating the month and year.

⑩ Drag the Date Area box up to the top so that it is centered over the orange stripe. Your Title Master should look something the one in the illustration to the right.

> **★4** *Do you remember how to insert a name on all regular (not title) slides?*

⑪ Because your company makes a product that attaches to cameras, your boss thinks it might be cute to stick a picture of a camera on every regular slide. Use the camera.wmf file that came with this book and position and size it fits in the upper-right corner.

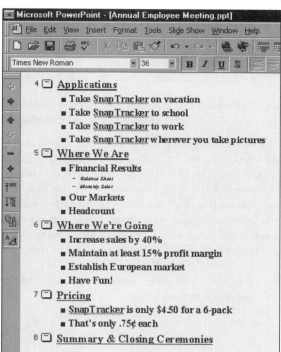

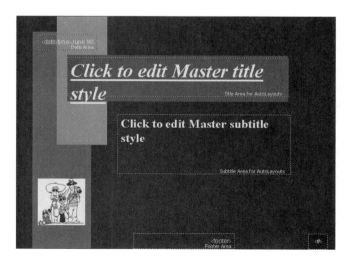

Skills challenge

12 Change the Handout Master to three slides per page so that your audience can make notes as they listen to the presentation.

5 *Do you remember how to insert a logo on a slide?*

13 Type the following in the Header area of the Notes Master using Arial, Bold Italic, 8: **SnapTracker Annual Employee Meeting**.

14 On the Notes page for the last slide (Summary & Closing Ceremonies) add the following in Arial, Bold, 18-pt text in the Click to Add Text area: **In conclusion, Ladies and Gentlemen, I want to thank you all for your time and attention today, but more important for your efforts and loyalty over the past year. Now, go enjoy the picnic and we'll all get back to work next week.** The Notes Page should look like the one in the illustration to the right.

6 *Do you remember how to insert a slide from another presentation?*

15 Save and close the presentation.

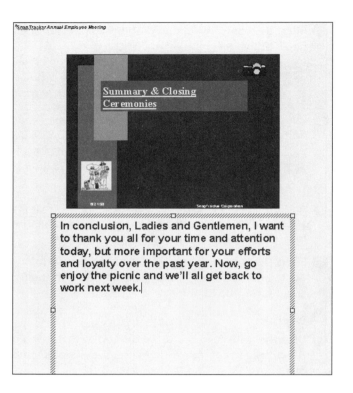

TROUBLESHOOTING

In this lesson you learned how to create a slide presentation using the AutoContent Wizard. Got questions? The following troubleshooting table may help.

Problem	Solution
When I was working through the AutoContent Wizard, the Presentation Styles dialog box never showed up.	You accidentally selected Internet, Kiosk in the AutoContent Wizard Output Options dialog box. Try again.
My AutoContent Wizard Presentations Options dialog box looks nothing like the one in the book. Mine includes copyright and e-mail information.	Same solution as previous.

Troubleshooting

Problem	Solution
The Office Assistant annoys me. How can I get rid of it?	Click its X box.
There is a Common Tasks toolbar open. How do I get rid of that?	Click its X box *or* click View ➢ Toolbars and click to deselect it or any other toolbars you want to get rid of.
I accidentally inserted a new slide in the wrong place in Outline view.	The easiest solution is to just click Undo. If you did it a long time ago and are just now getting help for it, tsk, tsk, tsk. . . . Position the cursor to the left of the unwanted slide and click Delete.
Why doesn't the Save As dialog box show up anymore?	Once you name a file when you save it the first time, PowerPoint assumes you want to keep that name. If you want to save a presentation under another name, click File ➢ Save As.
I accidentally added an extra bullet to a slide.	Backspace!
My computer doesn't have Times New Roman or Arial, the two fonts the book keeps telling me to use.	Choose your own fonts, but be consistent.
I can't move or resize clip art.	You must first select clip art before you can move or resize it.
What are the little squares between the slide number and the text of a slide in Outline view?	They are slide icons. If the icon is empty, there are no graphics on the slide. If you double-click one of those icons, you move immediately to Slide view for that slide.

Wrap up

WRAP UP

While you're not yet a Master PowerPointer, you have learned a lot in this lesson. For example, you learned how to

- Use AutoContent Wizard to create a new presentation
- Create a new presentation in Outline view
- Insert a new slide
- Enter text on slides
- Add footers
- Add logos and clip art
- Insert slides from other presentations
- Create masters (Title, Slide, Handout, and Notes Page)
- Add speaker notes

Feel free to go through the AutoContent Wizard again, making different choices and experimenting with the options.

In Lesson 2, you'll learn how to work with text and objects.

Working with a Presentation

GOALS

In Lesson 2, you'll work with text and objects. Specifically, you'll become expert in the following skills:

45 MINUTES

- Adding and deleting text
- Changing text case
- Formatting text
- Adjusting spacing
- Moving text or slides in Outline view
- Finding and replacing text
- Using AutoCorrect and checking spelling
- Adding text to objects
- Changing object colors
- Connecting, rotating, and flipping objects
- Grouping and ungrouping objects

Adding text

GET READY

To complete this lesson, you'll need to start PowerPoint 97 (refer to the Jump Start if you forgot how to do that) and open the Annual Employee Meeting presentation (refer to Lesson 1 if you forgot how to do that). You'll also need to copy the following files from the Lesson 2 folder on the CD-ROM to your own hard disk: AEM-EOL1.ppt and Diabetes97.ppt. Open the AEM-EOL1.ppt file and start from there. When you are finished, your presentations should look like the ones in AEM-EOL2.ppt and Diabetes97-EOL2.ppt.

WORKING WITH TEXT

OK. So now you know how to start PowerPoint 97 and even create a presentation. You're still no expert, but in a pinch, you could crank out something respectable. In this lesson, you're going to learn how to spiff up various elements of your presentation, starting with the text. While you won't learn *what* to say, you'll at least know how to say "it" effectively.

Adding text

Obviously your presentation requires text. In this lesson, you'll learn how to add a new slide and put text on it.

1 Start PowerPoint 97 so that the opening dialog box is displayed.

2 Double-click Open an Existing Presentation. The Open dialog box appears.

3 Navigate to the AEM-EOL1.ppt presentation and double-click it.

4 Select View ➤ Slide.

5 Scroll to display Slide #2 (Agenda).

There's a shortcut to Slide view that you might like. Instead of switching to Slide view and scrolling to a specific slide as directed in this exercise, switch to Slide Sorter view. Then just double-click the slide you want; the program automatically switches to Slide view. You can even insert new slides in Slide Sorter view more easily than anywhere else. Just click the slide you want to precede the new slide and then select Insert ➤ New Slide. Bingo!

6 Open the Insert menu.

7 Click New Slide. The New Slide dialog box appears, as shown in the illustration to the right.

8 Double-click Blank (lower-right corner). A blank slide formatted for this presentation automatically appears as shown in the illustration to the right.

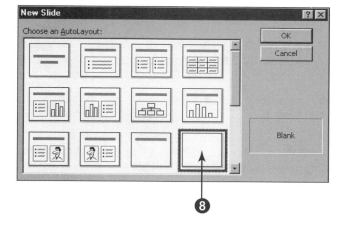

NOTE

When you single-click any of the formats, its name appears in the box in the lower-right corner of the dialog box.

9 Open the View menu.

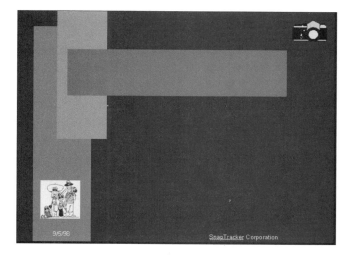

Changing text case

10 Select Outline. The new, blank slide should be in the third position, and the Promotions & Reassignments slide, as well as all the others, should have advanced one position, as shown in the illustration to the right.

11 At the new, empty third slide type the following: **New Corporate Logo**.

12 Press Enter.

13 Click Demote (or press Tab) to add a bullet.

14 Type the following text, in all caps, including "cut" for "cute": **WE WANTED SOMETHING CATCHY, WE WANTED SOMETHING KEEN, WE WANTED SOMETHING CUT, THAT ON A T-SHIRT WE COULD SCREEN.**

15 Press Enter to add a second bullet, as shown in the illustration to the right.

16 Type the following, also in all caps: **WE PICKED THIS HAPPY FAMILY, ON VACATION YOU CAN SEE, WITH CAMERA STRAPS A-CRYIN' OUT, FOR SNAPTRACKERS TO BE**.

17 Click View ➤ Slide.

18 Save, but do not close, the presentation.

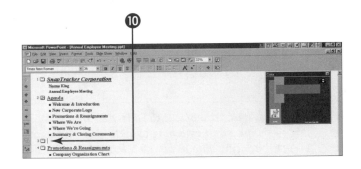

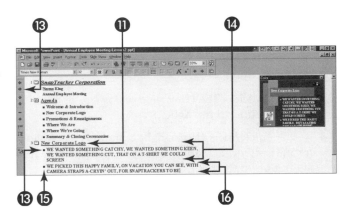

Changing text case

Yuck! Slide #3 looks awful! There's too much text on the slide, and all-caps text can be very hard to read (keep that in mind, by the way, as many presentation authors tend to over-use all caps). In this lesson, you'll learn how to change text case.

1 Select all the text you just typed in both bullets.

2 Open the Format menu, and select Change Case. The Change Case dialog box appears, as shown in the illustration to the right.

3 Make sure the Sentence Case button is already selected (if it's not, click to select it).

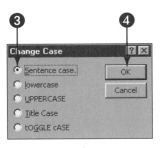

4 Click OK.

5 Save, but do not close, the presentation.

► *Formatting text*

If you're familiar with Microsoft Word, then you already know how to format text in PowerPoint 97. You can do most of the same things in the same way. In this exercise, you'll format the highlighted text so that it is easier to read and fits on the slide.

1 While the text is still selected, change the font size to 24, as shown in the illustration to the right.

2 Click anywhere to deselect the text.

3 Select the "w" of the word "we" that appears after the first comma.

4 Overtype it with a capital **W**.

5 Select the "w" of the word "we" that appears after the second comma.

6 Overtype it with a capital **W**.

7 Select the "t" that appears after the third comma.

8 Overtype it with a capital **T**.

9 In the second bullet, capitalize the first "S" and the "T" in "SnapTrackers."

10 Select the "o" that appears after the fourth comma.

11 Overtype it with a capital **O**.

12 Select the "w" that appears after the fifth comma.

13 Overtype it with a capital **W**.

14 Select the "f" that appears after the last comma.

15 Overtype it with a capital **F**.

16 In the first bullet, capitalize the "T" in "T-shirt."

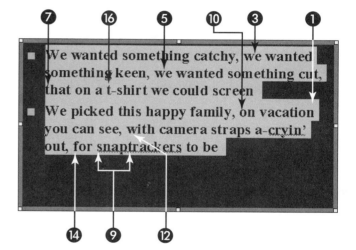

2

Working with a Presentation

17 In the first bullet, position the cursor in front of the second "We."

18 Press Tab twice.

19 Press the Spacebar once. This aligns the second line of our little ditty with the first line.

20 Still in the first bullet, position the cursor in front of the next "We."

21 Press Tab twice.

22 Press the Spacebar once.

23 Still in the first bullet, position the cursor in front of "That."

24 Press Tab twice.

25 In the second bullet, position the cursor in front of the word "On."

26 Press Tab twice.

27 Press the Spacebar twice.

28 Still in the second bullet, position the cursor in front of the word "With."

29 Press Tab three times.

30 Still in the second bullet, position the cursor in front of the word "For."

31 Press Tab.

32 Press the Spacebar. Your slide should now look like the one in the illustration to the right.

33 Save, but do not close, the presentation.

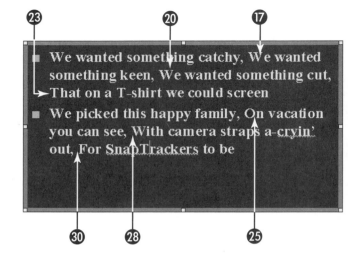

Deleting text

This slide is beginning to show promise, but it still has some problems. In this exercise, you'll delete some text.

1 At the end of the first line in the first bullet, click as close to the right side of the comma as you can get.

2 Press Backspace to remove the comma.

> **TIP**
>
> *Be careful to position the cursor immediately next to the comma about to be deleted. If you position the cursor too far away and then press Backspace, you may cause the text to become misaligned.*

3 Remove all commas in both bullets so that your slide looks like the one in the illustration to the right.

4 Save, but do not close, the presentation.

Adjusting spacing

There are several ways to adjust the spacing on a slide. You can modify line and paragraph spacing the same way you do in a word processor or you can insert a blank and invisible bullet.

1 Position the cursor at the end of the last line of the first bullet (that is, after "screen").

2 Press Enter.

> **NOTE**
>
> *Instead of inserting a regular bullet, PowerPoint 97 inserts a space–holding–but–invisible–when–printed– or–displayed bullet. This provides a wider separation between the two bullets, making them a little easier to read. When the text box is selected (that is, when you can see the box handles), the bullet will show up as black rather than tan like the visible ones.*

- We wanted something catchy
  We wanted something keen
  We wanted something cut
  That on a T-shirt we could screen
- We picked this happy family
  On vacation you can see
  With camera straps a-cryin' out
  For SnapTrackers to be

2

Working with a Presentation

Adjusting spacing

③ Switch to Outline view (select View ➤ Outline). Notice that the text for this slide looks really wacky in Outline view. Don't worry about it. Do not try to fix it.

④ Switch back to Slide view. You should still be on Slide #3 (New Corporate Logo).

⑤ Select all of the text in the two bullets you created.

⑥ Open the Format menu.

⑦ Select Line Spacing. The Line Spacing dialog box appears.

⑧ Click the down arrow in the Line Spacing text box.

⑨ Select Points.

⑩ Click the down arrow in the Line Spacing points box until you see the number 24.

⑪ Click OK.

⑫ Click anywhere to deselect the text so that you can better see how this looks.

⑬ Select all the text in the first bullet.

⑭ Select Format ➤ Line Spacing.

⑮ In the Line Spacing dialog box, click the down arrow in the After Paragraph text box.

⑯ Select Points.

⑰ Double-click the zero in the After Paragraph points box and replace it by typing **10.**

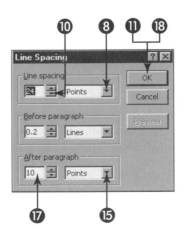

18 Click OK again. Your slide should now look like the one in the illustration to the right.

19 Save, but do not close, the presentation.

Moving text or slides in Outline view

Sometimes you'll create a presentation and then decide it works better if the slides are rearranged or even if some of the points on one slide are rearranged. In this lesson, you'll learn how to rearrange text and slides.

1 Switch to Outline view (select View ➢ Outline).

2 Position the cursor at the beginning of the fifth slide (Applications).

3 Press Enter to insert a new slide so that it falls after the Promotions & Reassignments slide and before the Applications slide.

4 Position the cursor at the new, blank slide.

5 Click the Move Up button twice so that the blank slide falls after the New Corporate Logo slide, as shown on the illustration to the right.

TIP

To rearrange bullets on a slide, you'd do the same thing. Position the cursor at the start of the bullet you want to move and click either the Move Up or Move Down button until the text is where you want it.

6 Leave this blank slide where it is for now. You'll use it later.

7 Save, but do not close, the presentation.

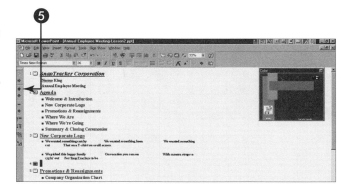

Positioning text on a slide

► Positioning text on a slide

Even after following all the basic rules for slide creation, you may find that the text just doesn't look quite right. Maybe you want to move it a little to the right or left or reposition it elsewhere on the slide. In this lesson you'll learn how to align and rearrange text.

❶ Position the cursor over the Slide View icon for Slide #3 (New Corporate Logo) so that it turns into a four-way arrow, as shown in the illustration to the right.

❷ Double-click the Slide View icon to switch to Slide view for the New Corporate Logo slide.

❸ Click anywhere in the text box containing the bulleted text but do not highlight any specific text.

❹ Click the down arrow of the Draw button on the Drawing toolbar.

❺ Select Align or Distribute ➢ Relative to Slide.

❻ Select Draw ➢ Align or Distribute ➢ Align Right.

NOTE

This moves the entire text box so that its right edge is flush with the right edge of the slide, but it seems a bit extreme.

❼ Select Draw ➢ Nudge.

❽ Click Left to move the entire text box ever so slightly to the left.

❾ Repeat step 8 two or three times until the slide looks something like the one in the illustration to the right.

- We wanted something catchy
  We wanted something keen
  We wanted something cut
  That on a T-shirt we could screen

- We picked this happy family
  On vacation you can see
  With camera straps a-cryin' out
  For SnapTrackers to be

Finding and replacing text globally

TIP

You can also reposition a word or group of words within a slide in Slide or Outline view.

⑩ With the New Corporate Logo slide still displayed in Slide view, position the cursor anywhere in the word "picked" (in the second bullet).

⑪ Double-click to select the whole word.

⑫ While "picked" is selected and the single-arrow cursor is pointing to it, drag the word to the end of the line so that it follows "family" (it should now read **We this happy family picked**).

⑬ Click anywhere to deselect the text. Your slide should look like the illustration to the right.

⑭ Save, but do not close, the presentation.

2

Working with a Presentation

Finding and replacing text globally

The SnapTracker Corporation is planning to introduce several new products in the coming years and is afraid that by keeping the name SnapTracker Corporation, they'll be thought of as a one-product company. Among other things at this employee meeting, they're planning to announce the new corporate name, FotoFriendly, Inc. Of course, no one bothered to tell you this until after you finished creating most of the presentation. Now you have to find all references to the SnapTracker Corporation and change them to FotoFriendly, Inc. (being careful, of course, not to change the name of the product, which remains SnapTracker).

First, you'll replace all instances of SnapTracker Corporation with FotoFriendly, Inc. Then you'll make sure all corporate references got changed, including those that don't include the word "Corporation."

❶ Open the Edit menu.

❷ Select Replace. The Replace dialog box appears.

Finding and replacing text globally

3 In the Find What text box, type the following: **SnapTracker Corporation.**

4 In the Replace With text box, type the following: **FotoFriendly, Inc.**

5 Click Replace All.

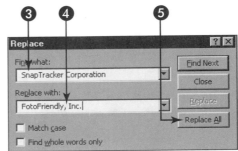

NOTE

If Office Assistant is installed, it will tell you how many replacements were made. If Office Assistant is not installed or is turned off, then a Microsoft PowerPoint 97 message box appears to tell you how many changes were made. In any event, in this case the number is two (one in the footer on the Slide Master and one on Slide #1).

6 Click OK in the message box that tells you how many changes were made.

7 In the Find What box, type the following: **SnapTracker**

8 Click Find Next. The first SnapTracker found refers to the product, and since you're not changing the product name, click Find Next again.

NOTE

You must be really careful in these next few steps because you don't want to accidentally change the product name — just references to the corporate name. That's why you can't just click Replace All.

9 Keep clicking Find Next until you come to the Pricing slide. So far, all references have been to the product, so you haven't had to make any change.

10 From the Pricing slide, click Find Next one more time. This time the search turns up an instance on the Agenda slide's Notes page where SnapTracker refers to the company name.

11 Click Replace. You now see another instance of SnapTracker that needs to be changed.

⑫ Click Replace again. The search automatically advances until it finds the next SnapTracker (in the header on the Notes Master), which is a reference to the company, not the product.

⑬ Click Replace. This time PowerPoint can't find any more instances of SnapTracker and tells you so.

⑭ Click OK in the message box (the one telling you that PowerPoint can't find any more items to change).

⑮ Click Close in the Replace dialog box.

⑯ Save, but do not close, the presentation.

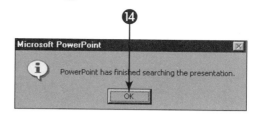

Using AutoCorrect

There is absolutely nothing more embarrassing than putting up a slide with a misspelled word (well, addressing your audience while wearing a big red clown nose might come close). Fortunately, there is also nothing easier to avoid (you're on your own with regard to the big red clown nose). PowerPoint 97 turns on the AutoCorrect feature by default when you install the program. You've probably already noticed that it corrects minor spelling errors and underlines with a squiggly line any words it doesn't recognize (like SnapTracker or FotoFriendly). By default, it is also set to correct your typing when you type two capital letters next to each other, ensure that the first word of a sentence starts with a capital letter, and see that each day of the week starts with a capital letter. It also corrects your typing if you accidentally misuse the Caps Lock key. If you don't like the way AutoCorrect works, you can turn it off or just correct its correction.

In this exercise, you'll turn AutoCorrect on and off and add a word to the AutoCorrect dictionary. You should still be on the Notes Master (if you're not, then select View ➢ Master ➢ Notes Master).

❶ Open the Tools menu.

❷ Select AutoCorrect. The AutoCorrect dialog box appears.

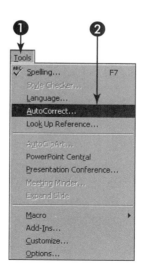

Using AutoCorrect

3 Click the Replace Text As You Type box to turn AutoCorrect off. It will still do all the other corrections that are marked (for instance, it will still correct two initial caps, capitalize the first word of a sentence, capitalize the days of the week, and correct the accidental use of the Caps Lock key).

TIP *If you were to click OK now, you'd leave AutoCorrect turned off. Since even the best typist or speller sometimes makes mistakes, it's a good idea to leave AutoCorrect turned on.*

4 Click the Replace Text As You Type box again to restore the check mark and turn it back on.

5 In the Replace box type the following: **snaptracker.**

6 In the With box type the following: **SnapTracker.**

7 Click Add.

8 Click OK to close the AutoCorrect dialog box.

9 Save your changes (File ➤ Save or click the little disk icon in the Standard toolbar).

10 Open the Tools menu.

11 Select Spelling. The Spelling dialog box appears.

12 Click Add to add FotoFriendly to PowerPoint 97's dictionary. From now on, when you type the company name, you won't see that squiggly line questioning its spelling.

13 The spell-checker next finds "Nosmo," which it doesn't recognize. Since this is not a "normal" word, you don't want to add it to your dictionary. Click Ignore.

14 The spell-checker automatically jumps to the next word it doesn't recognize: "cryin'." Since this is also not a normal word, you don't want to add it to your dictionary. Click Ignore.

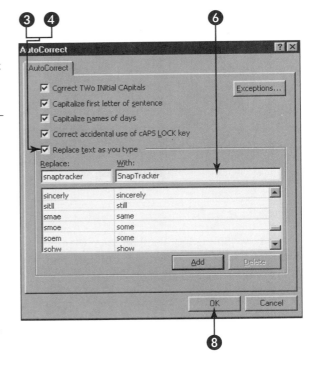

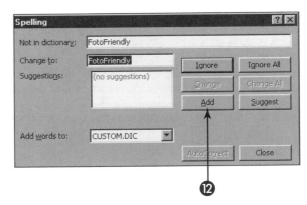

⑮ Next the spell-checker finds "SnapTrackers." Click Add again.

⑯ Next it finds "SnapTracker" (notice there's no "s" ending on this one), so click Add again.

⑰ Finish spell-checking the file.

⑱ Save and close the presentation.

Working with objects

Okay. You know what text is, but what is an object? Believe it or not, you've already worked with two kinds of objects! An object is any element of your presentation. It can be clip art or shapes you draw; it can be a chart or a graph; it can be a picture you import from another application; it can even be text.

You already know how to select and deselect objects and resize, move, and align them. In the following exercises, you'll learn how to add text to an object; change an object's color; connect, rotate, and flip objects; and group or ungroup them.

Adding text to an object

In this exercise, you'll be adding text to objects in the Diabetes presentation.

❶ Select File ➢ Open. The Open dialog box appears.

❷ Navigate to where you installed the practice presentations that came with this book.

❸ Double-click Diabetes97.ppt, as shown on the illustration to the right.

❹ Switch to Slide view if it doesn't come up in that view.

❺ Scroll to the last slide (#5). It should have a crude drawing of a syringe on it.

❻ Click anywhere in the long, skinny rectangle.

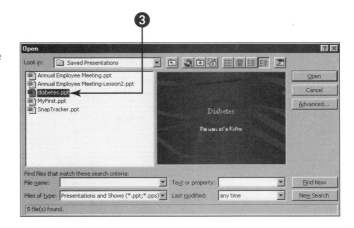

2

Working with a Presentation

7 Type the following: **Syringe**, as shown in the illustration to the right.

8 Click the Arrow button on the Drawing toolbar. The cursor turns into a big plus sign.

9 Drag the arrow line so that it points to the plunger.

NOTE *The pointy part of the arrow line will always be at the end opposite where you start. In other words, position the big plus sign cursor where you want the arrow line to begin, not where you want the arrowhead to be.*

10 Click once to deselect the arrow.

11 Click the Text Box button on the Drawing toolbar. The cursor turns into a down-pointing arrow, as shown.

12 Click at the non-pointy end of the arrow you placed on the slide in step 9 to open a text box.

13 Type the following in the box: **Plunger.**

14 Select the text you just typed.

15 Change its font size to 16 (Format ➤ Font ➤ 16).

16 Click anywhere to see how this looks. It should look something like the illustration to the right.

TIP *If you need to move the word or arrow so your slide looks like the illustration, just move the cursor over the text or arrow until the cursor turns into a four-way arrow and then drag the object.*

17 Save, but do not close, the presentation.

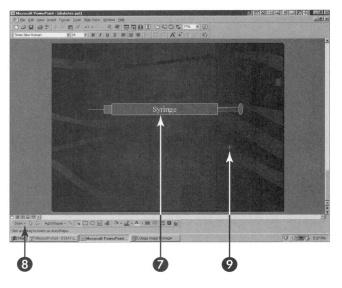

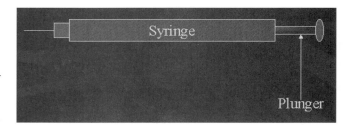

Changing the color of an object

Changing the color of an object

In this exercise, you will change the color pattern in the body of the syringe.

1 Click to select the part of the syringe drawing that contains the word "Syringe."

2 On the Drawing toolbar, click the down arrow of the Fill Color button, as shown in the illustration to the right.

3 Select Fill Effects. The Fill Effects dialog box appears.

4 On the Pattern tab, click "Large Confetti" (fourth from the right on the bottom row).

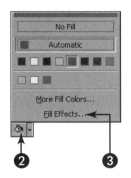

NOTE *Notice that when you click a pattern, its name appears under the patterns and a sample is displayed in the Sample box.*

5 Click OK.

6 Save, but do not close, the presentation.

2

Working with a Presentation

VISUAL BONUS

THE DRAWING TOOLBAR

In the next several exercises you'll be using the tools on the Drawing toolbar. There are a lot of them, so why not take a stroll through this Visual Bonus to become acquainted with them.

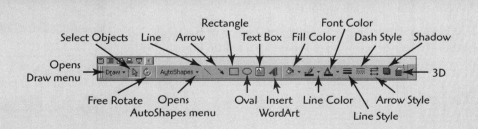

Connect, rotate, and flip objects

▶ Connect, rotate, and flip objects

In this exercise you will first add a bottle of insulin to the slide and then connect it to the syringe. You'll also tilt the insulin bottle slightly.

① Click the down arrow on the AutoShapes button on the Drawing toolbar, as shown in the illustration to the right.

② Point to Basic Shapes.

③ Click the can shape (immediately above the happy face). The cursor turns into a big plus sign.

④ Click in the middle of the syringe, but just beneath it. When you click, you drop the can shape into place, as shown in the illustration to the right.

⑤ Click on the diamond handle in the new can and drag it up just a bit to reduce the size of the top.

⑥ Click on the handle in the middle of the right side and drag it to the left to make the can a bit narrower (so it looks more like an insulin bottle).

⑦ Click the down arrow of the AutoShapes button and then point to Connectors.

⑧ Choose the Curved Arrow Connector (middle of bottom row). The cursor turns into a big plus sign.

⑨ Position the cursor near the middle of the top of the insulin bottle. The cursor turns into a square with a little box on each of its four sides.

⑩ Drag it to point at the syringe.

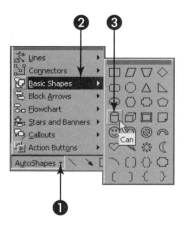

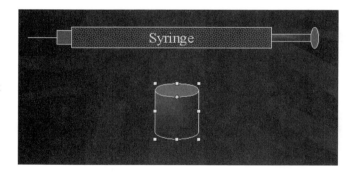

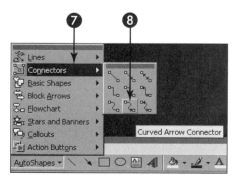

⑪ Click anywhere to deselect and see how the curved arrow connector connects the insulin bottle to the syringe, as shown in the illustration to the right.

Remember, you can always click the arrow to show its handles and then drag it where you want it.

⑫ Select the insulin bottle again.

⑬ Click the Free Rotate button on the Drawing toolbar. The cursor turns into a curved rotate symbol.

⑭ Center the cursor over the upper-right circle handle.

⑮ Drag it to the right slightly to tilt the insulin bottle, as shown in the illustration to the right.

⑯ Double-click outside the insulin bottle to deselect it and admire your work.

⑰ Select the insulin bottle again.

⑱ Click the down arrow of the Draw button on the Drawing toolbar.

⑲ Click Rotate or Flip.

⑳ Pick Flip Vertical. This turns the insulin bottle upside down, as shown in the illustration to the right.

㉑ Deselect the insulin bottle.

㉒ Save, but do not close, the presentation.

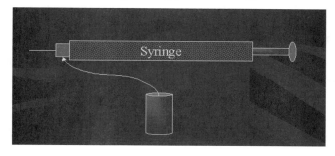

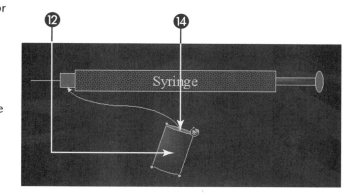

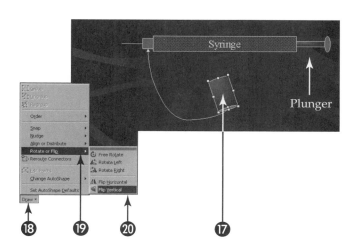

2

Working with a Presentation

Grouping and ungrouping objects

▶ Grouping and ungrouping objects

In this exercise you'll group all the objects on a slide, reposition them, and then ungroup them.

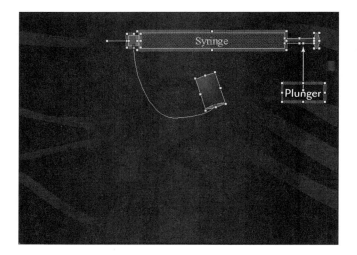

1. Still on Slide #5 of the Diabetes presentation, open the Edit menu.

2. Choose Select All. Handles appear on all objects on the slide.

3. Position the cursor inside any of the selected objects so that it turns into the four-way arrow.

4. Drag the entire slide contents up and to the right just a tad so that it looks like the illustration to the right.

5. Click anywhere outside the selected objects to deselect them.

6. Save and close the presentation.

SKILLS CHALLENGE

In this Skills Challenge you're going to fix some problems and polish up the two presentations: Annual Employee Meeting and Diabetes. First, you'll fix a number of problems with the New Corporate Logo slide in the Annual Employee Meeting presentation, and then you'll fix some of the problems that occurred as a result of the corporate name change.

Next you'll move to the Diabetes presentation where you'll add some callouts and some pizzaz, change colors, insert text, and add a shadow.

Do you remember how to add a new slide to a presentation in Slide view?

❶ Open the Annual Employee Meeting presentation in Slide view.

❷ Scroll to the New Corporate Logo slide.

 Do you remember how to change text case?

❸ Change "cut" to "cute" in the first bullet.

3 *Do you remember how to change font sizes?*

❹ Return "picked" to its proper place in the second bullet (it should read *We picked this happy family*).

4 *Do you remember how to delete text from a slide?*

❺ Nudge the entire bullet-text box to the left two or three times.

 Do you remember how to adjust line spacing?

❻ In the Notes Page for Slide #2, delete both instances of "Inc." (remember to delete the preceding comma, too). When you delete the second "Inc." be careful not to also delete the apostrophe+S. You want it to read "FotoFriendly's" when you're done, as shown in the illustration to the right.

6 *Do you remember how to move a slide from one position in the presentation to another?*

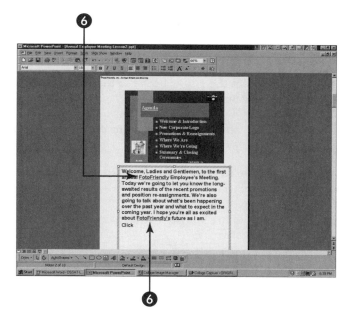

2

Working with a Presentation

Skills challenge

7 Add **fotofriendly** to the AutoCorrect list (replacing it with **FotoFriendly**).

 7 *Do you remember how to move a text box on a slide?*

8 Save and close the Annual Employee Meeting presentation.

 8 *Do you remember how to find and replace text globally?*

9 Open the Diabetes presentation in Slide view.

10 Scroll to the last slide.

 9 *Do you remember how to automatically correct what you type as you type it?*

11 Add a callout (Times New Roman, 16) identifying the needle as a needle.

 10 *Do you remember how to add a word to the AutoCorrect list?*

12 Flip and rotate the insulin bottle so that it looks like the one in the previous illustration.

 11 *Do you remember how to check the spelling in your presentation?*

13 Add the word **Insulin** (Times New Roman, 14) to the interior of the insulin bottle.

 12 *Do you remember how to change the color of an object?*

7

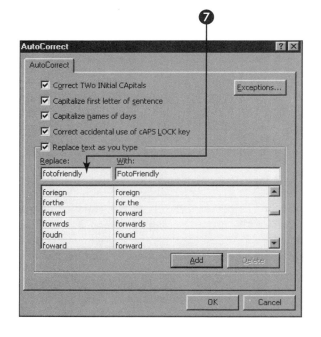

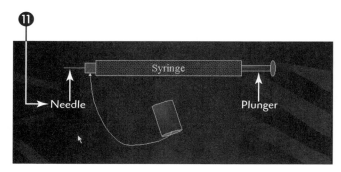

⑭ Assign Shadow Style 8 to the insulin bottle.

⑬ *Do you remember how to connect two objects?*

⑮ Use AutoShape to add a starburst (Explosion 1 from Stars and Banners) at the point of the syringe so that it looks like the one in the illustration to the right.

⑭ *Do you remember how to rotate an object?*

⑯ Make the starburst yellow.

⑮ *Do you remember how to flip objects?*

⑰ Save and close the Diabetes presentation.

⑯ *Do you remember how to group and ungroup objects?*

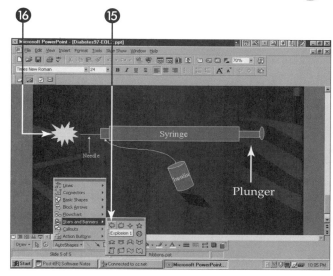

TROUBLESHOOTING

You covered a lot of territory in this lesson. Bet you've got some questions yourself. The following table may help.

Problem	Solution
I inserted a new slide in the wrong place. What do I do?	Switch to Outline view and use the Move Up or Move Down buttons to reposition the slide.
My bullets are too close together.	Insert a blank bullet *or* use the Format ➢ Line Spacing command to set the distance.
My text is too far apart (or packed too tightly).	Use the Format ➢ Line Spacing command to define the Line Spacing, Before Paragraph or After Paragraph.

Working with a Presentation

2

Wrap up

Problem	Solution
How do I stop a spell-check in progress?	Click Cancel or the × box.
My computer seems to be running more slowly than usual.	Sometimes the AutoCorrect function will slow older, slower-running computers. Try turning this feature off and see if that helps.
I selected the wrong object.	Click Esc or click somewhere else.
Drawing toolbar? What Drawing toolbar?	If you don't have the Drawing toolbar displayed, select View ➢ Toolbars ➢ Drawing.
I only want to select two or three objects — not all of them	Click the first object, then hold down the Shift key and simultaneously click whatever other objects you want to select. When you're done, click outside the objects to deselect them all at once.

WRAP UP

Tuckered out? Deservedly so! Before you run off for a full body massage, how about a quick review of what you've learned (and it's a lot!). In this lesson, you learned how to

- Add text to a slide
- Change text case
- Format text
- Delete text
- Adjust spacing
- Move text or slides in Outline view
- Position text on a slide
- Find and replace text globally

Wrap up

- Use AutoCorrect and the spell-checker
- Add text to an object
- Change the color of an object
- Connect, rotate, or flip objects
- Group and ungroup objects

In the next lesson you'll learn to work with special effects such as color schemes, backgrounds, embossed text, WordArt, and 3-D.

PART II

Dressing Up Presentations

This part shows you how to use the numerous special effects available in PowerPoint 97. It includes the following lessons:

Lesson 3: Adding Special Effects

Lesson 4: Advanced Special Effects and Hyperlinks

Adding Special Effects

50 MINUTES

GOALS

In Lesson 3 you get to start doing the really cool stuff — adding special effects. When you're through with this lesson, you should be an expert in the following skills:

- Working with color schemes
- Working with backgrounds (for example, gradient, texture, pattern, picture)
- Working with embossed text
- Working with WordArt
- Working with 3-D

Using a template's color scheme

GET READY

To complete this lesson, you still need to have PowerPoint 97 installed (big surprise) and ready to roll. You'll also need to copy the following files from the Lesson 3 folder on the CD-ROM to your hard drive: AEM-EOL2.ppt and Camera.wmf.

WORKING WITH COLOR SCHEMES

A color scheme is a set of eight coordinated colors. Each PowerPoint design template comes with its own unique color scheme as well as the tools for you to modify color schemes or even create your own.

PowerPoint design templates and their related color schemes were professionally created with visual effectiveness in mind. They take into consideration such things as the common occurrence of color blindness and avoid putting together colors that might be difficult to see for someone afflicted with this problem. They also employ basic color design techniques to avoid putting clashing or noncomplementary colors together. While you should feel free to modify or create color schemes to your heart's content, keep in mind that the main reason you're creating a presentation in the first place is to communicate some point. If you overwhelm your audience with clashing colors or underwhelm them with washed-out colors that allow for too little contrast, you will fail to make your point. Worse yet, if your presentation is hard on the eyes, you risk alienating your audience.

In the following exercises, you'll learn how to use the various color schemes that come with a design template as well as how to create your own custom color scheme.

Using a design template's default color scheme

Your boss peeked over your shoulder recently and saw the pukey green that was the dominant color in your presentation. Because your boss is an alum of UCLA, whose colors are blue and gold, and because in addition to a corporate name change, he's also planning to convert the company colors to his alma mater's colors, he's asked you to adjust the presentation accordingly. This is, of course, an excellent decision on his part.

Creating a custom color scheme

1 Start PowerPoint 97 and open AEM-EOL2.ppt in Slide Sorter view.

2 Open the Format menu, as shown in the illustration to the right.

3 Select Slide Color Scheme. The Color Scheme dialog box appears. The current color scheme is identified on the far left of the Standard tab.

NOTE *A slide must be selected in order for this to work.*

4 Double-click the middle choice to see how it would look on your entire presentation. It's actually not too far off from what your boss wants, but it's too wishy-washy, and the colors just aren't right.

TIP *Double-clicking, in this case, accomplishes the same thing as single-clicking the middle choice and then clicking Apply to All. If you want to see how the new color scheme will affect just one slide, or if for some reason you want to change just one slide, then single-click the middle choice and click Apply. The change will apply only to whatever slide is currently selected.*

5 Save, but do not close, the presentation.

Creating a custom color scheme

The secondary default color scheme that you selected in the previous exercise does use a powder blue, but there's no gold and the colors don't provide enough contrast to achieve any impact. In this exercise, you'll modify this scheme to create your own unique color scheme, and then you'll save it for future use.

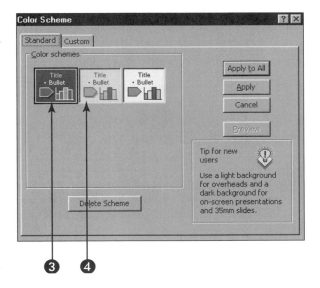

Creating a custom color scheme

① With the presentation open in Slide Sorter view and the bluish color scheme selected, click Format ➤ Slide Color Scheme. The Color Scheme dialog box appears again.

② Click the Custom tab, as shown in the illustration to the right.

③ Select Shadows.

④ Click Change Color. The Shadow Color custom spectrum appears, as shown in the illustration to the right.

⑤ Position the color selector and slide arrow so that they resemble the illustration (*if you can't figure out the illustration, just use the following settings and you'll get the right powder blue:* Hue = 143; Sat = 205; Lum = 183; Red = 125; Green = 200; Blue = 241).

⑥ Click OK. The Color Scheme dialog box reappears, still on the Custom tab.

⑦ Click Apply to All. This changes the blue background to make it a better powder blue on all slides in the presentation.

⑧ Select Format ➤ Slide Color Scheme again.

⑨ On the Color Scheme dialog box's Custom tab, click Text and Lines.

⑩ Click Change Color. The Text and Line Color dialog box opens to the Standard tab (*if it doesn't, then select the Standard tab*).

TIP *An even quicker way to get to the color dialog boxes is to double-click the Scheme Color box you want to change. For example, double-click Text and Lines.*

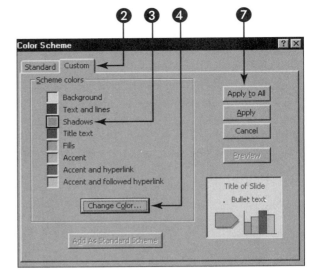

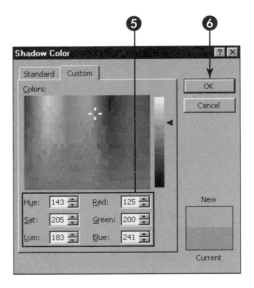

⓫ On the Standard tab of the Text and Line Color dialog box, select total black, as shown in the illustration to the right.

⓬ Click OK.

⓭ Click Apply to All in the Color Scheme dialog box.

⓮ Select Format ➢ Slide Color Scheme again.

⓯ On the Custom tab of the Color Scheme dialog box, double-click Accent.

⓰ On the Accent Color dialog box's Standard tab, select the center blue on the top row of blues, as shown in the illustration to the right.

⓱ Click OK.

⓲ Click Apply to All in the Color Scheme dialog box.

NOTE *Be sure to check the Slide Sorter results each time you click Apply to All.*

⓳ Select Format ➢ Slide Color Scheme yet again.

⓴ On the Color Scheme dialog box Custom tab, double-click Accent and Hyperlink.

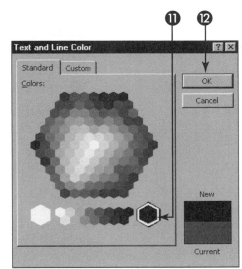

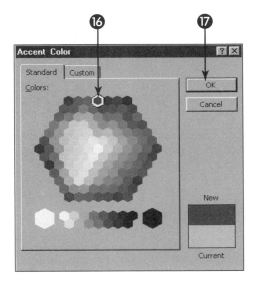

Adding a new color scheme

㉑ On the Accent and Hyperlink Color dialog box's Standard tab, select the center blue in the third row of blues, as shown on the illustration to the right.

㉒ Click OK.

㉓ Click Apply to All in the Color Scheme dialog box.

㉔ Select Format ➤ Slide Color Scheme one last time.

㉕ On the Color Scheme dialog box's Custom tab, click Accent and Followed Hyperlink.

㉖ Click Change Color.

㉗ On the Accent and Hyperlink Color dialog box's standard tab, select the fourth color (from the left) in the third row up from the bottom, as shown in the illustration to the right.

㉘ Click OK.

㉙ Click Apply to All.

㉚ Save, but do not close, the presentation.

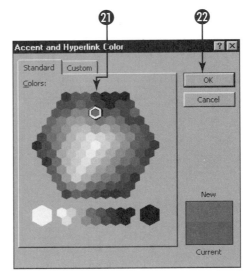

Adding a new color scheme to the standard list

Now that you've created this new color scheme, you should save it so that if your boss comes to you again and asks for a presentation using the new company colors, you don't have to try to figure out what you did. By saving it, you make it instantly available from now on.

❶ With the Annual Employee Meeting presentation still open in Slide Sorter view and now reflecting the blue and gold theme, select Format ➤ Slide Color Scheme one more time.

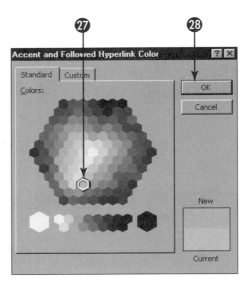

② On the Custom tab of the Color Scheme dialog box, click Add As Standard Scheme, as shown in the illustration to the right.

③ Click Apply to All. The next time you open the Slide Color Scheme dialog box, you will have four color schemes to choose from, including the blue and gold theme you just created. Go ahead and try it.

TIP

You can just as easily delete a color scheme. Say your boss's son decides to go to some other (inferior, of course) college and your boss wants to use those school colors and never see UCLA's colors again. You can delete the blue and gold color scheme by selecting it on the Standard tab and then clicking Delete Scheme. Quite frankly, however, I cannot imagine your ever wanting to do such a thing.

④ Save and close the presentation.

Applying a color scheme to a presentation

Your boss is so taken with your work so far and he loves the new blue and gold theme so much that now he wants you to interrupt your work on the Annual Employee Meeting presentation and apply this new color scheme to the SnapTracker presentation.

① Select File ➤ Open.

② Navigate to where you stored the practice presentations.

③ Open SnapTracker.ppt in Slide Sorter view, as shown in the illustration to the right.

④ Leave SnapTracker.ppt open and reopen the Annual Employee Meeting presentation in Slide Sorter view.

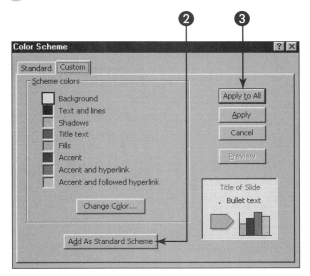

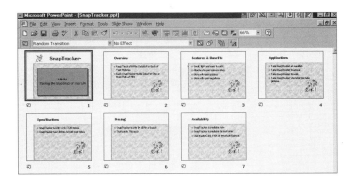

3

Adding Special Effects

Applying a color scheme

⑤ Select Window ➤ Arrange All. Both presentations appear simultaneously on your screen, as shown in the illustration to the right.

⑥ Select Slide #1 in the Annual Employee Meeting presentation.

NOTE

You don't really have to select Slide #1. You may select any slide, but you must select a slide.

⑦ Click the Format Painter button on the Standard toolbar. The cursor changes into a smaller version of the Format Painter icon invisibly attached to an arrow, as shown in the illustration to the right.

⑧ Move the Format Painter cursor into the portion of the screen that contains the SnapTracker presentation.

⑨ Click once anywhere in the white area (*not* on a slide) to transfer the active status to the window containing the SnapTracker presentation. No slides will be modified yet, and the Format Painter cursor remains.

⑩ Using the Format Painter cursor, open the Edit menu.

⑪ Choose Select All. All slides in the SnapTracker presentation should be selected.

⑫ Click the Format Painter cursor in any SnapTracker slide. The Format Painter cursor remains.

⑬ Press Esc to return to the normal cursor.

⑭ Because your boss stood hovering over your shoulder while you did this, he sees immediately that the newly formatted SnapTracker presentation doesn't really look very good using this color scheme and he doesn't want you to waste a lot of time fixing it, so just open the Edit menu.

⑮ Select Undo Apply Color Scheme.

⑯ Close, but do not save, the SnapTracker file.

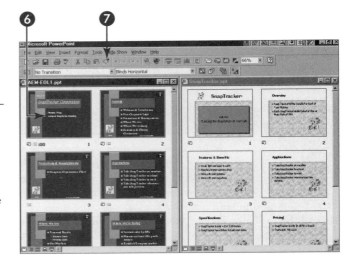

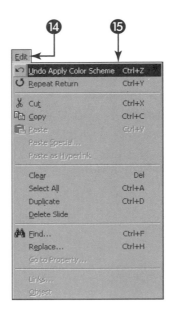

Choosing a preset gradient background ◀

TIP

You can also just close the SnapTracker file and when it asks if you want to save your changes, tell it no.

WORKING WITH BACKGROUNDS

You can change a slide's background so that it is not just plain, as yours is now. The background can consist of one or two colors, and you can choose them yourself or select one of the professionally designed backgrounds.

In addition, you can choose from among six shading styles for your background: horizontal, vertical, diagonal up, diagonal down, from corner, and from title.

You may also opt to make your background textured (there are 18 choices or you can import your own) or patterned (there are 48 patterns, but when you factor in the enormous color choices, the mind boggles at the possibilities). You can even insert a picture as a background for your slides.

In the following exercises, you will experiment with backgrounds for the Annual Employee Meeting presentation.

Whatever you choose to do here, however, may significantly alter whatever you specified in the Slide Color Scheme ➢ Custom/ Background dialog box.

Choosing a preset gradient background

In this exercise you will change the background of the Annual Employee Meeting presentation to one of the preset gradient backgrounds.

❶ If you are beginning this exercise right after completing the previous exercise, then you probably have the Annual Employee Meeting presentation visible on half your screen. Click the Maximize Window box in the upper right-hand corner, as shown in the illustration to the right.

❷ The Annual Employee Meeting presentation should now be displayed in Slide Sorter view. Click Slide #1 (it doesn't really matter which slide you select, but you must select a slide).

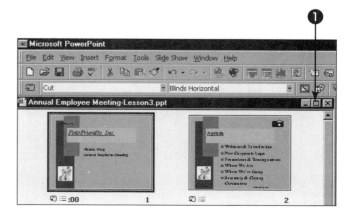

3 Select Format ➤ Background. The Background dialog box appears.

4 Click the down arrow to see the background fill options.

5 Click Fill Effects to open the Fill Effects dialog box, as shown in the illustration to the lower right.

6 Click Preset in the Colors section.

 NOTE *The Preset Colors option is visible only when you select Preset Colors from the Colors section. If you select One Color from the Colors section, then instead of Preset Colors, you'll see Col 1, from which you can select the desired color. If you choose Two Colors in the Colors section, then in addition to the Col 1 window, you'll also see Col 2, so you can define two different colors.*

7 Click the down arrow on the Preset Colors box. The default is Early Sunset.

8 Choose Daybreak.

9 Click Diagonal Up in the Shading Style section (the default is Horizontal).

 TIP *In addition to the six Shading Styles, you can also choose from four shading Variants. Once you've selected the background you want, you can choose one of the four ways in which it is implemented. Click any square and then check the Sample box to see how it will look on a slide.*

10 Click OK. The Background dialog box reappears.

11 Click Apply to All and watch as your entire presentation switches to this new background.

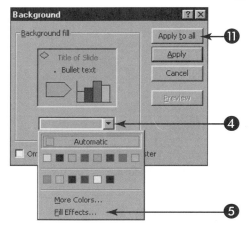

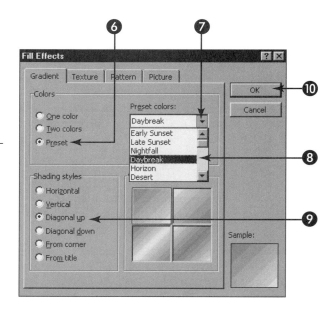

⑫ Feel free to experiment with the other preset choices and shading options, but when you're done, return to these settings for the sake of the rest of the exercises in this book.

⑬ Save, but do not close, the presentation.

Creating a one-color gradient background

Instead of choosing a preset background design, you can also create your own one-color background design.

① With the Annual Employee Meeting presentation still in Slide Sorter view and any slide selected, select Format ➤ Background.

② Click the down arrow to see the background fill options.

③ Click Fill Effects to open the Fill Effects dialog box. It should open to the Gradient tab.

④ Click One Color in the Colors section. The appearance of the Gradient tab changes, as shown in the illustration to the right.

⑤ Click to move the dark–light slide adjustment all the way to the right (light).

⑥ Click OK. The Background dialog box reappears.

⑦ Click Apply to All.

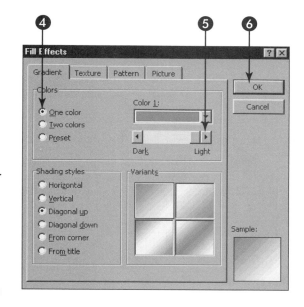

 NOTE

This change applied to the Annual Employee Meeting presentation is quite subtle. Since you should still be in Slide Sorter view, you can see how it affects all the slides. Personally, I don't think it enhances the background, so let's get rid of it.

⑧ Select Edit ➤ Undo Background.

You haven't made any changes that need to be kept, so don't bother to save the presentation. Leave it open, though, so it'll be handy for the next exercise.

3

Adding Special Effects

Creating a two-color background

Creating a two-color gradient background

Instead of choosing a preset or one-color background, you can also opt for a two-color background.

1 With the Annual Employee Meeting presentation still in Slide Sorter view and any slide selected, select Format ➤ Background.

2 Click the down arrow to see the background fill options.

3 Click Fill Effects to open the Fill Effects dialog box. It should still open to the Gradient tab.

4 Click Two Colors in the Colors section. The appearance of the Gradient tab changes, as shown in the illustration to the right.

5 Click the Color 2 down arrow.

6 Choose gold.

7 Click OK. The Background dialog box reappears.

8 Click Apply to All.

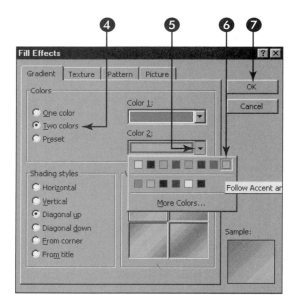

NOTE *Interesting though this is to look at, it was better before the change. As you can see, sometimes it takes a little hit-or-miss experimentation to come up with just the right color scheme.*

9 Select Edit ➤ Undo Background.

Again, since you didn't make any lasting changes, you need not save the presentation at this time. But keep it open for the next exercise.

TIP *If you want to change one of the two colors to something not in the default color scheme, you have to switch to Slide view first. If you try this in Slide Sorter view and choose More Colors, you get a message that says, "You Must Select a Shape." If you're in Slide view, when you click More Colors, you see the custom color palette as you're supposed to. Go figure.*

Choosing a pattern background ◀

Choosing a texture background

For some presentations, you'll find a textured background more appropriate (or maybe just more interesting) than the plain one you're using for the Annual Employee Meeting. In this exercise, you'll get to look at some of the possibilities.

❶ With the Annual Employee Meeting presentation still in Slide Sorter view, select Format ➤ Background.

❷ Click the down arrow to see the background fill options.

❸ Click Fill Effects to open the Fill Effects dialog box.

❹ Click the Texture tab to see the texture choices.

❺ Select the bluish texture in the lower right–hand corner (Bouquet).

❻ Click OK. The Background dialog box reappears.

❼ Click Apply to All.

❽ Select Edit ➤ Undo Background.

 NOTE

There are 18 textures to choose from. Take a few minutes to experiment with them on your own so that you'll have a more complete idea of what they look like and how they affect the slides in a presentation.

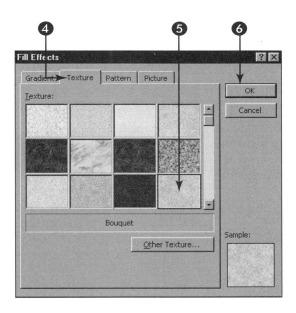

Choosing a pattern background

There are 48 different patterns to choose from, each one using up to two different colors. In this exercise, you'll be experimenting with the patterns.

❶ With the Annual Employee Meeting presentation still displayed in Slide Sorter view, select Format ➤ Background.

❷ Click the down arrow to see the background fill options.

❸ Click Fill Effects to open the Fill Effects dialog box.

3

Adding Special Effects

Using a picture for a background

④ Click the Pattern tab to see the Pattern choices, as shown in the illustration to the right.

⑤ Select the Outlined Diamond pattern (first column on the right, second one up).

 NOTE *When you position the cursor on a pattern and click once, the name of the pattern appears in the space under the pattern grid and a sample of it appears in the Sample box. These patterns will all use the color schemes you've already defined.*

⑥ Click the down arrow of the Foreground box.

⑦ Select the dark blue that is third from the right on the top row.

⑧ Click OK. The Background dialog box reappears.

⑨ Click Apply to All.

⑩ Ugh. Select Edit ➤ Undo Background.

 TIP *If you want to change either the Foreground or Background color to something not in the default color scheme, you have to switch to Slide view first. If you try this in Slide Sorter view and choose More Colors, you get a message that says "You Must Select a Shape." If you're in Slide view, when you click More Colors, you see the custom color palette as you're supposed to. Go figure.*

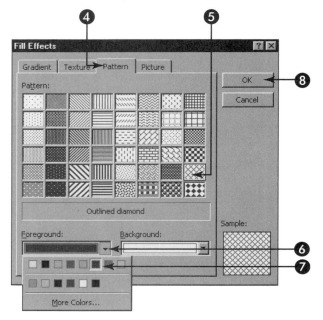

Using a picture for a background

In addition to all the colorful background choices you have, you may also choose to use a picture (such as a photograph or clip art) as your background. Although this may be an extremely tempting choice at times, remember that all text will lie on top of your picture, whatever it is. Be careful to choose a picture that will not overpower your text.

1 With the Annual Employee Meeting presentation still in Slide Sorter view, select Format ➤ Background.

2 Click the down arrow to see the background fill options.

3 Click Fill Effects to open the Fill Effects dialog box.

4 Click the Picture tab.

5 Click Select Picture. The Select Picture dialog box opens.

6 Navigate to where you installed the practice presentations and files.

7 Double-click Camera.wmf. The picture is plugged into the Fill Effects dialog box, as shown in the illustration to the right.

8 Click OK. The Background dialog box reappears.

9 Click Apply to All.

10 Now select Edit ➤ Undo Background.

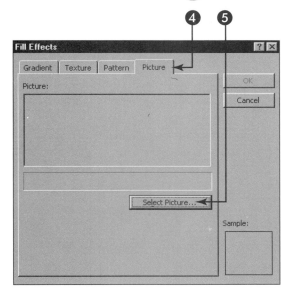

WORKING WITH EMBOSSED TEXT

Embossed text is raised text. You see it all the time on stationery and sometimes on business cards. You can feel it. Well, obviously on a slide you can't "feel" the raised text and just as obviously, the text can't actually *be* raised. But you can create the *effect* of raised text by choosing the emboss option when you format fonts. When you emboss text, it takes on the color of its background as well as the appearance of being raised.

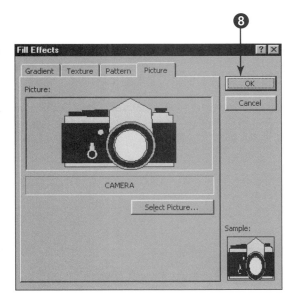

3

Adding Special Effects

Embossing text

Embossing text

In this exercise, you'll experiment with embossed text.

1. With the Annual Employee Meeting presentation still displayed in Slide Sorter view, double-click Slide #1. This switches that slide to Slide view.

2. Click on or close to your boss's name to reveal the handles on the text box.

3. Select Nosmo's whole name, as shown on the illustration to the right.

4. With Nosmo's name selected, select Format ➢ Font. The Font dialog box opens.

5. In the Effects area, click Emboss to put an check mark in its box.

6. Click OK.

7. Click anywhere outside the text box to see how it looks. Your boss's name should be blue and look slightly raised.

8. Select Edit ➢ Undo Font.

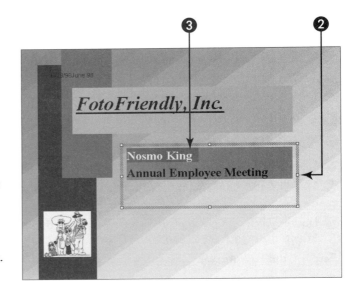

WORKING WITH WORDART

WordArt is a Microsoft tool that lets you create cool headlines and banners. You've decided that a simple "FotoFriendly, Inc." at the top of the Title slide is boring. With WordArt you can jazz it up.

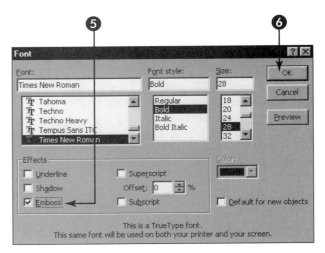

Adding WordArt to your presentation

Adding WordArt to your presentation

In this exercise, you'll convert the words "FotoFriendly, Inc." to WordArt to make a more powerful visual impact on the Title slide.

1 With Slide #1 still displayed in Slide view, switch to Title Master (View ➢ Master ➢ Title Masters).

2 Click just to the left of the first *C* in "Click."

3 Select all the text in that box (Click to Edit Master Title Style).

4 Press Delete.

5 Delete the Title Area for AutoLayouts box, as shown on the illustration to the right.

6 Click the Insert WordArt button on the Drawing toolbar. The WordArt Gallery automatically opens.

7 Double-click the second style from the right in the second row from the top, as shown in the illustration to the right.

8 On the Edit WordArt Text dialog box, type **FotoFriendly, Inc**.

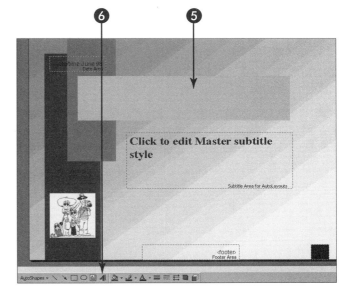

The default font on my computer is Impact, 36. If your computer does not have the Impact font, it will default to something else. Don't worry about it.

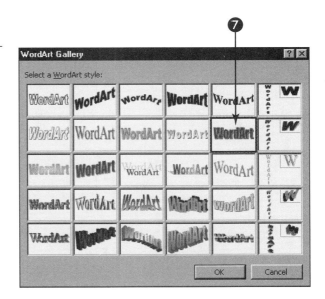

Adding 3-D effects

9 Click OK. The FotoFriendly, Inc., text box drops smack into the middle of your slide.

10 Position the cursor anywhere over the word "FotoFriendly," until the cursor turns into a four-way arrow.

11 Drag the word up to the Title Area for AutoLayouts.

12 Reposition the WordArt so that it looks similar to the illustration on the right.

13 Click anywhere in the light blue background to deselect the FotoFriendly box.

14 Save, but do not close, the presentation.

WORKING WITH 3-D EFFECTS

Making objects look three-dimensional can add real impact to your presentation. You can use shadows or 3-D effects to achieve similar results. For example, if you want to add dimension to the camera in the upper right-hand corner of the Annual Employee Meeting slides, you can use shadows but not 3-D effects. You can use 3-D effects only with objects you create, including text.

Adding 3-D effects

In this exercise, you'll further enhance the appearance of the words "FotoFriendly, Inc." on the Title slide, giving them a 3-D effect.

1 Select the new FotoFriendly, Inc., text you created in the previous exercise.

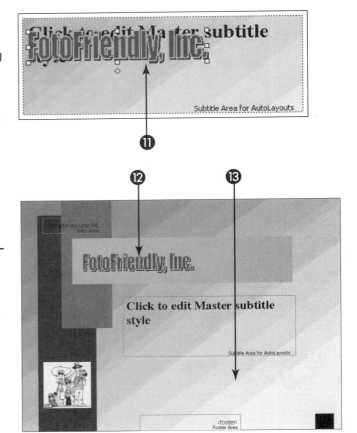

2 With the text selected, click the 3-D button on the Drawing toolbar, as shown in the illustration to the right.

3 Choose 3-D Style 8 (far right, second row from the top). This turns the phrase "FotoFriendly, Inc." slightly to the right and gives it more depth.

4 With the FotoFriendly, Inc., text still selected, click the 3-D button on the Drawing toolbar again.

5 Click 3-D Settings (at the bottom of the 3-D styles). The styles disappear, replaced by a 3-D toolbar.

6 On the 3-D toolbar, click the Lighting icon.

7 Click the center lighting option as shown on the illustration to the right.

8 Click the down arrow on the 3-D Color icon on the 3-D toolbar, as shown on the illustration to the right.

9 Select black from the 3-D palette, as shown on the illustration to the right. This turns the shadow behind the words "FotoFriendly, Inc." to black.

10 Click the × on the 3-D toolbar to close it.

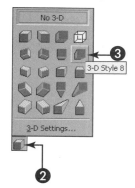

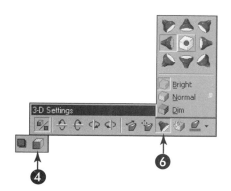

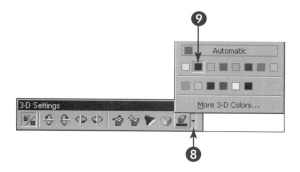

Skills challenge

The 3-D Toolbar

The 3-D toolbar includes several command buttons. To grow better acquainted with it before you embark on the next exercise, take a look at this Visual Bonus.

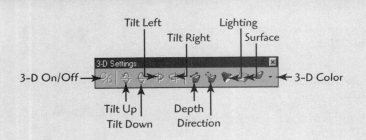

① Click anywhere to deselect the words "FotoFriendly, Inc." and observe the change, as shown on the illustration to the right.

⑫ Save and close the presentation.

SKILLS CHALLENGE

In this Skills Challenge you're going to dress up the presentation a little more. You'll change the bullets to gold, get rid of that useless blank slide, emboss the footer, change the background, and change the text color to dark blue.

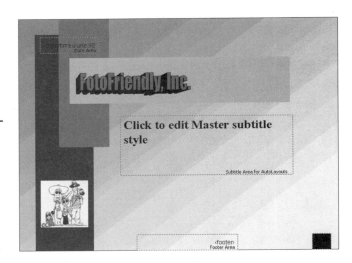

⭐**1** *Do you remember what a color scheme is?*

⭐**2** *Do you remember how to choose a different color scheme for your presentation?*

 Open the Annual Employee Meeting presentation with Slide #1 in Slide view.

 Click once to select the box containing "FotoFriendly, Inc."

3 Press Delete to remove the text box.

4 Change all bullets to the same gold you used in Accent and Followed Hyperlink (hint: bullets = Title Text).

 Do you remember how to apply a different color scheme to just one or two slides?

 Do you remember how to create your own color scheme?

5 Delete the blank slide (it should be Slide #4).

 Do you remember how to save a custom color scheme?

 Do you remember how to apply one presentation's color scheme to another presentation's slides?

6 Emboss the footer "FotoFriendly, Inc." in the Slide Master.

 Do you remember how to choose a preset gradient background?

 Do you remember how to create a one-color background?

7 Apply the Blue Tissue Paper background texture to all slides (hint: think Textures).

 Do you remember how to create a two-color background?

Do you remember how to select a pattern background?

3

Adding Special Effects

Troubleshooting

8 Make all Text and Lines dark blue (choose the far right end of the top line on the Text and Lines Color Standard dialog box).

 Do you remember how to use a picture for a background?

 Do you remember how to add WordArt to a slide?

9 Change the Date and Time to gold on all title slides.

 Do you remember how to give an object 3-D characteristics?

10 Save and close the presentation.

TROUBLESHOOTING

In this lesson you learned how to add some keen special effects to your presentation, but you may also have some questions. The following troubleshooting table may answer some of them.

Problem	Solution
I accidentally applied a color scheme to the entire presentation when I only meant to apply it to one slide.	If you realize your mistake immediately after committing it, just click Edit ➤ Undo. If it's too late for that, then select the original color scheme and Apply to All.
I copied the color scheme from one presentation into another, but the "other colors" didn't come with it.	That's right. And they won't. When you copy color schemes from one presentation to another, the "other colors" are not included.
I can't find Format ➤ AutoShape.	Format ➤ AutoShape is only available when you right-click an object *you* created. If you right-click clip art or an imported photograph, you'll get Format ➤ Picture instead.

Problem	**Solution**
I was minding my own business, switching between Outline view and Slide view, when all of a sudden PowerPoint stopped responding.	This means you are a very special person. This problem only occurs in PowerPoint 97 Version 7.0a and there aren't too many of those out. It was corrected in Version 7.0b. If you have Version 7.0a, you should upgrade to 7.0b, *or*, if you have access to the Internet, you can download a patch from the Microsoft Knowledge Base (see article ID Q136603, "Patch to Correct PowerPoint 7.0a Screen Redraw Problem").
Why can't I freehand draw something on top of clip art or a photograph?	You can. Click AutoShapes ➢ Lines and choose the Scribble option (far right, second row).
I tried to insert a slide from a PowerPoint 4.0 presentation into my PowerPoint 97 presentation, and I got a message telling me there were too many colors.	Here's why: PowerPoint stores all color information in 24–bit color definitions. This is fine so long as you display colors using the same 24–bit display driver. However, if you're using a 256–color display driver, then PowerPoint automatically uses its internal Palette Manager. When you run a slide using a color depth of 256 colors or more *and* it also contains graphics and gradients, you overwhelm the driver and will probably experience color loss; you may not even see an error message.

You can remedy this situation by changing the number of colors you want your monitor to display (provided your monitor supports this). For additional help, click the Windows 95 Start button ➢ Help and search under "Color, changing the number of." |

3

Adding Special Effects

Wrap up

WRAP UP

Let's sit a minute and review what you've learned. You learned
how to

- Use a design template's alternate default color scheme
- Create a custom color scheme
- Add a new color scheme to the standard list
- Apply the color scheme from one presentation to another
  presentation
- Choose a preset gradient background
- Create a one- or two-color gradient background
- Create a textured or patterned background
- Create a background from a picture
- Emboss text
- Work with WordArt
- Add 3-D effects

  Whew. Take five.

Advanced Special Effects and Hyperlinks

GOALS

In Lesson 4 you get to keep doing the really cool stuff — adding more cool special effects. When you're through with this lesson, you should be an expert in the following skills:

- Creating slide transitions
- Adding animation and sound effects
- Including action settings
- Hiding and unhiding slides
- Creating hyperlinks

Transitions, animation, and sound

To complete this lesson, you still need to have PowerPoint 97 installed and running. In addition, you'll need to copy the following files from the Lesson 4 folder on the CD-ROM to your hard drive: AEM–EOL3.ppt; SnapTracker.ppt; Diabetes97–EOL2.ppt; Snap-Fin.ppt. When you're finished with this chapter, your presentation files should be like the ones in AEM-EOL4.ppt, Diabetes97–EOL4.ppt, and SnapFin–EOL4.ppt.

SLIDE TRANSITIONS, ANIMATION, AND SOUND EFFECTS

Slide transitions are the effects that take place while the slide show moves from one slide to the next. In prehistoric days when Early Man had only a broken-down slide projector at his disposal, the clicking sound of the slide carousel was the only slide transition known (with the possible exceptions of the infamous burned-out-bulb transition and the melting-slide transition). For those diehards among you, PowerPoint 97 includes the sound of a clicking slide projector (as you'll see, or rather, hear, in a minute) in its arsenal of slide transitions, as well as many other, much cooler, effects.

In these modern days of computers, however, slide transitions are not limited to mere sounds. No, with PowerPoint97 you can enjoy visual transitions as well. In the following exercises, you'll be adding all kinds of transitions to the Annual Employee Meeting presentation.

Before you plunge headlong into the world of special effects, remember not to get caught up in the wonders of what you *can* do and forget about what you *should* do. I hate to be a nag, but you must keep in mind that your primary objective in creating any presentation is to inform your audience (and maybe entertain them a bit), not to knock them off their seats in amazement at the things *you* can do. Be prudent.

Exploring slide transitions

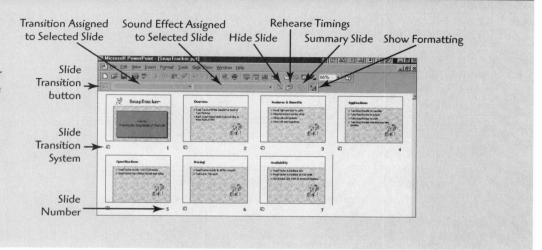

Slide Sorter View/Slide Transition Toolbar

The next several exercises will require you to be familiar with the buttons on the Slide Transition toolbar, which is part of Slide Sorter view. Use this Visual Bonus as a map to guide you through slide transitions.

Transition Assigned to Selected Slide
Sound Effect Assigned to Selected Slide
Hide Slide
Rehearse Timings
Summary Slide
Show Formatting

Slide Transition button
Slide Transition System
Slide Number

Exploring slide transitions

You're about to take a stroll down memory lane and review the SnapTracker.ppt presentation. It's fraught with different slide transitions and sounds.

1. Start PowerPoint 97 (if it isn't already started).
2. Open the SnapTracker.ppt presentation in any view.
3. If your computer system is equipped with sound, make sure the volume is turned up enough for you to hear and enjoy what's coming.
4. Open the Slide Show menu.
5. Select View Show. The Slide Show automatically displays the first slide, complete with sound and transitions, as appropriate.

Advanced Special Effects and Hyperlinks

4

Exploring slide transitions

6 Click each slide to move through the presentation.

7 When the slide show finishes, switch to Slide Sorter view (if it doesn't go there automatically, which it probably will).

8 Click the Transition Symbol under Slide #1 to see its transition. Since this presentation is set up for random transitions, you can click the Transition Symbol several times and see several different visual transitions. The whoosh sound will remain constant.

TIP *You can always click the Transition Symbol under an individual slide to preview its visual and audio transition. If there is no Transition Symbol under a slide, then no transition has been applied to that slide.*

9 Close the SnapTracker presentation.

The SnapTracker presentation uses random visual transitions, so I cannot "talk" you through each one. If you run through the presentation several times, you'll see different kinds of visual transitions. The sound transitions, however, are set per slide and do not change, as shown here:

- Slide #1: Whoosh

- Slide #2: Clicking camera

- Slide #3: Breaking glass

- Slide #4: Gunshot

- Slide #5: Clicking slide projector

- Slide #6: Drumroll

- Slide #7: Ka-ching of a cash register

Advancing slides automatically

When you choose a PowerPoint-provided template to create your presentation, it may come with a set of slide transitions. You can usually modify them, but you cannot remove them entirely. If you manually assign No Transition to such a presentation, it will revert to the original transition that was built into the template.

When you create a presentation from the Blank template or when you create your own template, you can modify any transitions that you apply to the presentation.

When you assign transitions, they may be specific or random, as you saw in the SnapTracker presentation (which had both kinds). You can even opt for no transitions in presentations you create from scratch. You are limited, however, to the transitions that come with PowerPoint 97. While you cannot assign random sounds to your slide transitions, you can import other sounds from your own library.

Advancing slides automatically

The idea of clicking your mouse to advance slides just drives you nuts, doesn't it? Well, there's a way out. In this exercise, you'll learn how to automatically advance slides. In later exercises, you'll learn how to time those advances to match your script, but for now, you're just giving your mouse a cheese break.

1 Open the File menu.

2 At the bottom of the File drop-down menu is a list of recently opened presentation files. Click AEM-EOL3.ppt.

This is a great shortcut for opening recently used files in any Microsoft Office product!

4

Advanced Special Effects and Hyperlinks

Assigning slide transitions

3 If the presentation doesn't automatically come up in Slide Sorter view, select View ➤ Slide Sorter.

4 Select Slide #1.

5 Open the Slide Show menu on the Standard toolbar.

6 Select Slide Transition to open the Slide Transition dialog box, as shown in the illustration to the right.

7 On the Slide Transition dialog box, click Automatically After to put a check mark in the box. This turns on the automatic advance process.

8 In the Seconds box, type the number **5**.

9 If there is still a check mark in the On Mouse Click box, click to deselect it.

10 Click Apply to All.

11 Save, but do not close, the presentation.

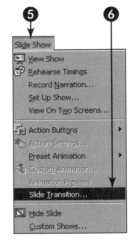

Assigning slide transitions to a presentation

In this exercise you will add visual transitions to the Annual Employee Meeting presentation. To add visual transitions, you need to be in either Slide Sorter view or Slide view.

1 With the Annual Employee Meeting presentation open in Slide Sorter view, select Slide #1.

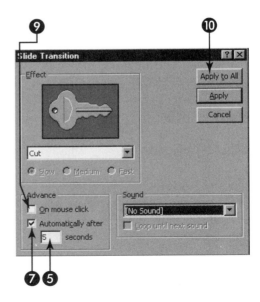

Assigning slide transitions

2 Select Slide Show ➢ Slide Transition. The Slide Transition dialog box appears, as shown in the illustration to the right.

3 Click the Effects down arrow to see the list of possible slide transitions.

NOTE *There are 42 different ways to visually switch from slide to slide, ranging from no visual transition at all (the slides are on, then gone, replaced by the next slide, much the way an old-fashioned slide projector would do it) to random transitions (where you let the computer choose the transition according to its own whim). With random transitions, of course, you never know what you're going to get or where you're going to get it, so if specific visual transitions are important, this would not be a good choice.*

4 Click the list's up arrow and scroll to Box Out. The transitions are listed alphabetically.

5 Select Box Out.

6 Click Apply to All; the transition is automatically applied to all slides in the presentation.

7 Select Slide Show ➢ View Show and observe the effect of these transitions.

TIP *If you don't want to sit through the whole show again, just click Esc to interrupt it and return to the previous view.*

8 Select Slide Show ➢ Slide Transition.

9 In the transition speed area under the visual effect selection box, click Slow, as shown in the illustration to the right.

10 Click Apply to All and observe the preview.

11 Save, but do not close, the presentation.

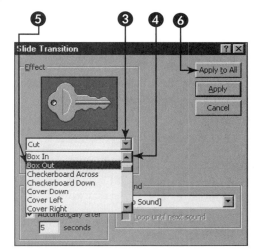

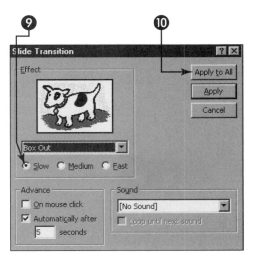

Advanced Special Effects and Hyperlinks

4

Assigning visual transitions to slides

Assigning visual transitions to individual slides

The Box Out transition might be a nice way to open the presentation, but it gets boring after a while. In this exercise, you'll assign different transitions to individual slides and to groups of slides.

1 With the Annual Employee Meeting presentation still open in Slide Sorter view, select the second slide.

2 Select Slide Show ➢ Slide Transition.

3 Click the down arrow of the Effects box to see the list of available transitions.

4 Scroll up until you see Blinds Horizontal, as shown in the illustration to the right.

5 Select Blinds Horizontal.

6 Click Apply to add this transition to only Slide #2.

NOTE *In addition to viewing the new transition in the preview box when you select it, you can also watch it affect the selected slide when you click Apply.*

7 Select the third slide.

8 Press and hold Shift while simultaneously clicking the fourth slide to select them both.

9 Click the Slide Transition button on the toolbar, as shown in the illustration to the right.

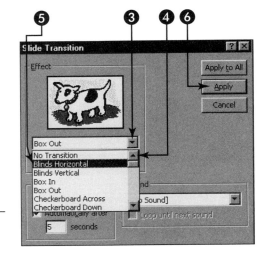

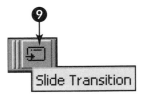

⑩ Click the down arrow of the Effects box to open the list, as shown in the illustration to the right.

⑪ Scroll down to Wipe Left.

⑫ Click Wipe Left to select it.

⑬ Click Apply. This transition will be applied to both Slide #3 and Slide #4.

⑭ Select Edit ➤ Select All to select all the slides in the presentation.

⑮ Press and hold Shift while simultaneously clicking Slide #1 to deselect it, since it already has a transition applied to it.

⑯ Repeat for Slides #2 through #4, inclusive. When you're through deselecting slides, your Slide Sorter view should look like the illustration to the right.

⑰ Select Slide Show ➤ Slide Transition.

⑱ Click the down arrow of the Effects box to open the list.

⑲ Scroll all the way to the bottom to find Random Transition.

⑳ Click Random Transition (bottom of the list) to select it.

㉑ Click Apply to apply random transitions to the remaining slides.

㉒ Select Slide #1.

㉓ Click the Slide Show View button.

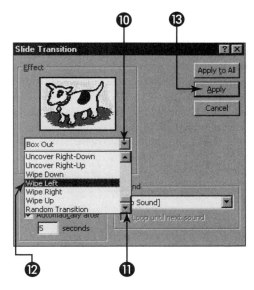

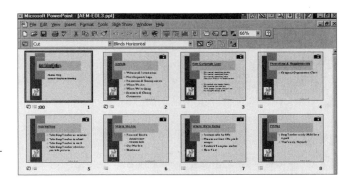

TIP

The Slide Show View button starts the presentation from whatever slide is selected, so if you only wanted to see how the last five slides looked after defining their transitions, you wouldn't need to do step 23. You could just click the Slide Show View button and watch the last five slides in the show (clicking to change slides and bring up text, of course).

㉔ Save, but do not close, the presentation.

4

Advanced Special Effects and Hyperlinks

Assigning sounds to slide transitions

Assigning sounds to slide transitions

As mentioned previously, Early Man was restricted to the sounds made by his prehistoric slide projector to provide audio accompaniment to his presentations. You, as a child of the Computer Age, have many more options at your fingertips. In this exercise, you will employ many of those options, some of them frivolously and just because you can. Of course, I'm sure I need not remind you that when you create a "real" presentation for your "real" boss, you should make your visual and audio slide transition choices with concern and consideration for their overall effect on your audience, not to mention your career.

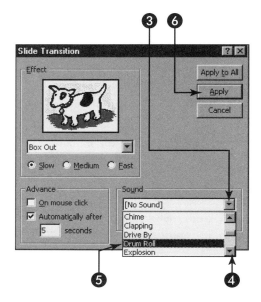

1 With the Annual Employee Meeting open in Slide Sorter view, select Slide #1.

2 Click the Slide Transition button on the toolbar.

3 In the Slide Transition dialog box, click the Sound down arrow, as shown on the illustration to the right.

4 Scroll down until you see Drum Roll.

5 Select Drum Roll.

6 Click Apply. You won't hear the sound, but you'll see the visual transition on the slide as you return to Slide Sorter view.

7 Click the Slide Transition Symbol under Slide #1 to see and hear the full transition.

8 Select Slide #2.

9 Click the Slide Transition button on the toolbar.

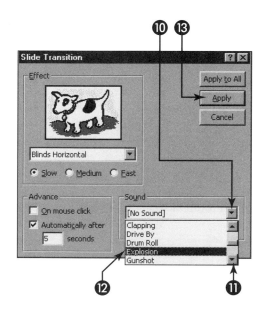

10 In the Slide Transition dialog box, click the down arrow of the Sound box, as shown on the illustration to the right.

11 Scroll down to Explosion.

12 Click Explosion.

13 Click Apply.

⑭ Click the Transition Symbol under Slide #2 to see the visual and hear the sound transitions.

⑮ Select Slide #3.

⑯ Click the Slide Transition button on the toolbar.

⑰ In the Slide Transition dialog box, click the down arrow of the Sound box, as shown on the illustration to the right.

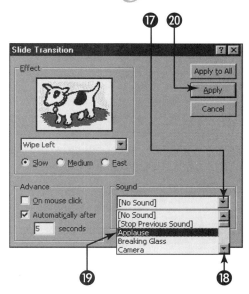

 NOTE *The Applause sound is the sound of a full audience, whereas Clapping is a smattering of applause.*

⑱ Scroll down to Applause.

⑲ Click Applause.

⑳ Click Apply.

㉑ Click the Transition Symbol under Slide #3 to see and hear the transitions.

㉒ Save, but do not close, the presentation.

 NOTE *If you have some special sound effects that you want to use in your presentation, no problem. Just click "Other Sound . . ." at the bottom of the sound effects list and navigate to where you've stored the sound you want to use.*

Animating slide text

In addition to controlling how slides change, you can even control how the text and other objects appear on slides. They can appear whole and complete, as you've seen so far in the various run-throughs, or you can have text or objects appear in any of several different ways. You can experiment with the possibilities at your leisure to see what each one does. In this exercise, you'll have the text appear in several different ways.

4

Advanced Special Effects and Hyperlinks

Animating title text

① With the Annual Employee Meeting presentation still open in Slide Sorter view, select Slide #1.

NOTE *Animations are available from an Animation toolbar (right-click in any open toolbar to see a drop-down list of other available toolbars, and then click to select the one you want) or from Slide Show ➢ Preset Animation. There are many more choices in the Preset Animation location.*

② Select Slide Show ➢ Preset Animation. A set of animation effects opens on a drop-down menu, as shown in the illustration to the right.

③ Click the Drive-In icon to apply it to Slide #1.

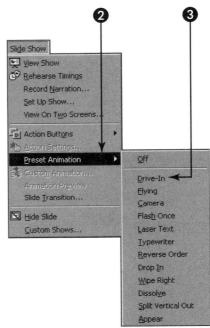

TIP *Before executing Step 5, you might want to adjust the automatic slide advance time downward to 0 or even 1 second. I am not a patient person and find waiting for the automatic slide changes to occur excruciating.*

④ Click the Slide Show button and enjoy Slide #1.

⑤ Save, but do not close the presentation.

⑥ Experiment with the other effects on either the Animation toolbar or Slide Show ➢ Preset Animations, but do not save your experiments.

Animating title text

In this exercise you'll animate the title on the first slide.

① With the Annual Employee Meeting presentation still open in Slide Sorter view, select View ➢ Master ➢ Title Master.

② Right-click anywhere in the text, "FotoFriendly, Inc." A drop-down editing menu appears.

③ Select Custom Animation. The Custom Animation dialog box appears.

④ On the Effects tab, click the down arrow in the top Entry Animation and Sound box.

⑤ Scroll down to Spiral.

⑥ Click Spiral to select it. The Effects list closes.

⑦ Still on the Effects tab, click the down arrow in the next Entry Animation and Sound box (labeled "No Sound").

⑧ Scroll down to Drum Roll.

⑨ Click Drum Roll to select it. The Effects list closes.

⑩ Click Preview to see this effect in action.

⑪ Click OK.

⑫ Click anywhere on the slide to deselect the title.

⑬ Switch to Slide #2 in Slide view.

⑭ Right-click inside the word "Agenda."

⑮ Select Custom Animation from the drop-down editing menu.

⑯ On the Effects tab, open the Entry Animation and Sound box, scroll up, and select Fly from Bottom. The Effects list closes.

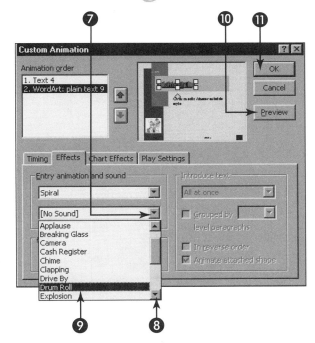

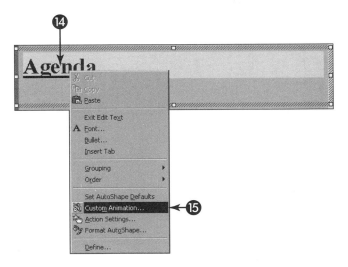

Animating text in groups

⑰ Click the down arrow for the No Sound box.

⑱ Scroll down to Breaking Glass.

⑲ Click Breaking Glass to select it.

⑳ Click the down arrow under Introduce Text, as shown on the illustration at the right.

㉑ Scroll to select By Letter.

㉒ Click OK.

㉓ Switch to Slide Show view and view the changes you made.

㉔ Save, but do not close, the presentation.

Animating text in groups

Some slides have more than one bullet level of text, and that means you have the option of animating each line or level individually. In this exercise, you'll animate the various bullet levels of the Where We Are slide (Slide #6).

❶ Switch to Slide #6 in Slide view.

❷ Right-click anywhere in the bulleted text area.

❸ Select Custom Animation. The Custom Animation dialog box appears.

❹ On the Effects tab, click the down arrow on the first Entry Animation and Sound box.

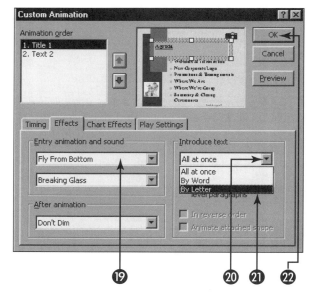

⑤ Scroll up to Fly From Top.

⑥ Click Fly From Top. Most of the other settings on the dialog box become available.

⑦ In the Introduce Text area, make sure the Grouped by Level Paragraphs box shows "1st."

> *Grouped by Level Paragraphs means that each bulleted grouping will appear per the defined effect, in this case, Fly from Top.*

⑧ Click Preview to see how this looks.

⑨ In the Introduce Text area, click the down arrow on the Grouped by Level Paragraphs box.

⑩ Select 2nd.

⑪ Click Preview to see how different this is from the one before.

⑫ Click OK to accept this setting.

⑬ Save, but do not close, the presentation.

Controlling text after animation

With PowerPoint 97 you can call special attention to important text by highlighting it as it appears on a slide and then returning it to its normal color. You can also hide it when you're done with it. In this exercise, you will control the text on the Applications slide (Slide #5).

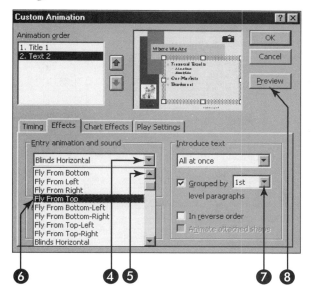

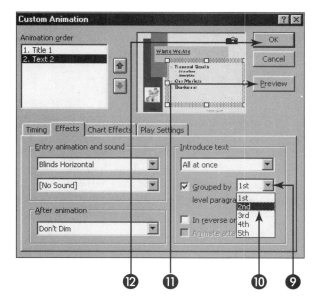

4

Advanced Special Effects and Hyperlinks

Controlling text after animation

1 Switch to Slide #5 in Slide view.

2 Right-click anywhere in the bulleted text to open the drop-down menu.

3 Select Custom Animation. The Custom Animation dialog box opens.

4 Click the down arrow on the first Entry Animation and Sound box.

5 Scroll to Crawl From Bottom.

6 Click to select Crawl From Bottom.

7 Click the down arrow on the After Animation box, as shown in the illustration to the right.

8 Select red.

9 Click Preview to see what you've done.

The blue text crawls up from the bottom, but as soon as it reaches position it turns red and stays red until the last text reaches position. Then everything returns to its original blue.

10 Click the down arrow in the After Animation box, as shown in the illustration to the right.

11 Select Hide After Animation.

12 Click Preview to see what this does.

This kind of animation is good for focusing your audience's attention on one point at a time. Each bullet crawls up the slide from the bottom, as you directed in the first Entry Animation and Sound box, but when it reaches its final position, it disappears, leaving only the next bulleted item visible on the slide. After all bulleted items have reached their positions, they all become visible again.

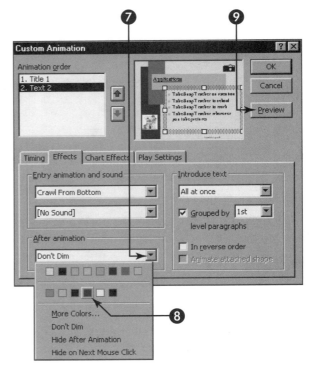

⑬ Click OK (to hold the Hide after Animation setting).

⑭ Save, but do not close, the presentation.

▶ De-animating slides

There are so many cool things to use in PowerPoint that it would be very easy to get carried away. Let's pretend that in your enthusiasm for creating this presentation, you add too many sound effects and text animations. You realize when you preview the presentation that you've overdone it. Do not panic. Remember, you are already something of a Master PowerPointer. In this exercise, you'll remove some of the animation from Slide #6 and make sure the title text appears all at once.

① Switch to Slide #6 in Slide view.

② Right-click anywhere in the title text (Where We Are) to open the drop–down editing menu.

③ Select Custom Animation. The Custom Animation dialog box appears, as shown in the illustration to the right.

④ On the Effects tab, click the down arrow in the first box under Entry Animation and Sound.

⑤ Scroll up to No Effect (top of the list).

⑥ Select No Effect. This immediately grays out all other choices. Since you're not animating the text, there would be no associated sound and the letters would not file in one at a time.

⑦ Click OK.

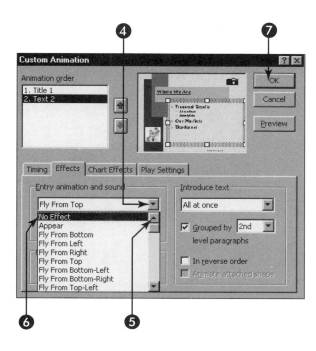

Advanced Special Effects and Hyperlinks

4

De-animating slides

TIP

By the way, at any time in Slide view, you can click Slide Show ➤ Animation Preview and see a preview of the slide's animation in a miniature slide. When it's done, you can click the ✕-close box on the miniature slide to get rid of it.

8 Switch to Slide #1.

9 Select Slide Show ➤ Custom Animation to open the Custom Animation dialog box.

10 In the Animation Order box, select "1. Text 1."

11 On the Timing tab, click Don't Animate under Start Animation. "Text 1" moves from the Animation Order box into the Slide Objects without Animation box because you've just turned off that animation, as shown in the illustration to the right.

12 Click OK.

13 Switch to the Title Master.

14 Select Slide Show ➤ Custom Animation to open the Custom Animation dialog box.

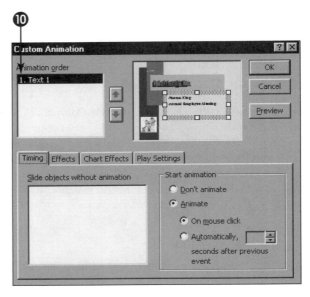

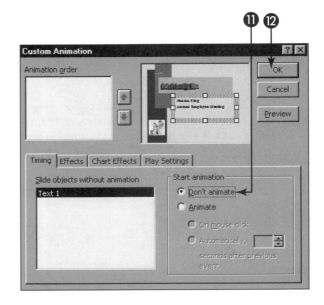

⑮ In the Animation Order box, select "2.WordArt: plain text 9."

⑯ On the Timing tab under Start Animation, click Don't Animate. This moves "2. WordArt: plain text 9" from the Animation Order box into the Slide Objects without Animation box, as shown on the illustration to the right. Now FotoFriendly will no longer be animated, but the two bulleted items will still skid onscreen.

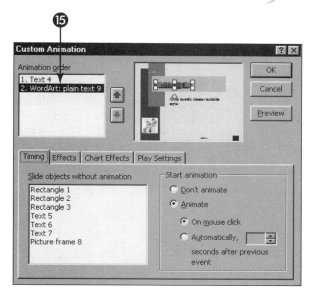

NOTE *Notice that when you click an item in the Animation Order box, that item is marked in the preview box so that you know exactly what object you're dealing with. This way, if you wanted to leave part of the slide animated but not all of it, you can selectively choose what to move into the Slide Objects without Animation box.*

⑰ Click Preview to see the total effect of your efforts.

⑱ Click OK to return to Slide view.

⑲ Save and close the presentation.

Animating text within an object

In some instances you may want to animate text within an object but not animate the object itself. At other times, you may want to animate both text and its object. In this exercise and the next, you get to do both.

❶ Open the Diabetes97–EOL2.ppt presentation to the last slide (Slide #5) in Slide view.

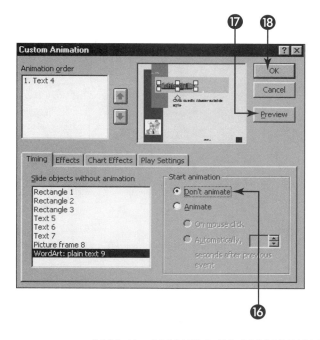

Advanced Special Effects and Hyperlinks

4

Animating text within an object

② Right-click anywhere in the word "Insulin" in the little bottle to select the text and simultaneously open the editing drop-down menu, as shown on the illustration to the right.

TIP

When you select either the insulin bottle object or the text within it, the entire bottle will be righted (not tipped). Don't worry about it. When you deselect it, the bottle returns to its tipped condition.

③ Select Custom Animation.

④ In the Entry Animation and Sound box on the Effects tab, select Fly from Left.

⑤ In the Introduce Text box, select By Letter.

⑥ Just below the Introduce Text area, click to deselect Animate Attached Shape. This allows only the text to fly from left, not the insulin bottle, too.

⑦ Switch to the Timing tab.

⑧ In the Start Animation box, click to select Automatically. The default is zero seconds, which is just fine.

⑨ Click OK.

⑩ Click the Slide Show view button to see this slide in action.

NOTE

That little flying disk that travels across the slide is part of the template. You need to wait for it to complete its journey cross-slide before the "insulin" text flies onscreen, but otherwise, you can ignore it.

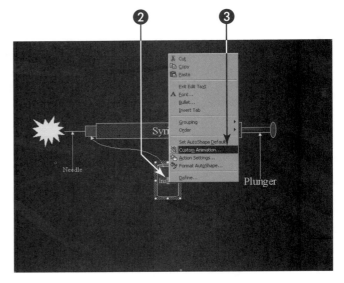

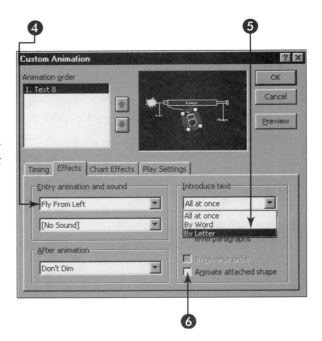

⑪ Press Esc to return to Slide view.

⑫ Save, but do not close, the presentation.

▶ Animating objects

Sometimes, to make a point, it's a good idea to animate an object. In this lesson, you'll animate the syringe in the Diabetes presentation.

❶ Position the cursor over the needle until you see the four-way arrow, as shown on the illustration to the right.

| TIP | *If you just point to the needle without the four-way arrow, you'll get the wrong menu. Be sure the four-way arrow is showing before you right-click.* |

❷ Right-click to open the familiar editing drop-down menu.

❸ Select Custom Animation.

❹ In the Entry Animation and Sound box, select Fly From Left.

❺ On the Timing tab, click Automatically 0 Seconds After Previous Event.

❻ Click Preview to see how this looks.

❼ Click OK.

❽ Click anywhere in the background to deselect the needle.

❾ Save and close the presentation.

Hyperlinking to a slide

WORKING WITH HYPERLINKS

What is a hyperlink? In a word, it's a connection. One of the really keen things about PowerPoint is that you can link to many other places from it even during a presentation. For example, you can go from one slide in your presentation to another in the same presentation or from one slide in one presentation to a slide in another presentation; you can even jump from a slide in your presentation into another program, such as Microsoft Excel. You can add a hyperlink action command to any text or other object within your presentation.

Hyperlinking to a slide

So far you've been working with fairly short slide presentations, so movement within the group of slides has been logical and progressive. Sometimes, though, you'll be working with longer presentations, and rather than recreate slides, you may find it more useful to jump around. For example, to keep the focus on your organization, you might want to return to the Agenda slide as you complete each item to see what's up next and where you stand in the overall presentation. In this exercise, you'll hyperlink from the Agenda slide to the Promotions and Reassignments slide.

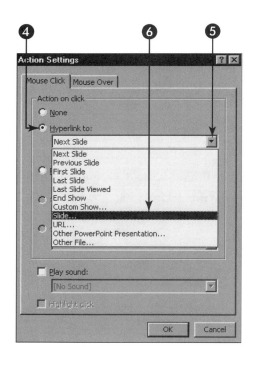

1 Open the Annual Employee Meeting presentation to the Agenda slide (Slide #2) in Slide view.

2 Select the bulleted text "Promotions and Reassignments."

3 With the text selected, select Slide Show ➤ Action Settings.

4 On the Mouse Click tab, click Hyperlink To.

5 Click the down arrow to open the list of Hyperlink To options.

6 Select Slide. The Hyperlink To Slide dialog box opens.

7 Select slide title 4 (Promotions & Reassignments).

8 Click OK. The Action Settings dialog box returns with the name of the selected slide inserted in the Hyperlink To box, as shown on the illustration to the right.

9 Click OK.

10 Click anywhere to deselect the text.

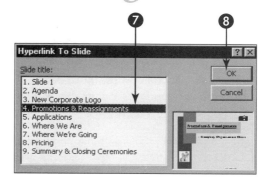

When you create a hyperlink, the text being linked becomes underlined and changes color as a signal to you that there's something more there than meets the eye. During a presentation, the cursor will turn into a little pointing-finger hand when it passes over hyperlinked text.

11 Click the Slide Show button to start a preview of this slide in the presentation.

12 When the hyperlinked text appears, position the cursor over it to observe the hand.

Unless you're extremely nimble-fingered, you may want to turn off the text animation for this slide in order to have enough time to position the cursor's pointing hand over the hyperlinked text before the presentation automatically moves on to the next slide.

13 Click and your presentation will jump to the Promotions & Reassignments slide.

14 Save, but do not close, the presentation.

That's all there is to it. The presentation will not automatically cut from the Agenda to the Promotions & Reassignments slide. If you don't click the hyperlinked text, then the slide show will progress normally.

4

Advanced Special Effects and Hyperlinks

Hyperlinking to another presentation

Hyperlinking to a slide in another presentation

From time to time you may want to include a slide from another presentation in your show, but you don't want to deal with the hassle of pulling and copying it into yours. For example, you may have a whole presentation prepared on company finances for the Board of Directors, yet you'd like to include one of the financial reports in another presentation. In this exercise, you'll hyperlink to a slide in another presentation.

1 Switch to the Where We Are slide (Slide #6) in Slide view.

2 Select the text "Our Markets."

3 Select Slide Show ➤ Action Settings to open the Action Settings dialog box.

4 On the Mouse Click tab, select Hyperlink To.

5 Click the down arrow of the Hyperlink To box.

6 Select Other PowerPoint Presentation. The Hyperlink to Other PowerPoint Presentation dialog box opens.

7 Navigate to where you installed the files that came with this book.

8 Double-click Snap-Fin.ppt. The Hyperlink To Slide dialog box opens.

9 Double-click Slide #6 (Revenue by Location). The Action Settings dialog box reappears.

10 Click OK.

11 Select Slide Show ➤ View Show.

12 When you get to the Agenda slide, do *not* hyperlink to the Promotions & Reassignments slide. Go onward.

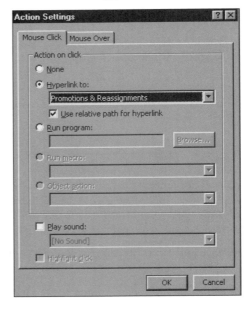

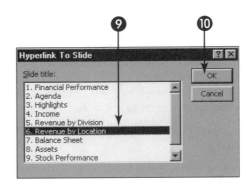

⑬ When you get to the Where We Are slide, *do* click Our Markets with the pointing finger cursor to hyperlink to the pie chart in the Snap-Fin.ppt presentation, as shown in the illustration to the right.

NOTE

Unless you're extremely nimble-fingered, you may want to turn off the text animation for this slide in order to have enough time to position the cursor's pointing hand over the hyperlinked text before the presentation automatically moves on to the next slide.

⑭ When you're through looking at the pie chart from the Snap-Fin presentation, click the action button in the lower left-hand corner.

TIP

You need to move the cursor before you can see the action button. It will be in the lower-left corner.

⑮ On the pop-up menu, click Go.

⑯ Select Previously Viewed to return to the Annual Employee Meeting presentation.

⑰ Finish the presentation (or press Esc to end it now).

⑱ Save, but do not close, the presentation.

Hiding slides during presentations

As you create presentations, you'll find that one audience may only need to see some of an already created presentation, whereas a different audience may need to see other portions of a presentation. You can create one presentation with several audiences in mind because you can hide slides so that your audience sees only what applies to them. In this exercise you'll hide a slide.

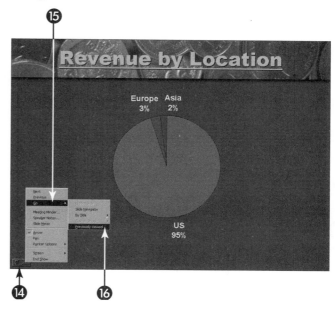

4

Advanced Special Effects and Hyperlinks

Unhiding slides

1 In Slide Sorter view, click between Slides #6 and #7 to insert a vertical line, as shown in the illustration to the right.

2 Open the Insert menu.

3 Select New Slide. The New Slide dialog box opens.

4 Double-click the Organization Chart format, as shown in the illustration at the bottom.

5 Select the new slide (if it's not already selected).

6 Click the Hide Slide button on the Slide Sorter toolbar. When you do this, the number 7 under the slide turns gray with a line through it to indicate that it's no longer active.

7 View the slide show to verify that there is no blank slide during the presentation.

8 Save, but do not close, the presentation.

Unhiding slides

There are a couple of ways to unhide a slide. The most obvious, of course, is to reverse the hide steps: select the hidden slide and click the Hide button (which is now the UnHide button). In this exercise, you'll learn another way to unhide a slide.

1 With the Annual Employee Meeting presentation open in Slide Sorter view, select Slide #6.

TIP

Before progressing any further with this exercise, you should read all the rest of the steps. You're going to have to act quickly to accomplish the task set before you, and it will be easier if you know what's coming.

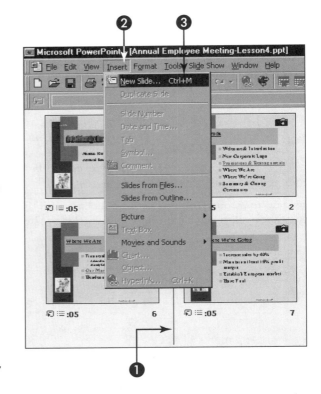

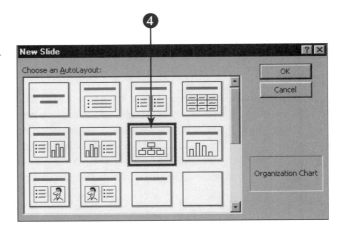

2 Click the Slide Show button to start the presentation from Slide #6.

3 When the Where We're Going slide appears, press P on your keyboard twice (or as many times as necessary to return to the Where We Are slide).

4 With the Where We Are slide displayed, right-click your mouse to open a drop-down menu.

5 Click Go.

6 Select Hidden Slide. The presentation advances to the hidden slide.

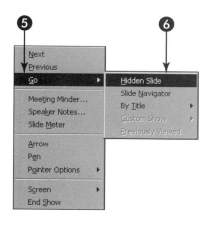

NOTE *The slide is still hidden. The next time you run this presentation, it will still hide the new, blank slide. You can perform the preceding steps 3–6 till you're blue in the face and that slide will remain hidden in a normal slide show. To permanently unhide the slide, select it in Slide Sorter view and then click the Hide Slide button on the Slide Sorter toolbar. You should see the normal number 7 under it in Slide Sorter view as your confirmation that it is no longer hidden. For now, leave it hidden.*

7 Save, but do not close, the presentation.

SKILLS CHALLENGE

In this Skills Challenge you're going to finish adding slide transitions to the Annual Employee Meeting presentation, change the automatic timing for the slide show, and set a couple of hyperlinks.

1 Set the automatic slide transition time to three seconds for all slides.

Skills challenge

2 In Slide Sorter view, assign the following visual transitions to the Annual Employee Meeting presentation:

Slide #1 = Blinds Vertical, fast

Slide #2 = Cover Down, fast

Slide #3 = Cover Left, fast

Slide #4 = Cover Right, fast

Slide #5 = Cover Up, fast

Slide #6 = Wipe Down, fast

Slide #7 = Wipe Up, fast

Slide #8 = Fade Through Black, slow

Slides #9-10 = Random, medium

 Do you remember where to find the Slide Transition button on the toolbar?

3 De-animate the title on Slide #2 so that its text just appears.

 Do you remember how to activate a hyperlink?

4 Hyperlink the title of Slide #6 in the Snap-fin.ppt presentation so that you can automatically return to Slide #6 in the Annual Employee Meeting presentation when you're through viewing the chart (hint: choose Last Slide Viewed).

5 Insert a new blank Organization Chart slide (second from the right, middle row on the New Slide dialog box) so that it falls after Promotions and Reassignments.

6 Assign the following title to the new slide: **FotoFriendly Organization Chart**.

7 Use Times New Roman, 32, Centered for the Organization Chart font.

8 Hyperlink the Org Chart back to the Agenda slide.

 Do you remember how to stop (or escape) from a slide show in progress?

9 Unhide the hidden Slide #7 (which is now Slide #8).

10 Title the previously hidden slide as follows: **Balance Sheet 1997** (use Times New Roman, 36).

11 Assign the following transition to the new Balance Sheet 1997 slide: Split Vertical Out, Chime, Medium, and 3-second automatic advance.

4 *Do you remember the difference between Slide Show ➢ View Show and the Slide Show view button?*

12 Animate the title text on the new Balance Sheet 1997 slide so that it dissolves "on."

 Do you remember how to show a hidden slide during a presentation?

13 Swivel the title text on the last slide.

14 Change the visual effect of the text on the Applications slide so that it reads Spirals (with a Whoosh sound).

15 Animate the bulleted text on the Applications slide so it's Fly From Top-Right, Laser, Don't Dim, and By Letter.

16 Save and close the presentation.

Troubleshooting

TROUBLESHOOTING

In this lesson you learned how to add slide transitions, sounds, some special effects, and hyperlinks. If you encountered any problems or thought up any questions, maybe the following troubleshooting table will help.

Problem	Solution
There are no slide transition symbols under the slides in my presentation.	No problem. That just means there are no slide transitions assigned to those slides.
When I run a slide show, the slides advance automatically as they should until I get to this one particular slide, and then, even though there are more slides in the presentation, the show stops.	There could be a couple of reasons for this. First, check the timing for this slide. Maybe instead of 5 seconds you accidentally set it to 5 minutes. Another possibility is that the Advance instruction for this slide is set to On Mouse Click. In either event, click Slide Show ➢ Slide Transition and make whatever adjustment is necessary.
Even though all the other slide animations work fine, on one slide I have to click the mouse four times to get all four lines of text to appear.	Click Slide Show ➢ Slide Transition and make sure Advance is set to Automatically and includes some reasonable number of seconds. After you fix this, click Apply (be careful not to click Apply to All or all attributes of this particular slide will be applied to all slides in the presentation, regardless of their previous settings).

Problem	Solution
When I click the hyperlinked text, nothing happens.	First of all, the hyperlink feature only works in Slide Show view, so if you're clicking on the hyperlinked text in any other view, nothing is supposed to happen. If you're running the slide show and still nothing happens, then it's possible that the destination file has been renamed, moved, removed, or otherwise changed from when the hyperlink was originally established.
When I click the hyperlinked text or object, I get an error message.	In Slide view, select the hyperlinked text or object and then click Slide Show ➢ Action Settings and make sure there are no special settings applied.
Yikes! I can't find "drumroll" or "explosion" or "applause" (or some other referenced transition).	You probably installed PowerPoint 97 using the "Typical" installation option. Un-install it and reinstall it using the Custom/Complete option.

WRAP UP

Specifically, you learned a lot of neat things in this lesson, such as how to

- Assign visual transitions to an entire presentation all at once

- Assign visual transitions to individual slides or groups of slides

- Assign sounds to slide transitions

4

Advanced Special Effects and Hyperlinks

Wrap up

- Advance slides automatically
- Animate slide text
- Animate title text
- Animate slide text in groups
- Control what happens to text after it's animated on a slide
- De-animate slides
- Animate text within an object
- Animate objects
- Hyperlink to a slide within your presentation
- Hyperlink to a slide in another presentation
- Hide slides during a presentation
- Unhide slides during a presentation

In the next lesson, you'll learn how to work with charts, worksheets, tables, and graphs.

PART III

Beefing Up Presentations

This part teaches you how to use PowerPoint with many other Microsoft products and applications. It includes the following lessons:

Working with Charts, Worksheets, Tables, and Graphs

GOALS

In Lesson 5 you'll learn how to create and add organization charts, Microsoft Excel charts, tables, and graphs. When you're through with this lesson, you'll be the master of the following skills:

- Inserting an organization chart slide
- Editing organization charts
- Inserting Microsoft Excel charts
- Editing Microsoft Excel charts
- Working with Microsoft Excel worksheets
- Inserting tables
- Entering data into and modifying tables
- Working with Microsoft Graph

Starting an organization chart

GET READY

To complete this lesson, you still need to have PowerPoint 97 installed and running and you must also have Word 97 (or later) available. In addition, you'll need to copy the following files from the Lesson 5 folder on the CD-ROM to your hard drive: AEM-EOL4.ppt, Chart97.xls, and Fin97.xls. When you're finished, your presentation should look like the one in AEM-EOL5.ppt.

ORGANIZATION CHARTS

An organization chart is a blueprint to a company's structure, and as part of the upcoming employee meeting, your boss wants to include an organization chart reflecting all the new promotions and reassignments. You're actually already ahead of the game, since you inserted an org chart slide in the previous lesson's Skills Challenge. Up to now, however, it's just been a blank slide. In the following exercises, you'll learn how to convert it into a full organization chart.

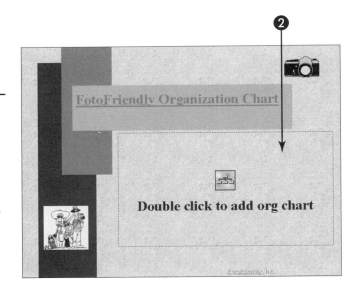

Starting an organization chart

In this exercise, you'll use the blank slide you inserted at the end of the Skills Challenge for Lesson 4 and create the new FotoFriendly Organization Chart.

1 Open AEM-EOL4.ppt to the blank FotoFriendly Organization Chart slide (Slide #5) in Slide view.

2 Double-click anywhere inside the "Double click to add org chart" area. The Microsoft Organization Chart application appears (albeit quite slowly).

3 Maximize the Microsoft Organization Chart window.

4 Select "Chart Title."

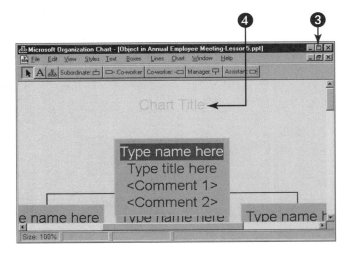

5 Replace it with the phrase **FotoFriendly Folks**, as shown in the illustration to the right.

6 Select "Type name here" in the box directly underneath the new Organization Chart title.

7 Type this phrase in the "Type name here" box: **Nosmo King**.

8 Press Enter.

9 Under Nosmo's name, type **President/CEO**.

10 Press and hold the Ctrl key while pressing the down cursor control key. This moves the cursor to the leftmost "Type name here" box.

11 Replace "Type name here" with **Huey T. Duch**.

12 Press Enter.

13 In place of "Type title here," type **Vice President, Sales**.

14 Press and hold the Ctrl key while pressing the right cursor control key. This changes the active box to the middle one.

15 In the middle box replace "Type name here" with **Dewey T. Duch**.

16 Press Enter.

17 In place of "Type title here," type **Vice President, Operations**.

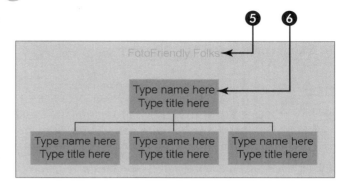

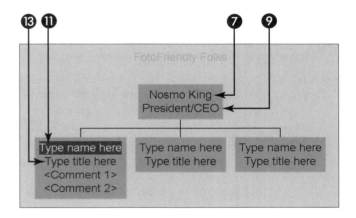

5

Working with Charts, Worksheets, Tables, and Graphs

Adding chart boxes to an org chart

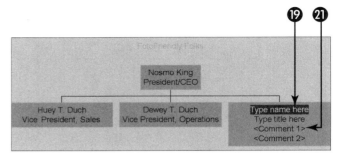

18 Simultaneously press Ctrl and the right arrow to move to the next box. Your org chart should look like the one in the illustration to the right.

TIP *There are a couple of ways to move between boxes. You've already seen one way (simultaneously press Ctrl and the appropriate cursor control key). You can also just click anywhere in the box you want to edit.*

19 In place of "Type name here," type **Louie T. Duch**.

20 Press Enter.

21 In place of "Type title here," type **Vice President, Finance**.

22 Click anywhere outside the name boxes. Your chart should look like one in the illustration to the right.

23 Click Zoom on the toolbar. The cursor turns into a mini-version of the Zoom icon (that is, a magnifying glass or mini-org chart).

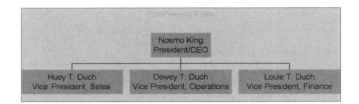

NOTE *When the cursor is a magnifying glass, clicking in the org chart's background expands the org chart (makes it bigger). When the cursor is a mini-org chart, clicking in the org chart's background shrinks it to fit on your screen.*

24 Click anywhere to magnify the view. Then click the Zoom button again and click outside the boxes. The org chart shrinks to fit the screen.

Adding chart boxes to an organization chart

Obviously there's more to the FotoFriendly organization than a big boss and three underbosses. In this exercise, you'll add a sales crew of three subordinates to Mr. H. Duch and an assistant to Mr. King (you, of course).

Adding chart boxes to an org chart

1 Click Assistant in the Org Chart toolbar. The cursor turns into a miniature Assistant chart box.

2 Click anywhere in the Nosmo King box. A new box branches off of the Nosmo King box, as shown in the illustration to the right.

3 Type your name in the "Name" area.

4 Press Enter or Tab.

5 Type your true title (OK, you can keep "The True Power," if you want it but business cards are your responsibility).

6 Click anywhere in the background area, and your org chart should now look like the illustration to the right.

7 Open the View menu and select 50% of Actual. The org chart shrinks a bit to fit better on your screen. The choice has no effect on how it will look on the slide.

8 Click Subordinate in the Org Chart toolbar. The cursor changes into a miniature version of the Subordinate chart box.

9 Click anywhere in Huey's box. A Subordinate chart box attaches directly beneath Huey's box.

10 Type this phrase in the new box: **Penny Sears**.

11 Press Tab.

12 Replace Title with **Sales Rep**.

13 Click anywhere outside the boxes. Your Org Chart should now look like the one in the illustration to the right.

14 Click Subordinate in the toolbar again.

15 Click anywhere in Huey's box again. This opens a second Subordinate box beneath Huey's box. The two Subordinate boxes are equal (that is, they both report to Huey).

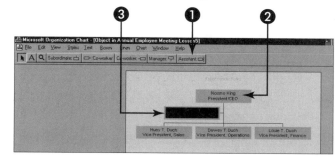

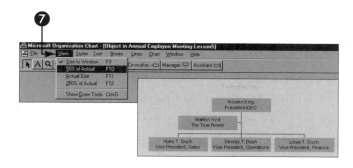

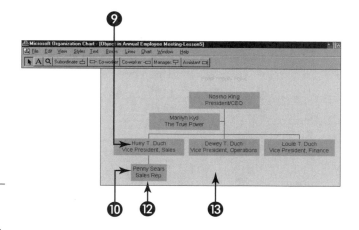

TIP
You don't really have to click inside the black box in order to type text. With the black box staring you in the face, just start typing; your text will automatically go into the right place.

5

Working with Charts, Worksheets, Tables, and Graphs

Adding chart boxes to an org chart

16 Type this phrase in the new box: **Monty Ward**. Press Enter.

17 Replace "Title" with **Sales Rep**.

18 Click Right Co-Worker in the toolbar. The cursor changes into a miniature version of the Right Co-Worker chart box.

19 Click anywhere in Monty's box; a new, equal box opens immediately to its right.

20 Replace "Name" with **Pete Barnum** and press Tab or Enter.

21 Replace "Title" with **Sales Rep**.

22 Click anywhere outside the boxes.

23 Click Subordinate in the toolbar.

24 Click inside Dewey's box to open a new subordinate box.

25 Replace "Name" with **Eric Torset** and press Enter.

26 Replace "Title" with **Manufacturing Manager**.

27 Click Subordinate in the toolbar again.

28 Click inside Eric's box to open a new box subordinate to his, as shown on the illustration to the right.

29 Type this name: **Rennie Sanse** and press Enter.

30 In place of "Title," type this: **Builder**.

31 Click the Subordinate button again.

32 Click in Eric's box again to open another subordinate box.

33 Type this: **Frank Legeau** and press Enter.

34 Replace "Title" with **Builder**.

35 Click the Right Co-Worker.

36 Click anywhere in Frank's box to open another, equally subordinate box, as shown in the illustration to the right.

37 Type **Lloyd Wright** and press Tab.

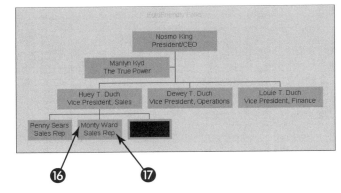
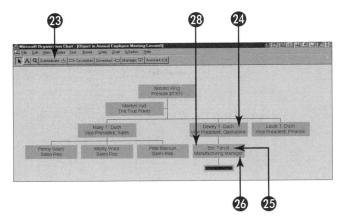
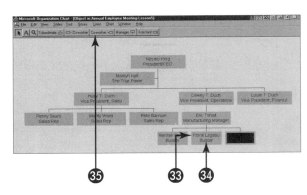

38 Replace "Title" with **Builder**. Your org chart should look like the one on the right.

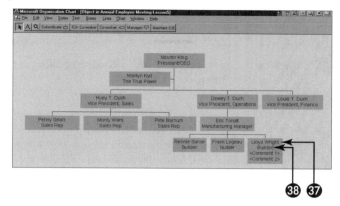

NOTE *You don't have to, but you could click anywhere outside the boxes to close Lloyd's box.*

39 Open the File menu and select Exit and Return to Annual Employee Meeting. A system dialog box appears.

40 Click YES.

41 Position the cursor anywhere in the org chart area so that the cursor turns into a four-way arrow; reposition the org chart up and to the left just a bit.

42 Click anywhere outside the org chart to see how it will look. It should look like the illustration at the bottom.

Save, but do not close, the presentation.

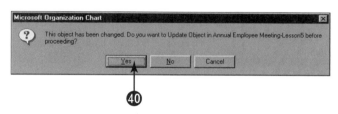

Editing an organization chart

No sooner had you finished creating the org chart than your boss came to you and reminded you that Penny Sears got married last weekend and changed her name to Penny Bloomingdale. And, confidentially, your boss lets you know that Lloyd Wright will be leaving the company before the annual employee meeting, so you need to delete his name from the chart. In this exercise, you'll edit text in one box and delete another box.

1 With the Org Chart slide open in Slide view, double-click anywhere in the org chart area. This returns you to the Microsoft Organization Chart application.

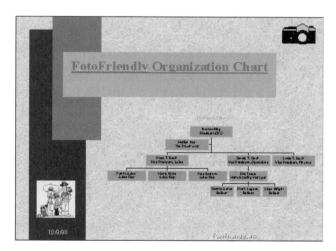

Working with Charts, Worksheets, Tables, and Graphs

5

Changing an org chart style

2 Maximize the Microsoft Organization Chart window.

3 Single-click twice in Penny Sears's name (do not double-click).

4 Select "Sears" and replace it with **Bloomingdale**, as shown in the illustration to the right.

NOTE *The easiest way to select a name is to double-click it. Of course, you can always click at the start of the name and drag the cursor to the end of the name, too.*

5 Click anywhere in Lloyd's box.

6 Press Delete.

7 Open the File menu and select Exit and Return to Annual Employee Meeting.ppt.

8 Click Yes in the system dialog box.

9 Reposition the org chart on the slide so that it is better centered, if necessary.

10 Save, but do not close, the presentation.

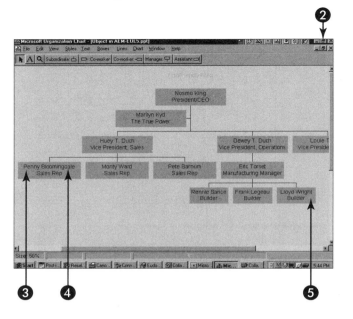

Changing an org chart style

The organization chart on your slide now is in the traditional format, but it's too spread out to fit neatly on a slide and be readable. In this exercise, you'll change the format to one that it fits more compactly on a slide.

1 Double-click anywhere in the chart area of the Organization Chart slide to return to the Microsoft Organization Chart application.

2 Maximize it.

3 Press Shift and while holding it down, click once each in Penny's, Monty's, and Pete's boxes to select all three, as shown in the illustration to the right.

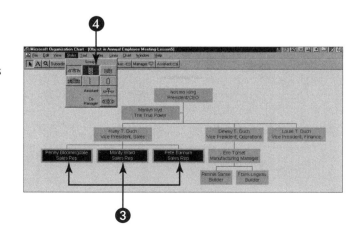

Reassigning positions on an org chart

④ Open the Styles menu and select the middle style in the top row. This changes the three selected boxes from a horizontal to a vertical position, as shown in the illustration to the right.

⑤ Select File ➢ Exit and Return to Annual Employee Meeting.ppt.

⑥ Answer YES to the system dialog box.

⑦ Save, but do not close, the presentation.

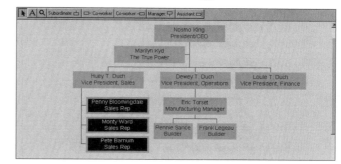

Reassigning positions on an organization chart

Your boss has been under a lot of stress lately. He keeps forgetting to tell you things. He just remembered that Penny Bloomingdale is being named Manager of U.S. Sales with Monty and Pete working for her. You need to change the org chart to reflect this. In this exercise, you'll introduce a new chart box and rearrange boxes to reflect the correct subordination.

① Double-click anywhere in the org chart area to return to the Microsoft Organization Chart application.

② Maximize it.

③ Click Subordinate on the toolbar.

④ Click in Penny's box to open a subordinate chart box directly beneath hers.

⑤ Drag Monty's box into the new, empty box that is subordinate to Penny's box. There will still be an empty box subordinate to Penny, as shown on the illustration to the right.

⑥ Drag Pete's box into the empty box that is subordinate to Penny's box.

When you drag a box, the cursor changes. It may be a four-way arrow (to show that you're in a dragging mode), or it may show a fat arrow pointing in the direction you've moving the box (up, down, right, left).

⑦ Click the empty box under Penny's and press Delete.

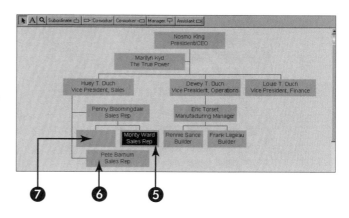

Working with Charts, Worksheets, Tables, and Graphs

5

Prettying up an organization chart

8 Select Monty's box.

9 Press and hold Shift while clicking Pete's box to select it also.

10 Open the Styles menu and choose the same vertical style you picked earlier (middle choice, top row).

11 Select "Sales Rep" under Penny's name.

12 Replace it with **Sales Manager, U.S.**

13 Click anywhere outside the boxes. Your org chart should now look like the one in the illustration at the bottom.

14 Select File ➤ Exit and Return to Annual Employee Meeting.ppt.

15 Answer YES to the system dialog box.

16 Save, but do not close, the presentation.

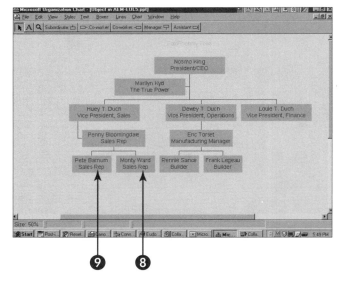

Prettying up an organization chart

OK. You've created a functional organization chart that reflects a lot of your company's recent moves and reassignments, and it all makes sense, but it's not very aesthetically pleasing. For one thing, it incorporates a jumble of styles. The title is hard to read, too. In this exercise, you'll change the title and use formatting tools to make the boxes more appealing.

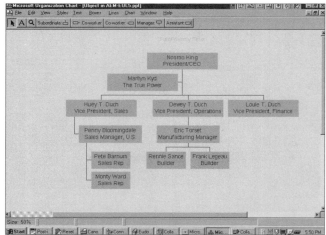

1 Double-click anywhere in the chart area to return to the Microsoft Organization Chart application.

2 Maximize it.

3 Select the title ("FotoFriendly Folks").

4 Select Text ➤ Font. The Font dialog box opens.

5 Choose Times New Roman.

6 Set style as Bold.

7 Pick 18 for size.

8 Click OK.

9 With the text still selected, open the Text menu and select Color.

10 Choose dark blue (top row, far left) as shown.

11 Click OK.

12 Select Nosmo's box.

13 Select Boxes ➤ Shadow. A drop-down menu shows the available shadow options.

14 Click the only shadow choice in the top row.

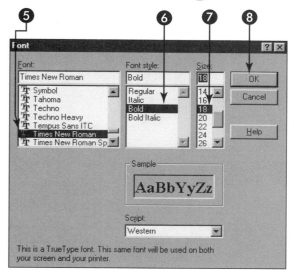

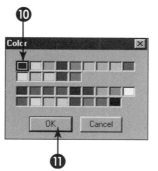

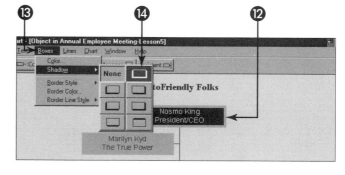

Working with Charts, Worksheets, Tables, and Graphs

5

Prettying up an organization chart

⑮ With Nosmo's box still selected, choose Boxes ➤ Border Style.

⑯ Choose the last style (bottom right).

⑰ With Nosmo's box still selected, choose Boxes ➤ Border Color. The Color dialog box opens.

⑱ Choose black.

⑲ Click OK.

⑳ Click anywhere outside the boxes to deselect Nosmo's box. This sets off his box quite distinctly, as you can see in the illustration to the right.

㉑ Select Chart ➤ Background Color.

㉒ Choose light blue (third from the right, top row).

㉓ Click OK. The entire background color changes to the light blue.

㉔ Right-click anywhere in the background.

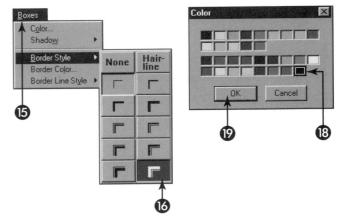

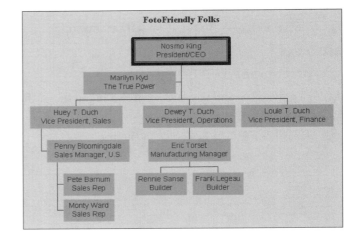

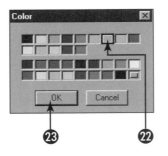

25 Choose Select ➤ All. All boxes in the org chart are automatically selected.

26 Simultaneously hold down the Shift key and click Nosmo's box to deselect it.

27 Select Boxes ➤ Border Color.

28 Choose black (far right, bottom row) and click OK.

29 Click anywhere in the background to deselect all the boxes. Each box should now have a black outline, as shown in the illustration to the right.

30 Return to PowerPoint. Don't worry. You'll adjust the way it looks on the slide later.

31 Save, but do not close, the presentation.

MICROSOFT EXCEL CHARTS

Microsoft Excel may be used to introduce charts into your PowerPoint 97 presentations. This is cool because the Bean Counters can do all the work and just present you with a file. In this exercise, you'll add an Excel chart created by my own personal staff of bean counters (my husband) and format it.

Adding an Excel chart

In this exercise, you'll insert a Microsoft Excel chart that shows the past year's headcount: Budget vs. Actual.

1 Switch to Slide Sorter view.

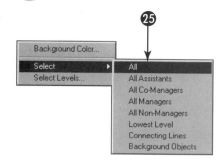

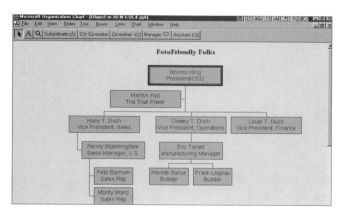

Adding an Excel chart

2 Position the cursor between Slides #8 and #9, as shown in the illustration to the right.

3 Open the Insert menu and select New Slide. The New Slide dialog box opens.

4 On the New Slide dialog box, double-click the Title Only format (second from right, bottom row).

5 Double-click the new slide to switch to Slide view.

6 In the "Click to add title" area, type: **See How We've Grown**!

7 Click anywhere to deselect the title.

8 Open the Insert menu and select Object. The Insert Object dialog box opens.

9 In the Insert Object dialog box, click Create from File. The dialog box changes.

10 Click Browse.

11 Navigate to where you installed the files that came with this book.

12 Double-click Chart97.xls.

13 Click OK on the Insert Object dialog box. The chart will drop onto the slide, but it will be too big and not properly positioned.

14 Grab the top-right handle and drag diagonally to the left to reduce its size proportionally.

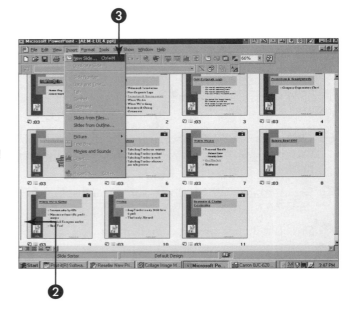

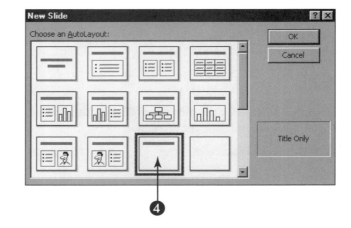

⑮ Drag the chart into position beneath the title. The slide should resemble the one in the illustration to the right.

⑯ Save, but do not close, the presentation.

▶ *Editing an Excel chart*

Well, the chart is in its proper place, but who can read it — even a literate eagle would have trouble with this. In this exercise you'll modify the legend and chart labels so that they are readable by regular people.

❶ With the See How We've Grown! slide still open in Slide view, double-click anywhere in the chart. The chart opens in Excel with the Chart toolbar superimposed over it, as shown.

❷ Click the Value Axis on the chart. The words "Value Axis" appear in the Chart Objects portion of the Chart toolbar.

❸ Click Format Axis on the Chart toolbar. The Format Axis dialog box appears.

❹ On the Font tab of the Format Axis dialog box, resize the Value Axis font to 36 and click OK.

❺ Click the Category Axis on the chart. The words "Category Axis" appear in the Chart Objects portion of the Chart toolbar.

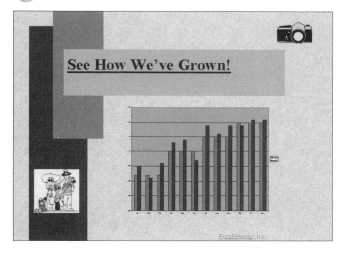

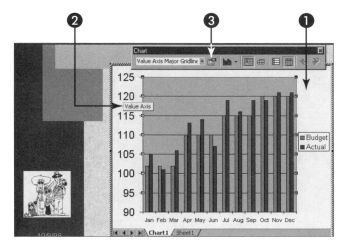

Editing an Excel chart

6 Click Format Axis on the Chart toolbar.

7 On the Font tab of the Format Axis dialog box, resize the Category Axis font to 20 and click OK.

TIP

If you size the Category Axis font any larger, there won't be enough room for all the months, so the program will automatically list only every other month, beginning with January. Feel free to experiment with font sizes.

A Microsoft Excel Chart

The following Visual Bonus is a map of a Microsoft Excel chart. It should help you locate items as you insert and edit a Microsoft Excel chart in the following exercises.

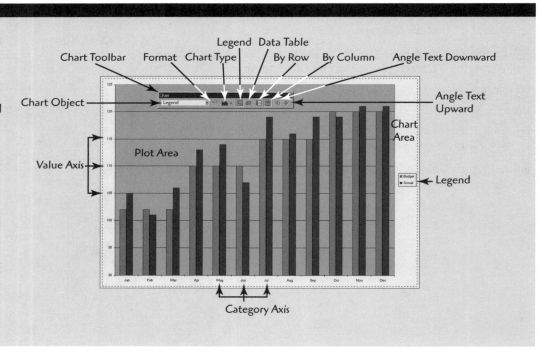

Adding an Excel worksheet

8 Click anywhere in the legend. The word "Legend" appears in the Chart Objects portion of the Chart toolbar.

9 Click Format Legend on the Chart toolbar (don't let the name change fool you — it's the same as Format Axis).

10 On the Font tab of the Format Legend dialog box, resize the Legend font to 24 and click OK.

11 Click anywhere on the slide outside the chart area (except the title area, of course) to see the results of your handiwork. It should look like the one in the illustration at the bottom.

12 Save, but do not close, the presentation.

MICROSOFT EXCEL WORKSHEETS

You can also use Microsoft Excel worksheets in you presentation. In this exercise, you'll insert a worksheet into the Balance Sheet slide and format it for the presentation.

Adding an Excel worksheet

A long time ago you inserted a new org chart slide and called it Balance Sheet. What were you thinking? (I know, I know — I told you to do that — what was *I* thinking?) You had intended to insert a Microsoft Excel worksheet showing the company's 1997 balance sheet, but the Corporate Bean Counters hadn't finished it yet. Well, it's ready for you now, but the slide is the wrong type. In this exercise, you'll change the layout of the slide and then insert the worksheet they prepared for you.

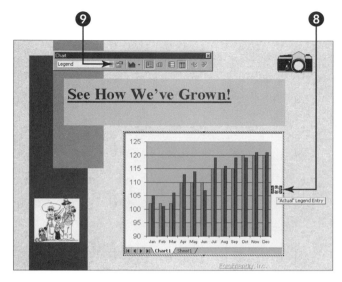

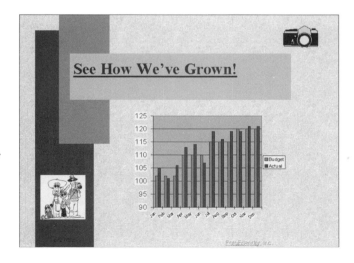

Adding an Excel worksheet

1 Switch to Slide #8 (Balance Sheet 1997) in Slide view.

2 Click the Slide Layout button on the standard toolbar, as shown in the illustration to the right. The Slide Layout dialog box opens (it's almost identical to the New Slide dialog box).

3 Double-click the Title Only layout (second from the right, bottom row).

4 Open the Insert menu and select Object.

5 Choose Create from File.

6 In the Insert Object dialog box, click Browse.

7 Navigate to where you installed the files that came with this book.

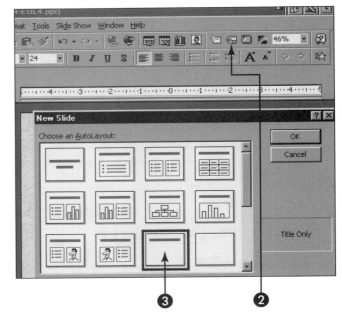

TIP *For this exercise, you will not check the Link box, but if you wanted your presentation to be linked to the Excel file, and thus reflect real-time data, then you would check this box. If linked, your slide show would always reflect up-to-date information. By leaving this box unchecked, you are embedding the chart "as is" and if changes are made later, then you will have to delete it and insert the updated worksheet.*

8 Double-click Fin97.xls.

9 Click OK on the Insert Object dialog box. The Balance Sheet will plop down rather unceremoniously in the midst of the slide and look something like the illustration to the right.

10 Use the handles to resize and reposition the Balance Sheet in the blank area.

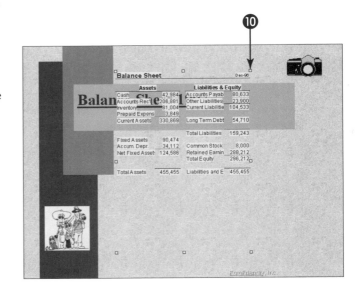

Editing an embedded Excel worksheet ◄

⑪ Click anywhere outside the worksheet to best see the result.

⑫ Save, but do not close, the presentation.

► Editing an embedded Excel worksheet

Even though the worksheet is embedded, you can still edit it. It will never reflect updated information, though, unless you either key it in by hand or insert it as a linked object rather than an embedded object. As with other embedded objects, you can pretty it up. In this exercise, you'll modify its appearance so that it's more readable.

❶ Double-click anywhere within the Balance Sheet.

❷ Select the cell containing "Dec-96."

TIP *Do not highlight the date text. To select the cell, just click in it once.*

❸ Resize Dec-96 to 12 points.

❹ Set the font to Bold.

❺ Move the cursor to the separator line between A and B at the top.

❻ When the cursor changes to a plus sign with a left/right arrow through the middle, move the line to the right until you can read all of the assets completely.

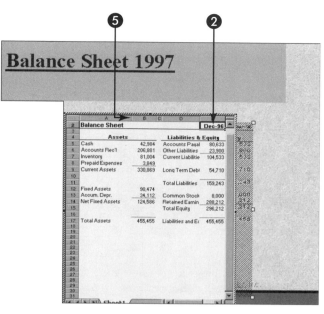

Adding a table

7 Click anywhere outside the worksheet. Your slide should look like the one in the illustration to the right.

8 Save, but do not close, the presentation.

TABLES

When you created the Organization Chart, you actually slipped into another application, Microsoft Organization Chart, and then added the chart as an embedded object in your presentation. Then, when you added the See How We've Grown chart, you slipped into Microsoft Excel. When you work with tables, you use Microsoft Word In the next couple of exercises, you'll use Microsoft Word to create and edit a table.

 NOTE *In order to complete the following exercise, you must have Microsoft Word 97 (or later) available on your system.*

Adding a table

Your boss has decided the best way to show the employees how well the SnapTracker product is doing is to insert a table for December's monthly sales. In this exercise, you will insert a new slide and add a table.

1 In Slide Sorter view, position the cursor between Slides #8 and #9.

2 Open the Insert menu and select New Slide.

3 Choose Table AutoLayout from the New Slide dialog box, as shown in the illustration to the right.

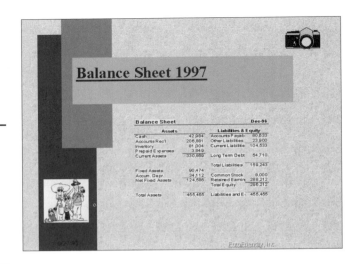

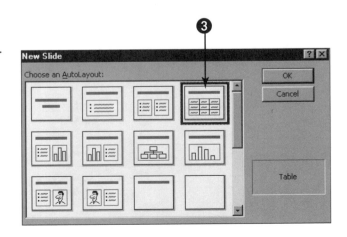

Remember, you can single-click Table AutoLayout and see its name in the ID box under OK and Cancel.

4 Double-click the new slide to switch to Slide view.

5 Replace Click to Add Title with **Monthly Sales: December 1997**.

6 Double-click anywhere in the area that says "Double click to add table." The Insert Word Table dialog box opens.

7 Click the up arrow on the Number of Columns box to change it to 3.

8 Click the up arrow on the Number of Rows box to change it to 5.

9 Click OK. A blank table opens ready for your input.

10 At the blinking cursor type **Sales Region**.

11 Press Tab.

12 Using Tab to move from cell to cell, fill in the table so it looks like the illustration to the right.

Your table may not include the dots that precede the last two dollar amounts in the Year-to-Date column. They represent blank spaces. It's a feature I like turned on in Word 97, but a lot of people find it annoying.

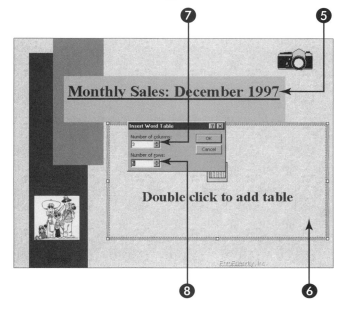

Monthly Sales: December 1997

Sales Region	December 1997	Year-to-Date
West	$7,711	$103,720
MidWest	$5,223	$.96,423
East	$3,431	$.84,093
South	$4,435	$.72,059

5

Working with Charts, Worksheets, Tables, and Graphs

Formatting a table

⓭ Click anywhere outside the table. The slide should now look like the one in the illustration to the right.

⓮ Save, but do not close, the presentation.

Formatting a table

Now that you've got the table inserted, you need to fix it up so that it's not so ugly. In this exercise, you'll use the Table AutoFormat tool to do that.

❶ Double-click anywhere in the table to return to the Microsoft Word application.

❷ Select all the title text in row 1 (Sales Region, December 1997, and Year-to-Date).

❸ Resize it to 22.

❹ Set the text to Bold.

❺ Center the text.

❻ Select all the text under the December 1997 and Year-to-Date columns.

❿ Resize the font to 20.

⓫ Center the text.

⓬ Select all the text under the Sales Region column.

⓭ Resize it to 20 (leaving it left aligned). The table should look like the one in the illustration to the right.

⓮ Click the Tables and Borders button in the Standard toolbar. The Tables and Borders toolbar opens.

> **NOTE**
> The table must be open in Word.

⓯ Click the Table AutoFormat button on the Tables and Borders toolbar. The Table AutoFormat dialog box opens.

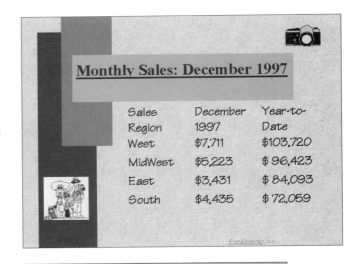

Sales Region	December 1997	Year-to-Date
West	$7,711	$103,720
MidWest	$5,223	$ 96,423
East	$3,431	$ 84,093
South	$4,435	$ 72,059

16. In the Formats Box, select "3D Effects 3."

17. In the Formats to Apply area, deselect "AutoFit."

18. Click OK.

19. Click a blank area on the slide to close the Tables and Borders toolbar.

20. Position the cursor anywhere in the table so that it becomes a four-way arrow and drag the table down and to the left a bit to better place it on the slide. It should look something like the illustration to the right.

21. Save, but do not close, the presentation.

GRAPHS

So far you've inserted data into your presentation using Microsoft Organization Chart, Microsoft Excel, and Microsoft Word. When you create a graph in PowerPoint 97 (as opposed to importing data from Excel), you create it in Microsoft Graph.

Inserting a graph

In this exercise, you will insert a new slide to follow the Where We Are Going slide and on it you'll create a graph showing projected European sales.

1. Switch to Slide Sorter view.

2. Position the cursor between Slides #11 and #12.

3. Select Insert ➤ New Slide.

4. Double-click Chart AutoLayout from the New Slide dialog box, as shown in the illustration to the right.

5. Double-click the new slide to switch to Slide view.

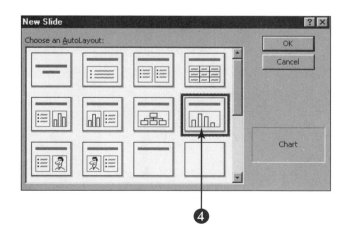

Inserting a graph

6 Replace Click to Add Title with **Projected European Sales: '98**.

7 Double-click in the area that says "Double click to add chart." The default graph opens, as shown in the illustration to the right.

8 Select the cell containing the word "East" and replace it with **England**.

9 Replace the default data under 1st Qtr with the **1500**.

10 Replace the default data under 2nd Qtr with the **1700**.

11 Replace the default data under 3rd Qtr with the **1900**.

12 Replace the default data under 4th Qtr with the **2100**.

13 Replace "West" with **Italy**.

14 Replace the default data under 1st Qtr with **1000**.

15 Replace the default data under 2nd Qtr with **1100**.

16 Replace the default data under 3rd Qtr with **1250**.

17 Replace the default data under 4th Qtr with **1400**.

18 Replace "North" with **Spain**.

19 Replace the default data under 1st Qtr with **500**.

20 Replace the default data under 2nd Qtr with **575**.

21 Replace the default data under 3rd Qtr with **650**.

22 Replace the default data under 4th Qtr with **700**.

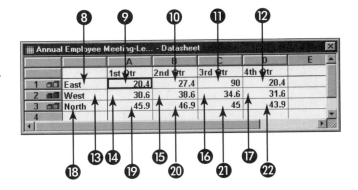

		A	B	C	D	E
		1st Qtr	2nd Qtr	3rd Qtr	4th Qtr	
1	East	20.4	27.4	90	20.4	
2	West	30.6	38.6	34.6	31.6	
3	North	45.9	46.9	45	43.9	
4						

Annual Employee Meeting-Le... - Datasheet

㉓ In the blank cell (row 4) in the title column, type **France**.

NOTE *Notice that when you enter **France**, Microsoft Graph automatically assigns it a color from the color scheme and adds it to the Legend.*

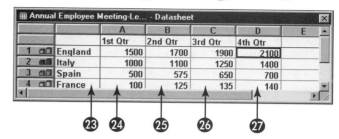

㉔ In the 1st Qtr column, type **100**.

㉕ In the 2nd Qtr column, type **125**.

㉖ In the 3rd Qtr column, type **135**.

㉗ In the 4th Qtr column, type **140**. The datasheet window should now look like the one to the right.

㉘ Click anywhere outside the graph. The slide should now look like the one in the illustration at the top.

㉙ Save, but do not close, the presentation.

Formatting a graph

You have the graph now showing a 40 percent projected increase in European sales, but it's just not spiffy enough. In this exercise, you'll format various elements of the graph.

❶ Double-click anywhere in the graph to open Microsoft Graph.

❷ Right-click anywhere in the Chart area of the graph (the cursor will say "Chart Area") to open a formatting menu.

❸ Select Format Chart Area. The Format Chart Area dialog box opens to the Patterns tab.

❹ Click Fill Effects to open the Fill Effects dialog box.

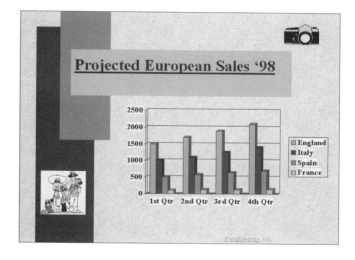

5

Working with Charts, Worksheets, Tables, and Graphs

Formatting a graph

⑤ Switch to the Texture tab.

⑥ Double-click Blue Tissue Paper (far left, third row from the top). The Format Chart Area dialog box returns with the Blue Tissue Paper pattern plugged into the Sample box.

⑦ Click OK. The chart now appears on the slide with the same background as the slide.

⑧ Verify that the graph is still selected. If it's not, double-click anywhere within it.

⑨ Right-click in the Chart area to reopen the formatting menu.

⑩ Select Chart Type.

⑪ Switch to the Custom Types tab.

⑫ Click the Chart Type down arrow to scroll through the list.

⑬ Double-click Tubes (at the bottom of the list). This reformats the chart to the Tubes type.

⑭ Right-click in the Chart (though it will say "Plot," instead of "Chart") area to open the formatting menu.

⑮ Select Chart Options. The Chart Options dialog box appears.

⑯ Switch to the Legend tab.

⑰ Click Corner to move the legend to the upper-right corner.

⑱ Click OK.

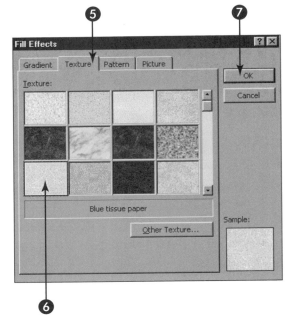

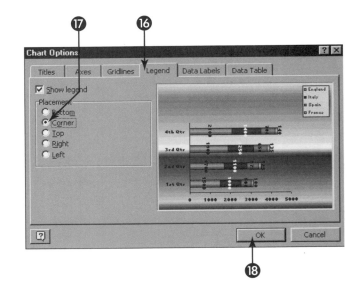

⑲ Click anywhere in the slide to deselect it and see what you have so far. It should look like the illustration on the right.

TIP *You can animate and modify this graph just as you would any other object. With the graph not selected, right-click anywhere in it and you'll open a formatting menu that includes Custom Animation, Action Settings, Format Object, and so on.*

⑳ Double-click anywhere in the graph area.

㉑ Double-click the 4th Quarter tube area representing England. The Format Data Series dialog box opens.

㉒ Switch to the Data Labels tab.

㉓ Click None.

㉔ Click OK. The dialog box closes and returns you to the slide. At the same time, the labels on the 4th Quarter for all countries have disappeared (thus reducing visual clutter).

NOTE *When you modify the label for one element of the 4th quarter tube, you modify it for all.*

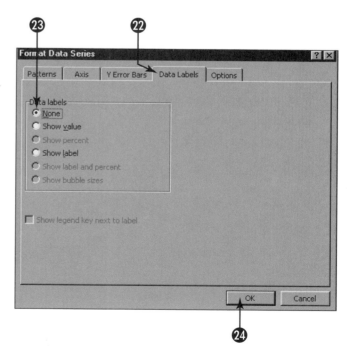

Formatting a graph

25 Right-click anywhere within the Legend to open the Formatting drop-down menu.

26 Select Format Legend. The Format Legend dialog box opens to the Patterns tab, as shown.

27 On the Patterns tab, select light blue (third from right, third row up from Fill Effects).

28 Switch to the Font tab.

29 Choose Times New Roman for the font.

30 Resize it to 9 (leaving it in the "regular" style).

31 Click OK.

32 Right-click the Category Axis.

33 On the pop-up menu, select Format Axis.

34 On the Font tab, change the Category Axis font to Times New Roman.

35 Set the font size to 20.

36 Choose Bold for the style.

37 Click OK. The slide should now look like the one in the illustration on the right.

38 Right-click the Value Axis.

39 On the pop-up menu, select Format Axis.

40 On the Font tab, change the Value Axis font to Times New Roman.

41 Set the font size to 11.

42 Choose Bold for the style.

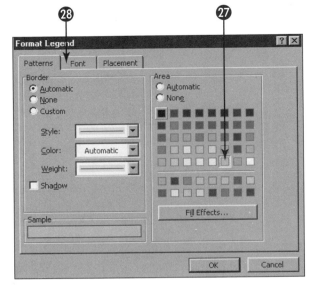

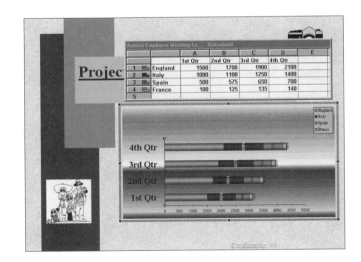

Click OK.

Click anywhere outside the graph area. The slide should now look like the one in the illustration to the right.

Save, but do not close, the presentation.

▶ Editing a graph

Your boss has just come in with new projections for the European market. He and his underbosses have decided to include Scotland in the mix. You suspect one of them just wants an excuse to go there, but you keep that to yourself. In this exercise, you will add Scotland, along with its projected numbers.

❶ Double-click anywhere in the graph area.

❷ On line 5 of the datasheet, directly under France, type **Scotland**.

> **TIP**
>
> *You may have to gain access to line 5 by clicking France and then the down arrow on your keyboard.*

❸ In the 1st Qtr cell, type **15**.

❹ In the 2nd Qtr cell, type **35**.

❺ In the 3rd Qtr cell, type **50**.

❻ In the 4th Qtr cell, type **60**.

❼ Click anywhere outside the graph. It should now look like the one in the illustration to the right.

❽ Save, but do not close, the presentation.

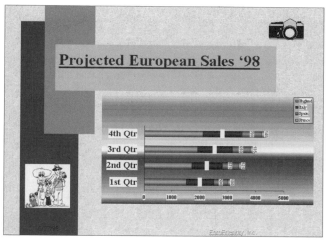

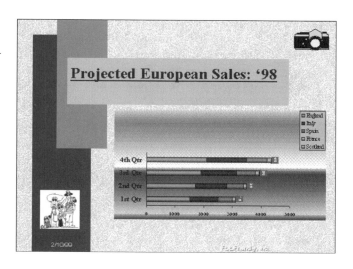

Skills challenge

SKILLS CHALLENGE

In this Skills Challenge you'll fix the Org chart so that its boxes are consistent in appearance, add a Head Bookkeeper and her subordinates, and edit the Org chart so that it's more attractive. You'll assign transitions to the new slides and replace the Headcount chart with a quarterly, rather than monthly, Headcount.

1 On the Org chart slide, change Frank Legeau's and Rennie Sance's boxes so that they are presented in the same style as Monty Ward's and Pete Barnum's.

 Do you remember how to insert an organization chart slide?

2 Add **Drucilla Wolfinpickle, Head Bean Countress** as a subordinate to Louis T. Duch.

3 Show the following three Bean Counters as subordinates to Drucilla and in the same style as Monty and Pete: **Fred Barney, Fred N. Ethle, Fred A. Stere.**

 Do you remember how to change box styles in an organization chart?

4 Change Nosmo's box border so that it is more modest. Use the second border down under None on the Boxes/Border Style option box.

5 Change the text "Nosmo King" to Bold 16.

 Do you remember how to add a table to a slide?

6 Reposition and resize the org chart, as necessary, so that it looks better on the slide

7 Assign the following slide transition characteristics to the Monthly Sales slide: Checkerboard Across, Advance Automatically after 3 Seconds, and Cash Register Loop until Next Sound.

 4 *Do you remember how to change the width of a column in a spreadsheet on a slide?*

8 Assign the following slide transition characteristics to the See How We've Grown! slide: Random Bars Vertical, Advance Automatically after 3 Seconds, and Drum Roll (no loop).

 5 *Do you remember how to format the two axes or the legend on a chart?*

9 Reposition and expand the chart on the See How We've Grown! slide so that it is centered and easier to read.

10 Widen the "D" column on the Balance Sheet so that you can read all the liabilities.

 6 *Do you remember how to insert a graph?*

11 Remove the numeric labels from the England, Italy, and Spain tubes on the Projected European Sales slide.

12 Change the font size on the Category Axis to 16 on the Projected European Sales slide.

 7 *Do you remember how to change the background of a graph legend?*

13 Change the Legend font to size 12.

14 Change Scotland's color to red (hint: on that Format Data Labels/Patterns tab, choose red).

Troubleshooting

TROUBLESHOOTING

In this exercise, you learned how to insert and edit an organization chart, a Microsoft Excel chart, a table, and a graph. Did you get stumped by anything? Look it up in this table.

Problem	Solution
When I tried to add an organization chart, the Microsoft Organization Chart application didn't open.	It's probably not installed. Rerun the setup program.
I accidentally deleted the wrong person in the org chart.	If you *just* did it, click Edit ➢ Undo. If it's too late for that, you'll have to recreate the person's box.
When I tried to paste a Microsoft Excel 97 chart onto a slide, the object came in cropped and missing its legend.	That means you're using Microsoft NT, since this problem doesn't exist with Windows 95. You can fix it by just resizing the chart in Excel so that it's smaller before you copy it. You can enlarge it after everything gets copied into the PowerPoint slide.
There's not enough room on my chart for all the labels.	Then you've got some decisions to make. You can resize the fonts, of course, but if they're too small to read, what's the point? Probably the best choice is to angle the labels, as that allows for more of them to fit in a limited space.
The datasheet is too small.	Grab the lower-right corner and drag to resize it till you're happy.

WRAP UP

Before you take a much-deserved break, let's review what you've learned in this lesson. You learned how to

- Insert an organization chart slide
- Add boxes with the proper subordination to an organization chart
- Edit an organization chart
- Change an organization chart's box style
- Reassign positions in an organization chart
- Make an organization chart more attractive
- Add a Microsoft Excel chart
- Edit a Microsoft Excel chart
- Add a Microsoft Excel spreadsheet
- Edit an embedded Microsoft Excel spreadsheet
- Add a table
- Format a table
- Insert a graph using Microsoft Graph
- Format a graph
- Edit a graph

In the next lesson, you'll learn how to insert pictures, including scanned images, into the presentation. You'll also learn how to insert audio clips (including music) and movie clips.

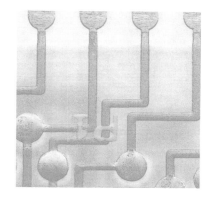

Using Multimedia Elements

35 MINUTES

GOALS

In Lesson 6 you will learn how to insert pictures, scanned images, media clips (movies), and sounds and then use them in a presentation. When you're through with this lesson, you'll be in command of the following skills:

- Inserting photographs
- Inserting movies
- Playing movies
- Inserting sounds
- Playing sounds

Inserting a picture into a presentation

GET READY

To complete this lesson, you need to have PowerPoint 97 installed and running. In addition you'll need the following files from the Lesson 6 folder on the CD-ROM: AEM-EOL5.ppt, Diabetes97-EOL4.ppt, Globe.avi, Bottles.jpg, Scan1.bmp, Huey.bmp, Louie.bmp and LACool.wav. When you're finished with this lesson, your presentations should look like the ones in AEM-EOL6.ppt and Diabetes97-EOL6.pt.

PICTURES

From time to time you may find it useful to include a photograph in a presentation. For example, you may want to illustrate a product, show a product in its natural environment, or introduce a new, key employee. You may even choose to use pictures simply to beautify your presentation.

Some graphics formats may be used without filters: Enhanced Metafile (.emf), Joint Photographic Experts Group (.jpg), Portable Network Graphics (.png), Windows Bitmaps (.bmp, .rle, .dib), and Windows Metafile (.wmf). That means that when you try to insert them into a presentation, everything will be hunky-dory. All others will require the appropriate filter. Even the first mentioned files may require a filter if you plan to use the Photo Editor with them. If you didn't install a filter and you need it later, just rerun the installation program and follow the onscreen instructions. You can always click HELP on the PowerPoint 97 Menu Bar, too.

Inserting a picture into a presentation

In this exercise, you'll insert a photograph of insulin bottles into the Diabetes presentation.

❶ Open the Diabetes presentation in Slide Sorter view.

Inserting a picture into a presentation

② Position the cursor between Slide #4 and Slide #5.

③ Open the Insert menu and select New Slide. The New Slide dialog box opens.

④ Double-click Title Only AutoLayout.

⑤ Double-click the new slide in Slide Sorter view to switch to Slide view.

⑥ Replace Click to Add Title with the following: **Insulin Types**.

⑦ Click anywhere outside the Title Area to deselect it. The slide should look like the one at the bottom.

⑧ Open the Insert menu, select Picture, then choose From File. The Insert Picture dialog box opens.

⑨ Navigate to where you installed the files that came with this book.

⑩ Double-click Bottles.jpg. A photo of insulin bottles drops onto the slide.

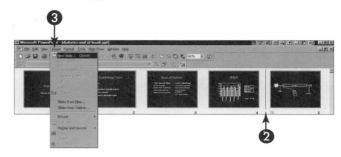

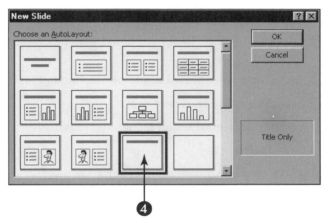

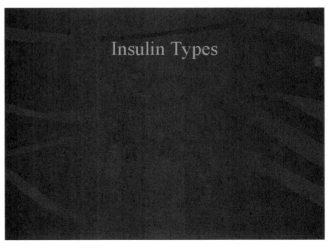

Inserting a picture into a presentation

⑪ Drag the picture to the lower right-hand corner of the slide.

TIP

When you insert a picture in this way, the Picture toolbar automatically opens.

⑫ Open the Insert menu and select Text Box. The cursor changes into a down-pointing arrow.

⑬ Click under the title and on the left to open a text box, as shown in the illustration to the right.

⑭ Click the Left Alignment button on the standard toolbar, if necessary.

⑮ Type **There are several kinds of insulin**, and press Enter.

⑯ Enter **The most common are . . .**

⑰ Click the Bullet button on the standard toolbar.

⑱ Enter **R (Regular)**.

⑲ At the next bullet, enter **NPH (Long Lasting)**

⑳ At the next bullet, enter **Humalog (Extremely Fast)**.

㉑ Click the bullet button to turn off bullets.

㉒ Type **They come in bottles that look similar to the ones in this picture**.

NOTE

Notice that the box automatically adjusts its size to accommodate the text you enter.

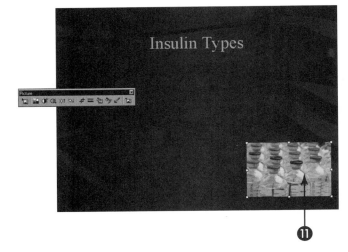

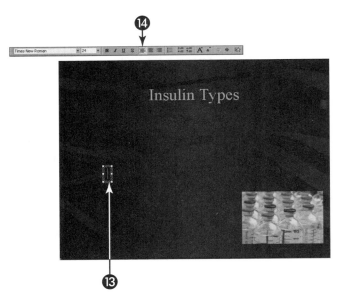

㉓ Grab the middle handle on the right side of the Text Box and move the box to the left so that none of the words are in the picture (but keep "There are several kinds of insulin" all on one line), as shown on the illustration to the right.

㉔ Select the text in all three bullets.

㉕ Open the Format menu and select Line Spacing. The Line Spacing dialog box opens, as shown in the illustration to the right.

㉖ Verify that the line spacing default is 1 (if it's not, scroll until 1 appears in the box).

㉗ In the Before Paragraph box, scroll to put 1 in the box. Click OK.

㉘ Select the text in just the last bullet.

㉙ Select Format ➢ Line Spacing. The Line Spacing dialog box opens again.

㉚ Verify that a one is in both the Line Spacing and Before Paragraph boxes (if not, fix it).

㉛ Select the zero in the After Paragraph box.

㉜ Replace the zero by typing **1** (the number "one"). Click OK.

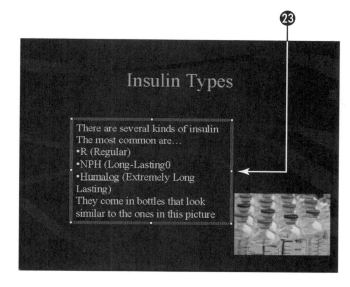

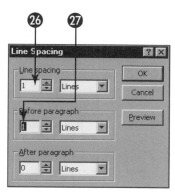

Inserting a picture into a presentation

㉝ Position the Text box so that your slide looks similar to the one in the illustration to the right.

㉞ Save, but do not close, the presentation.

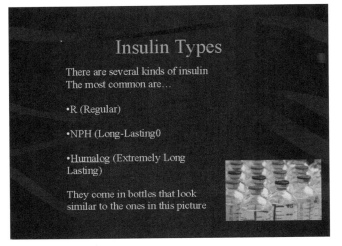

THE PICTURE TOOLBAR

The Picture toolbar contains tools that allow you to control the final appearance, size, shape, and position of your pictures. Here's an up-close and personal look at its elements.

Insert Picture from File   More Brightness   Recolor Picture

Image Control   Less Brightness   Format Picture

Picture

More Contrast   Crop

Less Contrast   Line Style   Set Transparent Color

Reset Picture

Editing a picture in a presentation ◄

► Editing a picture in a presentation

When you insert a photograph into a presentation, you have several editing options. You can adjust its brightness and contrast. You can control the image so that it looks like a regular photograph, is gray only, or is pure black and white. You can make a picture a watermark. You can crop pictures. You can even define the thickness of framing lines; recolor, resize, reposition, and even reshape some pictures. You should experiment with these features so that you are familiar with all their effects. In this exercise, you will change the picture to grayscale, enhance its contrast and brightness, and crop it.

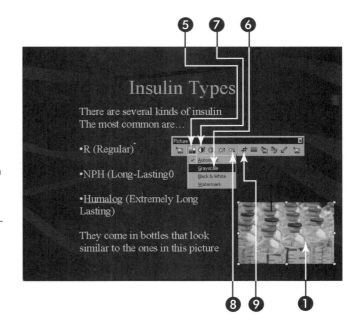

❶ With the Diabetes presentation still open in Slide view to the new slide, click anywhere in the picture to select it.

❷ If the Pictures toolbar is not visible on the screen, click the View menu.

❸ Select Toolbars.

❹ Choose Picture to turn on the Picture toolbar.

❺ Click Image Control, as shown in the illustration to the right.

❻ Select Grayscale. The picture blinks off and on quickly, and when it blinks back on, it is no longer in color. It is a grayscale picture.

NOTE *You may be tempted to call this picture "black and white," but it's not really black and white. If you want to see what true black and white looks like, try this. Select the picture and instead of clicking Grayscale,* click Black & White. See? I never lie. Now switch back to Grayscale and read on. (Of course, if you do not have a color monitor, this is all moot.)

❼ Click More Contrast three times. After each click, the picture will blink on and off, showing more contrast each time (assuming your eyes are sharp enough to catch it).

❽ Click Less Brightness twice.

❾ Click Crop. The cursor changes into a cropping tool.

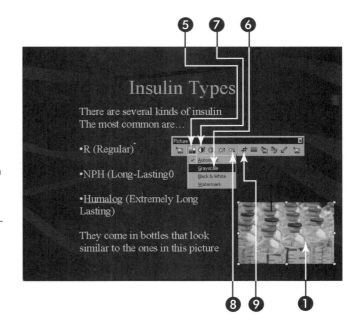

Inserting a movie clip

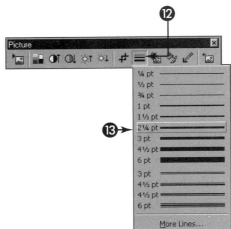

⑩ Position the cropping tool over the left-center handle of the picture.

⑪ Drag the picture to the right to cut out an entire row of bottles, as shown in the illustration to the right.

⑫ Click Line Style to open the line thickness choices.

⑬ Select the 2¼ pt line. This puts a black line frame around the insulin-bottle picture.

⑭ Click anywhere in the slide to deselect the picture and turn off the Picture toolbar (you may have to click twice).

⑮ Save and close the presentation.

MEDIA CLIPS

If you really want to liven up·your presentation, you can insert an actual movie. Be aware, however, that when you do this a couple of things happen. First, you make your presentation *enormous* in size and if RAM is a consideration, you might want to think twice about inserting movie clips.

Second, when you run the movie it will be restricted to a fairly small area on the slide, which may make it difficult to see in a large room or even in a small room if there are a lot of people. However, there's no denying the potential power of its impact.

Inserting a movie clip

Your boss has decided it would be cool to include a circling globe on the Where We're Going slide to emphasize the fact that the company is taking on the world. In this exercise, you'll insert the globe media clip and then format the slide so that you can activate it during the presentation.

1 Switch to the Where We're Going slide in Slide view.

2 With nothing selected, choose Insert ➤ Movies and Sounds.

3 Choose Movie from File. The Insert Movie dialog box opens.

4 Navigate to where you installed the files that came with this book.

5 Double-click Globe.avi. The unmoving globe will appear in the middle of the slide.

6 Drag the globe to the lower-right corner.

7 Resize it so that it fits between the footer (FotoFriendly, Inc.) and the word "Market," as shown in the illustration to the right.

8 While it's selected, double-click the globe so that you can see what it does (be patient). It twirls for 4.1 seconds.

9 Switch to Slide Sorter view.

10 With the Where We're Going slide still selected, choose Slide Show ➤ Slide Transition. The Slide Transition dialog box opens, as shown on the illustration to the right.

11 Click Automatically After to deselect it.

12 Click On Mouse Click.

13 Click Apply. Now you will have to click to display the slide's text and click to advance this slide during a presentation. It will not advance on its own. This gives you time to spin the globe as many times as you want.

14 Save, but do not close, the presentation.

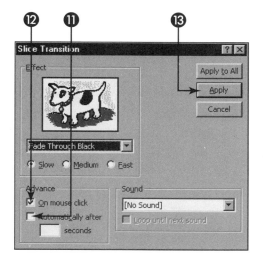

Inserting sounds

SOUNDS

If you think the movie clips are neat, wait till you see (or, more accurately, hear) the effect of sounds. In addition to assigning slide transition sounds, which you've already done, you can actually insert music (or other sounds) into a presentation.

Inserting sounds

Well, your boss is so impressed with what you've done so far that he wants you to keep dressing up this presentation. He thinks it would be cool to insert some jazzy music while the first slide is showing and let it play while people are taking their seats. In this exercise, you'll insert that jazzy music then retime the slide.

1 Switch to the first slide in Slide view.

2 With nothing selected, choose Insert ➢ Movies and Sounds.

3 Choose Sound from File.

4 Select the LACool.wav file in the Lesson 06 folder.

5 Click OK.

6 A little speaker will appear on the slide, probably in the middle.

7 Drag the speaker to the lower-left corner so that it's beneath the kid in the dark pants.

8 Double-click the little speaker to hear it again (if you want to).

9 Select Slide Show ➢ Slide Transition.

10 In the Effect box, select No Transition (you'll have to scroll to the top of the list).

11 Click On Mouse Click to put a check mark in its box (this means you'll have to click to advance to the next slide).

12 In the Advance box, click Automatically After to deselect it.

13 Verify that No Sound shows in the Sound box.

14 Click Apply.

15 Save and close the presentation.

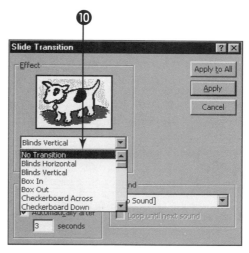

SKILLS CHALLENGE

Your Annual Employee Meeting presentation is shaping up quite nicely, but you can still do a few things to fix it up. The Diabetes presentation is also looking pretty good, but like the Annual Employee Meeting presentation, it could still use a little attention.

In this Skills Challenge, you'll restore the picture of insulin bottles to color and un-crop it. You'll also change the text on the insulin picture slide so that it's more aesthetically pleasing.

In the Annual Employee Meeting presentation, you'll fix the SnapTracker image so that it's not so yellow (the original was actually more green), change slide transitions to accommodate the things you've added in this lesson, and add more music.

1 Open the Diabetes presentation to the Insulin picture slide and restore color to the photograph (hint: use Automatic on Image Control).

 Do you remember how to adjust the contrast and brightness of a photograph?

Skills challenge

2 Restore the insulin photograph to its full image.

 2 *Do you remember how to adjust the line spacing on a slide that holds a picture?*

3 Resize the text box on the Insulin Types slide, as necessary, to make it look like the one in the illustration to the right. Be sure the text does not slop over onto the photo.

 3 *Do you remember how to turn the Picture toolbar on and off?*

4 Save and close the Diabetes presentation.

5 Open the Annual Employee Meeting presentation to the Org Chart slide in Slide view.

6 Change the text in Huey's name box so that it is Text-Right (hint: you will have to go inside the Org Chart application).

7 Change the text in Louie's name box so that it is Text Left.

8 Drag Huey's photo so it's partially in the name box.

9 Insert and crop the picture of Louie (Louie.bmp) so that your Org Chart slide looks like the one shown here.

 4 *Do you remember how to create a border around a picture or photograph?*

10 Remove all visual transitions from the Where We're Going slide.

 5 *Do you remember how to play a tune when the little speaker is on a slide?*

11 Add the same music that's on Slide #1 to the last slide (and position the little speaker in the same place).

 6 *Do you remember how to "play" a movie clip?*

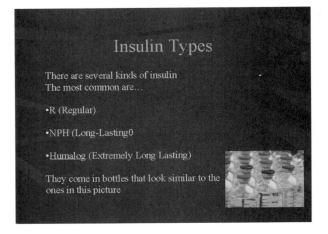

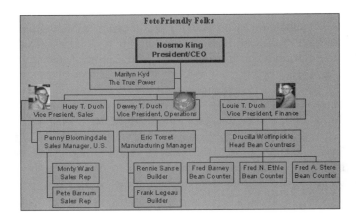

⑫ Make the Projected European Sales slide advance automatically after three seconds, if it didn't automatically default to that setting.

⑬ Save and close the presentation.

TROUBLESHOOTING

You probably thought dealing with music and movies and pictures and such was going to be really hard, didn't you? Turned out to be a breeze, didn't it? Well, you may still have some questions, so here's a little troubleshooting guide to help you.

Problem	Solution
When I was in the Custom Animation dialog box, I got an error message that told me to save, exit and restart PowerPoint 97. Yikes! What's going on?	Don't panic! Yes, this is a problem, but it's really minor and as long as you did save before exiting, you've lost nothing, including whatever you were doing in the Custom Animation dialog box. Microsoft knows about this and as of mid–March 1997, they were working on it. If you have access to the Internet, you should check in periodically at their Knowledge Base and see if they've fixed it.
I don't have the same selection of photos or sounds or movies shown in the illustrations. I can't find the ones called for in the exercises.	No problem. Whether you purchased PowerPoint as a standalone product or are using it as part of Office 97, you have on your installation CD a folder called Valupack. Load its contents onto your hard drive and you'll have all this and more. If you don't want to do that, just substitute something you do have.
One of my slides doesn't stay visible long enough for the sounds assigned to it to play.	Reset the Slide Transition timing.

Wrap up

WRAP UP

This was a fun lesson that even included a few minutes of toe-tapping. Here's a review of what you learned, which included how to

- Insert pictures
- Crop photos
- Insert movie clips
- Play movie clips
- Resize and reposition movie clips
- Insert sound clips
- Position sound clip markers
- Play sound clips

In the next lesson, you'll learn how to set up custom options, change bullets, save presentations as templates, and do other neat stuff.

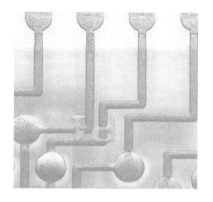

Odds & Ends — An Eclectic Collection of Tips and Tricks

55 MINUTES

GOALS

In Lesson 7, you'll pick up skills that will allow you to tweak and fine tune your presentation. When you're through with this lesson, you'll master these skills:

- Setting up custom options
- Customizing Page Setup
- Changing the appearance of bullets
- Working in black and white
- Expanding and collapsing slides
- Showing outline formatting
- Saving a presentation as a template
- Applying templates
- Working with AutoClipArt and the ClipArt Gallery
- Using the Multiple Undo feature
- Recovering files lost to power failure (AutoRecover)

Setting custom options

GET READY

To complete this lesson, guess what? You need to have PowerPoint 97 installed and running. Of course, you also need to copy the following files from the Lesson 7 folder on the CD-ROM to your hard drive: Logo.bmp (if you haven't already done it), Camera.wmf (if you haven't already done it), AEM-EOL6.ppt, Diabetes97-EOL6.ppt, Bottles.jpg, LACool.wav, Globe.avi.

SETTING CUSTOM OPTIONS

You have two ways to customize the performance and appearance of PowerPoint. You can modify the default settings on the Tools ➤ Options dialog box, or you can specify settings on the Page Setup dialog box. You can also choose to do both.

Many application programs come with a number of setup options preset. While the default settings are the right ones most of the time, there are always times when you need to customize them. Most of the PowerPoint options are self-explanatory (take for instance the Startup dialog on the View/Show tab — if you deselect this, you'll no longer see the PowerPoint start-up dialog box when you start the program), but some require more explanation. If you see one you don't understand, right-click it to open a What's This? box, and then click the What's This? box. PowerPoint automatically provides a brief explanation.

Setting custom options

A table immediately preceding this lesson's Skills Challenge identifies the many default settings used in PowerPoint 97. In this exercise you'll learn how to change the default settings. In all cases except the Print tab, the settings you specify in this dialog box will apply to *all* presentations. On the Print tab, a few choices apply only to the "current" presentation.

Setting custom options

① Start PowerPoint 97.

② Click Cancel in the PowerPoint dialog box. The PowerPoint dialog box disappears.

③ Select Tools ➢ Options. The Options dialog box appears.

 NOTE

If this is the first time you've used the Tools ➢ Options feature, it will appear with the View tab. If Options have been used before, it will come up with the most recently used tab selected.

④ Switch to the General tab.

⑤ Click the up arrow of the Recently Used File List to change it to 9.

⑥ Switch to the Save tab.

⑦ Click Allow Fast Saves to deselect it (that is, turn that feature off).

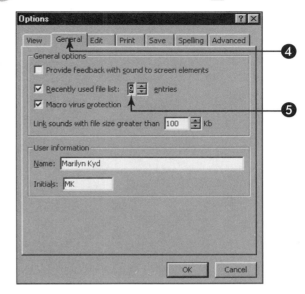

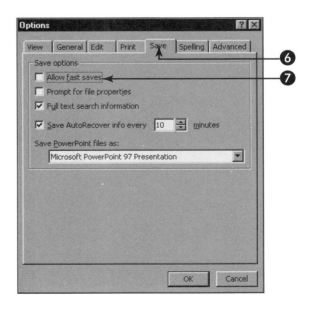

Customizing the page setup

⑧ Switch to the Advanced tab.

⑨ Click Render 24-Bit Bitmaps at Highest Quality to deselect it (that is, to turn off the feature).

 TIP *Turning this feature off may allow pictures to display more quickly on your screen.*

⑩ Click OK.

Customizing the page setup

The Page Setup dialog box is the place to define the shape and size of your presentation. There are a number of predefined choices, plus an option enabling you to set the parameters yourself. The standard choices are On-Screen Show, Letter Paper, A4 paper (mostly used in Europe), 35mm Slides (more on this choice later), Overhead (more on this choice later), Banner, and Custom.

In addition, the Page Setup dialog box is also where you tell PowerPoint whether your presentation should be in landscape or portrait orientation and whether your printed handouts should be in landscape or portrait orientation. The default for both, by the way, is Portrait.

In this exercise, you'll create a banner for the Annual Employee Meeting.

❶ Open the File menu and select New. The New Presentation dialog box appears, probably with the General tab open (if the General tab is not selected, then click to select it).

❷ Double-click Blank Presentation. The New Slide dialog box appears.

❸ Double-click Blank (lower right-hand corner). A completely blank slide opens.

❹ Open the File menu and select Page Setup. The Page Setup dialog box appears.

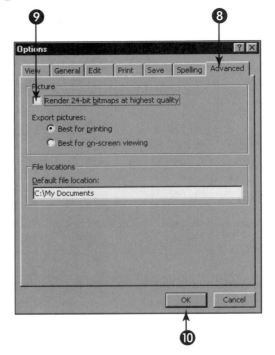

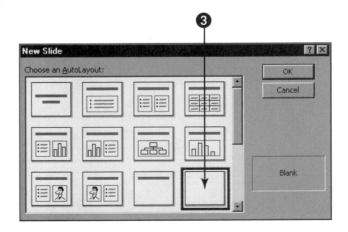

Customizing the page setup

⑤ Click the down arrow in the Slides Sized For box to open the list of possibilities.

⑥ Select Banner. The default settings automatically change to the following: Width from 10 inches to 8 inches; Height from 7.5 inches to 1 inch.

NOTE

This is obviously not the kind of banner you hang over the railing at a baseball game. This is a banner that fits across a presentation slide. The maximum measurements are 56 inches × 56 inches.

TIP

If you were creating a slide presentation to be combined with another presentation, you might want this new one to start with a slide number other than 1. The Number Slides From box allows you to specify what slide number you want to be used on the first slide of this presentation. Other slides will fall into place after that.

⑦ Click OK to accept the Banner default settings (including Landscape as the Slide orientation and Portrait as the Notes, Handouts & Outline orientation). The slide working area changes to resemble the one in the illustration to the right.

⑧ Open the Format menu and select Background. The Background dialog box opens.

⑨ Click the down arrow to open a drop-down menu.

⑩ Click Fill Effects. The Fill Effects dialog box opens to the Gradient tab.

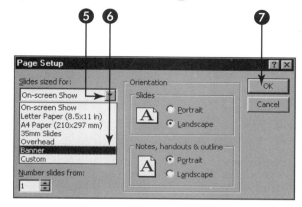

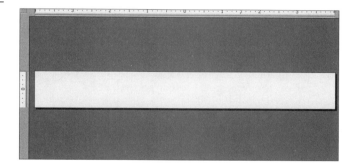

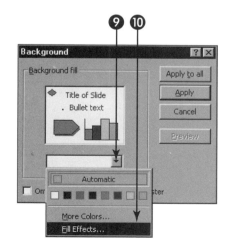

Customizing the page setup

⓫ Switch to the Texture tab.

⓬ Select the blue tissue paper texture.

⓭ Click OK. The Background dialog box returns with the blue tissue paper displayed as a sample.

⓮ Click Apply.

⓯ Open the Insert menu and select Text Box. The cursor turns into a down-pointing arrow.

⓰ Click anywhere in the slide to open a text box.

⓱ Type the following inside the text box: **Welcome SnapTrackers.**

⓲ Select the text you just typed.

⓳ If the font is not Times New Roman, click the down arrow of the font box on the Standard toolbar and select Times New Roman.

⓴ If the font size is not 24, click the down arrow of the font size box on the Standard toolbar and select 24.

㉑ Click the Bold button to make the text Bold.

㉒ With the text still selected, click open the Slide Show menu and select Custom Animation.

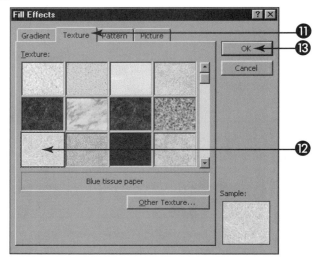

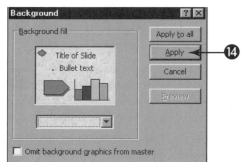

㉓ Switch, if necessary, to the Effects tab.

㉔ Click the down arrow of the Entry Animation and Sound box.

㉕ Scroll down and select Swivel.

㉖ Switch to the Timing tab.

㉗ Set Automatically – Seconds after Previous Event to zero (it may already be set at zero).

㉘ Click OK.

㉙ Open the Insert menu, select Picture, and then choose From File. The Insert Picture dialog box appears.

㉚ Navigate to where you stored the files that came with this book.

㉛ Double–click Logo.bmp. It plops itself down on top of the banner.

㉜ Grab one of the corners and resize the logo.

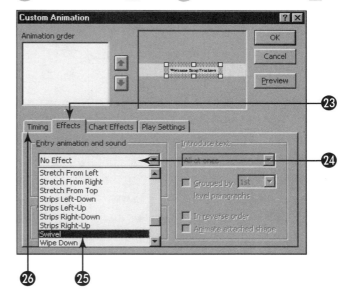

7

Odds & Ends – An Eclectic Collection of Tips and Tricks

㉝ Drag the logo to the lower-left corner of the banner so that it looks like the illustration to the right.

㉞ With the logo still selected, select Edit ➢ Copy.

㉟ Click anywhere outside the logo to deselect it.

㊱ Select Edit ➢ Paste. A copy of the logo appears, probably on top of the original.

㊲ Drag the copy to the upper-right corner of the slide.

㊳ Click anywhere outside the logos and text boxes. The slide should look like the illustration to the right.

㊴ Open the Insert menu, select Picture, and then choose From File. The Insert Picture dialog box opens before in this exercise.

㊵ Double-click Camera.wmf. A huge camera plops down on top of the banner.

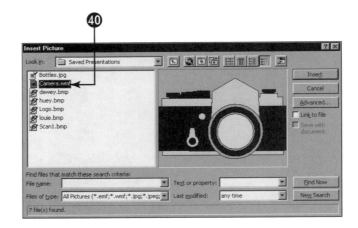

41 Resize the camera so that it will fit on the banner, and then position the camera as shown in the illustration to the right.

42 With the camera still selected, select Edit ➤ Copy, as before.

Click anywhere outside the camera to deselect it and then select Edit ➤ Paste. A copy of the camera appears on the banner, probably on top of the original camera.

Drag the copy to the other side of the greeting and then click anywhere outside the boxes and pictures. The slide should look like the one in the illustration to the right.

Open the Slide Show menu and select Set Up Show. The Set Up Show dialog box opens.

Click Browsed at a Kiosk (Full Screen).

Click OK.

Save, using the name **Banner**, and close the presentation.

WORKING WITH INDIVIDUAL SLIDES

Sometimes you'll find that your color scheme is fine, the order of the slides is fine, the text is fine and so on, but you want to make changes to individual slides — not all-encompassing changes. You can change bullets (you can even make them smiley faces!), switch to black and white, expand or collapse slides, or hide formatting.

Changing bullets

Most bullets are your typical (and boring?) black dots. Of course, you can always change the color of the bullets to complement your color scheme, but a big round bullet is a big round bullet. In this exercise, you'll change bullets in the Annual Employee Meeting presentation to something more fun.

1 Open the Annual Employee Meeting presentation to the Agenda slide (#2) in Slide view.

2 Select all of the bulleted text.

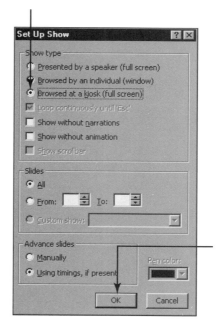

Changing bullets

③ Select Format ➤ Bullet. The Bullet dialog box appears.

④ Make sure the Use a Bullet box has a check mark in it (if it doesn't, click the box to put a check mark in it).

⑤ The default font is probably Monotype Sorts. Click the down arrow of the Bullets From box to open a list of bullet sources.

⑥ Scroll to and select Wingdings.

⑦ Double-click the happy face.

⑧ Click anywhere outside the text are to deselect the text box. The bullets on the slide are now cheerful little faces, but they are very hard to see.

⑨ Select all the bulleted text again.

⑩ Select Format ➤ Bullet.

⑪ Click the down arrow of the color box.

⑫ Click Automatic. The color changes to a scheme-matching dark blue.

⑬ Click OK.

⑭ Click anywhere outside the text box to see the reformatted bullets. Your slide should look like the one to the right.

⑮ Save, but do not close, the presentation.

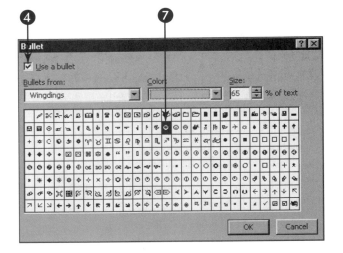

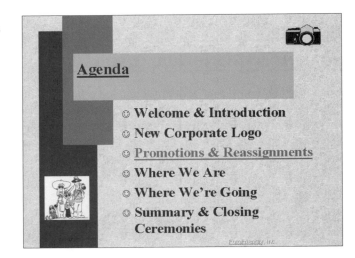

Working in black and white

Working in black and white

Picture this. You've slaved over a hot keyboard to produce a gorgeous and colorful presentation. You modestly admit to everyone you see (including strangers on the street), that this presentation is a masterpiece. You're hoping for nomination into the Master PowerPointer's Hall of Fame. Then you print 100 copies of it for your audience. Uh oh! Much of it is unreadable! How can this be?

What happened was, you created a beautiful presentation *onscreen* but forgot that you'd be printing it *in black and white!* While your color combinations may be lovely to look at onscreen, they may blend into each other and become unreadable when printed in grays.

In this exercise, you'll learn the two ways to preview the Annual Employee Meeting in black and white to make sure it'll print so your audience can read it.

① Switch to Slide #1 in Slide view.

② On the Standard toolbar, click the Black and White View button.

③ The entire presentation switches to a black and white appearance, but lest you forget, includes a color version of the active slide in the upper right-hand corner, as shown in the illustration to the right.

④ Scroll through the presentation checking the readability of each slide.

TIP *If the color slide miniature does not appear automatically and you do want to see it, click View ➤ Slide Miniature. When you switch to Slide Sorter view, all slides will remain black and white.*

Expanding and collapsing slides

5 Select File ➤ Print. The Print dialog box opens.

 NOTE *Of course, your Printer dialog box may look different from mine, depending on your printer configuration.*

6 Click OK to print one copy of the entire presentation.

7 Review the printout to make sure it is all readable.

8 Click the Black and White View button again to restore color to your working presentation.

9 Save, but do not close, the presentation.

Expanding and collapsing slides

Just like people, slides can be expanded. The main difference is that when a slide expands, it's so-called friends don't start snickering behind its back. The Expand feature creates new slides from the text on one slide, including any bulleted text or text under a bullet. In this exercise, you'll expand the Where We Are slide.

1 Switch to the Slide Sorter view.

2 Select the Where We Are slide (Slide #7).

3 Select Tools ➤ Expand Slide. Each bullet on the Where We Are slide becomes the title of a new slide. The first one (Financial Results) includes as bullets the information that was subordinate to the bullets on the original slide. The others are blank slides, except for the title.

4 Switch to Outline view, as shown in the illustration to the right.

5 Click Collapse All on the Outline toolbar. The entire outline collapses to show only each slide's title — no bullets, no text, as shown in the illustration on the next page.

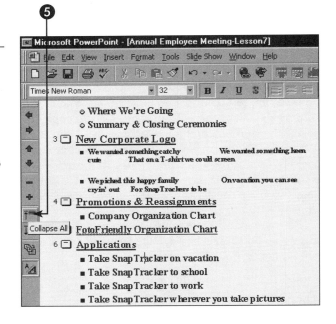

Outline formatting

TIP

You may have to scroll to see the entire outline.

NOTE

The Expand, Expand All, Collapse, and Collapse All buttons on the Outline toolbar allow you to see, in Outline view, all of your outline by Slide title (up to 26 slides—anything more than that and you'll have to scroll through it) and then to Expand individual slides or all slides or even create new slides with titles borrowed from the original slide's bullets.

❻ Save, but do not close, the presentation.

Outline formatting

For some people seeing how the text will look while they're creating the slide can be distracting. For others, it's imperative. PowerPoint 97 allows you to decide whether you want to concentrate on content or a combination of content and appearance. In this exercise, you'll examine the Show Formatting function.

❶ Still in Outline view, click Expand All.

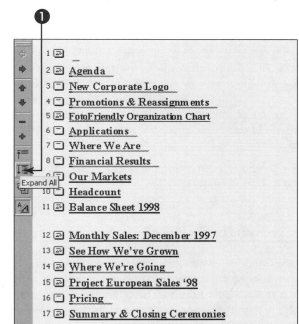

7

Odds & Ends — An Eclectic Collection of Tips and Tricks

② Click Show Formatting on the Outline toolbar.

NOTE

This turns off the formatting for the slides in the presentation, as shown in the illustration to the right. What you see now is raw slide data — all using the same font and font size. Subordination is retained.

The Slide Miniature never wavers, however, so you can still see how the slide looks.

③ Click the Show Formatting button again to display the outline with its true formatting.

WORKING WITH TEMPLATES

You've already done some work with templates, but in these exercises you'll learn how to save a presentation as a template, and then how to apply it to your presentation. Use all the tools you've learned so far to modify it, as necessary.

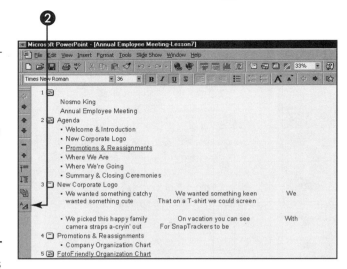

Saving a presentation as a template

You know your boss to be a devoted UCLA fan, so you expect you may need to use this blue and gold template again in the future. Rather than recreate it from scratch, you can save loads of time by just saving this one as a template.

① With the Annual Employee Meeting presentation still displayed (in any view except Slide Show), select Edit ➢ Select All to select all text.

② Press the Delete key to delete all the text. If you get a warning message that all notes and graphics will also be deleted, relax and click OK.

③ Select File ➢ Save As. The Save As dialog box appears.

I can guarantee that your Save As dialog box will not look exactly like the illustration; however, I present this one to give you an idea of what to expect.

4 Click the down arrow of the Save As Type box to reveal the list of saving options.

5 Scroll down to and select Presentation Template (*.pot).

6 Navigate to the Presentation Designs folder.

7 In the File Name box, type the following: **Blue and Gold Template**.

8 Click Save. The Save As dialog box disappears and you now have a new template.

9 Select File ➢ New. The New Presentation dialog box opens.

10 Click the Presentation Designs tab. The Blue and Gold template should be included as a choice.

11 Click Cancel, since you don't really want to start a new presentation (you were just peeking to make sure the template did what it was supposed to do).

12 Select File ➢ Close.

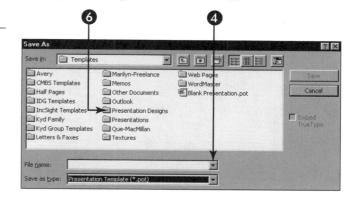

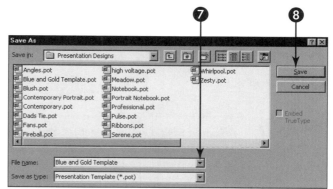

Applying templates

OK. You've knocked yourself out creating this Annual Employee Meeting presentation for your boss so that it incorporates UCLA's blue and gold motif. Then, the day before the presentation is scheduled to be given, Huey, Dewey, and Louie stroll by your desk. Huey, Dewey, and Louie did not go to UCLA. They ask you if you wouldn't mind changing the template to something a little less, um, partisan.

You gulp. Of course you wouldn't mind. After all it's three vice presidents versus only one president. Besides, you know that if your boss really gets into a snit over the change, you can revert back quickly and easily. In this lesson, then, you'll apply a different

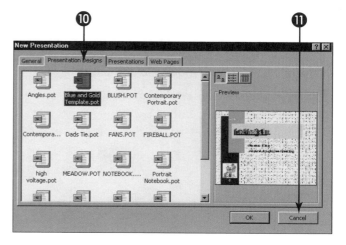

Applying templates

template to the Annual Employee Meeting (with any luck, of course, your boss will come along soon and turn Huey, Dewey, and Louie into duck soup).

1 Open the Annual Employee Meeting presentation to the first slide in Slide Sorter view.

2 Click Apply Design on the Standard toolbar.

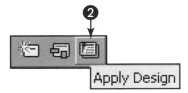

NOTE *If the design templates don't appear in the Apply Design dialog box, then navigate to where you installed PowerPoint (or MS Office 97) and further navigate to the Templates folder. Inside the Templates folder, you should find the Presentations and Presentation Design subfolders.*

3 In the Apply Design dialog box, select Meadow.pot.

4 Click Apply.

NOTE *This could take a while, so get up and stretch, run a lap, or whatever. As soon as you click Apply, you should see a message that says:* Charts are being updated with the new color scheme." *This is what takes so long.*

5 Examine each slide closely to see which ones are going to demand some reformatting. For example, on the Title slide, the speaker that starts the music is sitting smack dab on top of the date. You'd want to move one or the other.

6 Save, but do not close, the presentation.

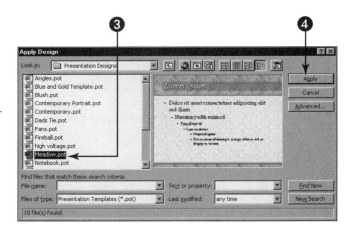

WORKING WITH THE MICROSOFT CLIP GALLERY

PowerPoint 97 comes with a great collection of more than 1,000 pieces of clip art (more than 3,000 if you install the Valupack). They're stored in the Microsoft Clip Gallery, where you can see thumbnail previews of them. You can use the AutoClipArt feature to suggest appropriate images for your presentation or the Find feature to search for clips that include keywords that you specify.

The Microsoft Clip Gallery also includes about 400 sound clips, movie clips, and photographs.

Of course, you can add or delete files to the Microsoft Clip Gallery.

THE MICROSOFT CLIP GALLERY

Most of the functions on the Microsoft Clip Gallery are clearly labeled or explained in the following exercises; however, there are some whose functions are important but unannounced. Use this Visual Bonus to better acquaint yourself with the Microsoft Clip Gallery.

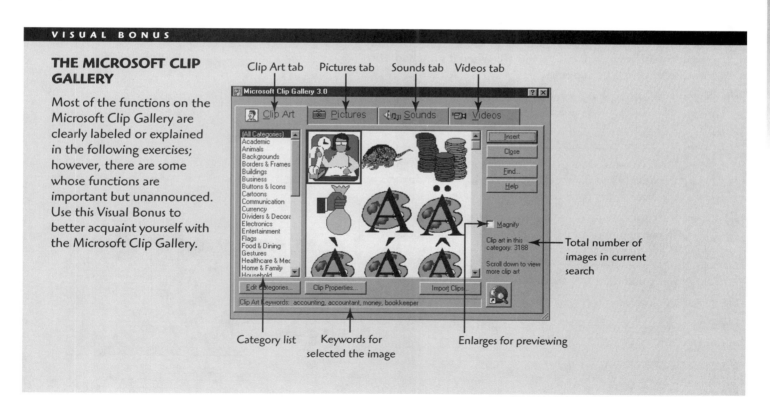

Clip Art tab   Pictures tab   Sounds tab   Videos tab

Total number of images in current search

Category list   Keywords for selected the image   Enlarges for previewing

Odds & Ends — An Eclectic Collection of Tips and Tricks

7

Using AutoClipArt

Using AutoClipArt

The AutoClipArt feature searches through the Microsoft Clip Gallery for clip art that may be appropriate to your presentation, based on the presentation's content. When you use the AutoClipArt feature and it cannot find appropriate clip art for you, it displays a message like the one shown to the right.

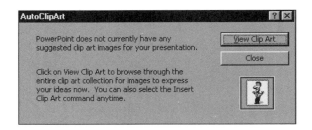

When it fails to find something, it invites you to visit the Clip Gallery and search for something on your own. While it's a keen feature, you'll find that it occasionally misses the mark even when it does find possibilities.

1 Switch to Slide #1 in Slide view.

2 Select Tools ➢ AutoClipArt. PowerPoint scans the presentation and then searches for applicable clip art. When it's finished, the AutoClipArt dialog box appears.

3 Click the down arrow of the Happy box to see if PowerPoint used any keywords other than "Happy" in its search for clip art.

NOTE *Four words were used in the search: Happy, Organize, Result, and Balance. The first one, Happy, appears on Slide 3, the New Corporate Logo slide.*

4 Click View Clip Art twice (do *not* double-click). The Microsoft Clip Gallery opens to a selection of clips PowerPoint thought might be appropriate for this slide. Perhaps you'll find something there worth using. Much as I enjoy Screen Beans, I find nothing useful for this presentation.

5 Click Close on Microsoft Clip Gallery.

6 Repeat steps 3–5 until you've checked all the clip art suggestions.

7 Click Close on the AutoClipArt dialog box.

8 Save and close the presentation.

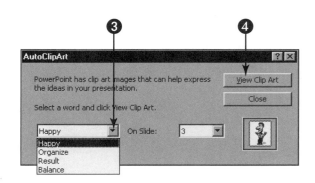

Inserting clip art

Inserting clip art from the Microsoft Clip Gallery

When AutoClipArt doesn't work for you but you still want to insert clip art, you can go search the Microsoft Clip Gallery yourself. In this exercise, you'll look for something medical to use as an illustration on the first slide of the Diabetes presentation.

TIP *Listen up! This is very important. Read it out loud so that you get the benefit of not only seeing and reading it, but hearing it. Even though there are hundreds of clips available in the Microsoft Clip Gallery and you're free to use those clips in your presentations whenever and however you want, you are not free to distribute those clips to anyone without Microsoft's written permission. (This applies just to the clip files). Microsoft holds the copyright (or has licensed the rights from third-party vendors) on all the Microsoft Clip Gallery images and clips. If you're not sure whether or not you need permission to use or distribute an image, contact Microsoft. Better safe than sorry!*

① Open the Diabetes97-EOL6.ppt presentation to the first slide in Slide view.

② Select Insert ➢ Picture ➢ Clip Art. The Microsoft Clip Gallery appears.

③ Select Healthcare & Medicine from the Category list.

④ Click the down arrow of the images list until you come to a mostly white caduceus.

⑤ Double-click the caduceus. It plops onto the slide and automatically opens the Picture toolbar.

NOTE *If your list of images doesn't match the illustration, don't worry. If you've installed the ValuPak, it should be pretty close. If you can't find a caduceus like the one in the illustration, just choose some other image so that you can proceed with the exercise.*

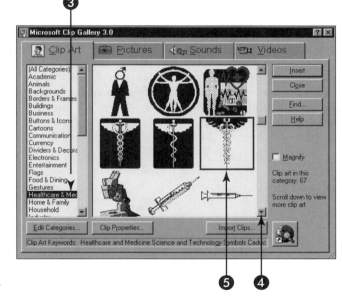

Inserting clip art files

6 Click Recolor Picture on the Picture toolbar. The Recolor Picture dialog box opens.

7 Click the down arrow on the New Color box to see the color choices. The selection has been matched to the presentations color scheme.

8 Double-click Gold (Follow Title Text Scheme Color). The New Color box closes, returning you to the Recolor Picture dialog box with the newly colored caduceus in the display window.

9 Click OK. The caduceus is still selected and still in the middle of the slide, but now it's the same gold as the title.

10 Drag the caduceus to the lower right-hand corner, as shown in the illustration at the bottom.

11 Save, but do not close, the presentation.

Inserting clip art files into Microsoft Clip Gallery

From time to time you may come across neat clip art you'd like to add to the Gallery, making it available any time you search for appropriate illustrations. In this exercise, you'll insert the FotoFriendly, Inc., logo into the Microsoft Clip Gallery.

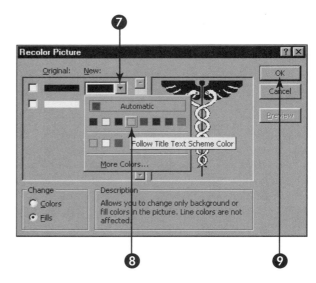

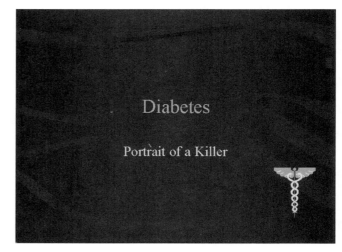

Inserting clip art files

1 With any presentation open to any slide in Slide view and nothing selected, click Insert ➢ Picture ➢ Clip Art. The Microsoft Clip Gallery appears.

2 Click Import Clips.

3 On the Add Clip Art to Clip Gallery dialog box, navigate to where you stored the files that came with this book.

4 Double-click Logo.bmp. The Clip Properties dialog box appears.

5 In the keywords box, type the following: **SnapTracker, family, camera, vacation, photograph, FotoFriendly**.

TIP

You can use these keywords to find this particular piece of clip art later. If you can think of any other relevant keywords, go ahead and add them. Generally speaking, you want to include as many keywords as you can possibly think of so that you will find the clip art easily when it is appropriate to your need.

6 In the Categories box, click to select the following Categories: Business, Cartoons, People, Seasons, Special Occasions, Sports & Leisure, Travel, and Weather.

7 Click New Category. The New Category dialog box opens.

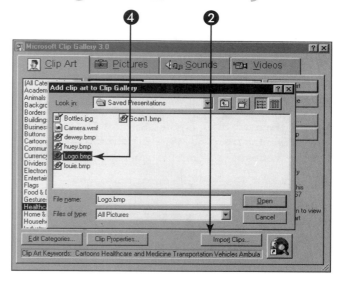

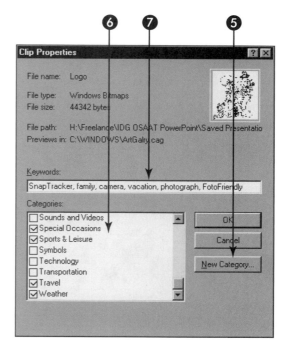

Inserting clip art files

8 Type the following in the New Category Name box:
SnapTracker.

9 Click OK on the New Category dialog box.

10 Click OK on the Clip Properties dialog box.

11 Click Close on the Microsoft Clip Gallery dialog box.

12 Test the new art. Open the Microsoft Clip Gallery to the Pictures tab (remember, the Clip Art tab takes only *.wmf files, and the logo is a *.bmp file, which puts it on the Pictures tab).

13 Click Find. The Find Clip dialog box opens.

 NOTE *Different keywords will result in different groupings of images. Experiment.*

14 Type the following in the Keywords box: **vacation**.

15 Click Find Now. The Microsoft Clip Gallery returns to the Pictures tab with the Logo image displayed.

16 Click Close.

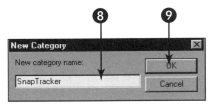

▶ Editing clip art in the Microsoft Clip Gallery

Things change. Stuff happens. Time marches forward. Annoying cliches never die. And clip art needs vary. What do you do if you don't want outdated clip art cluttering your Microsoft Clip Gallery? Or what do you do if you realize you need to change the keywords for an image? What you do is this . . . .

① Switch to Slide #1 in Slide view, if necessary.

> **TIP**
>
> *Actually, it doesn't really matter what presentation you open for this exercise, but you must have a presentation open in order to successfully edit clip art in the Microsoft Clip Gallery.*

② Select Insert ➤ Picture ➤ Clip Art. The Microsoft Clip Gallery dialog box opens.

③ Switch to the Pictures tab, if necessary.

④ Click Edit Categories.

⑤ On the Edit Category List, select SnapTracker.

⑥ Click Rename Category.

⑦ In the Rename Category box, type **FotoFriendly**.

⑧ Click OK on the Rename Category box.

⑨ Click Close on the Edit Category List.

⑩ Click Close on the Pictures tab of the Microsoft Clip Gallery.

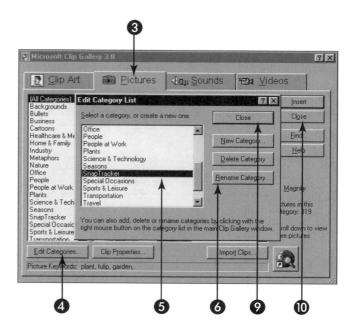

Deleting clip art files

Deleting clip art files from Microsoft Clip Gallery

What goes up, must come down. And what you add to the Microsoft Clip Gallery, you may eventually wish to remove. It can be done, but not with your eyes closed. For this exercise, you're going remove a file: the logo file.

1 With the Annual Employee Meeting presentation still open to Slide #1 in Slide view, select Insert ➢ Picture ➢ Clip Art.

2 Switch to the Pictures tab.

3 Click Find. The Find Clip dialog box opens.

4 On the Find Clip dialog box, type the following in the Keywords box: **Vacation**.

5 Select the SnapTracker logo.

6 With the logo selected, click Clip Properties. The Clip Properties dialog box opens.

7 Write down the complete pathname for the Logo.bmp file.

8 Click Cancel on the Clip Properties dialog box.

9 Click Close on the Microsoft Clip Gallery.

10 Open Windows Explorer.

11 Navigate to the file you wrote down.

TIP *It might be easier to just use the Tools ➢ Find ➢ Files or Folders feature, just type in **logo.bmp**, and let Windows Explorer find the file. You choose.*

12 Select that file in Windows Explorer.

13 Press Delete. (If prompted to make sure, click Yes.) It's history.

14 Close the Diabetes presentation.

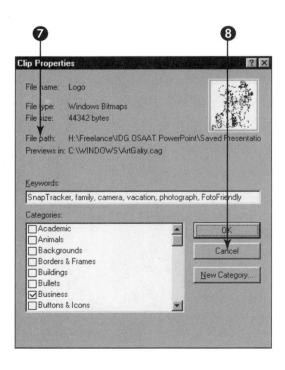

ODDS AND ENDS

There are a couple of other tricks you can use whenever you work with PowerPoint, but they don't fit neatly into any chapter groupings. The first is Multiple Undo, which allows you to undo one or several previous actions all at once. The other is AutoRecover, which you will not use voluntarily, but for which you will be immensely grateful.

Using multiple undo

When you use Multiple Undo, you effectively erase a series of actions. If you just want to undo the most recent action, you can just click Undo on the Standard toolbar or click Edit ➤ Undo. When you realize that you've performed a whole series of incorrect tasks or functions, you could still click Undo on the Standard toolbar, reading the name of each undo function till you are caught up — *or*, you could do it like this (first you have to create stuff you don't want) . . . .

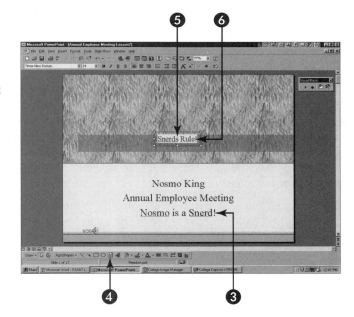

1 On Slide #1 of the Annual Employee Meeting presentation, click in the text box, at the end of the Annual Employee Meeting line.

2 Press Enter.

3 Add a third line, as follows: **Nosmo is a Snerd!**

4 Click the Insert Text box on the Drawing toolbar.

5 Click in the center of the slide to open the text box.

6 Type the following in the text box: **Snerds Rule!**

7 Select AutoShapes, as shown in the illustration to the right.

8 Select Basic Shapes.

9 Click the Sun shape.

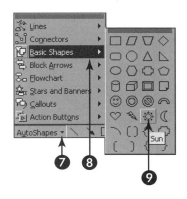

Using AutoRecover

⑩ Position the sun shape on the slide as shown in the illustration to the right.

⑪ Okay. You've just inserted a bunch of junk onto the slide, and you want to get rid of it. Click the down arrow of the Undo button on the Standard toolbar.

NOTE *Your Undo list may not be exactly the same as mine, but you should be able to figure out which actions you want to undo. On the illustration the first action (Move Object) refers to my positioning the sun;* "Insert AutoShape" *refers to the insertion of the sun shape on the slide;* "Move Object" *refers to when I moved the Snerds Rule box so it was centered (I didn't tell you to do that, assuming that you'd be better at centering the text box, but don't worry about it);* "Typing" *refers to the typing of the words* "Snerds Rule!"; "Insert Text Box" *refers to inserting the box into which I typed Snerds Rule; and* "Typing" *refers to the line* "Nosmo is a Snerd!"

⑫ Select all five or six actions that relate to Nosmo's snerdiness. A little box at the bottom of the list tells you how many items you've selected.

⑬ Click the bottom item. Voilà! Back to normal.

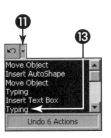

TIP *When you click the last task (or any midlist task), you are, in effect, clicking it and everything above it. When you click to delete, you delete it and everything above it. Use this valuable tool, but use it carefully.* The same applies to the ReDo tool.

⑭ You didn't do anything worth saving, so just close the presentation.

Using AutoRecover

The AutoRecover feature is one that will make you fall down on your knees and kiss your PowerPoint 97 CD. Picture this. It's 2 in the morning. You missed your kid's karate demonstration. It's your anniversary and your spouse's birthday. Yet, at 4 in the afternoon, your boss said he needed a presentation by 8 o'clock tomorrow morning. You've been chained to your computer ever since. You're almost done when (the very thought of this horror makes my arms get all goosebumpy), the power fails and your computer shuts off.

Do not despair. You needn't chain your computer to your ankle, drive to the nearest dock, and fling yourself into the deep. Although I am sympathetic to the home situation created by an insensitive boss (this would have to be your *real* boss, as Nosmo King would never do such a thing, by the way), you are on your own with that one. The computer problem, however, can be easily remedied. By the way, the AutoRecover feature must be defined and turned on *before* the power failure if you have any hope of recovering the data. Do it now!

❶ Select Tools ➢ Options. The Options dialog box opens.

❷ Click the Save tab.

❸ Make sure there is a check mark in the Save AutoRecover Info Every box. If there is no check mark, click to put one there.

❹ Think about how much work you're willing to lose. The default is 10 minutes, but you can change that. I keep the default, but you can choose whatever you want. Now, if there's a power or equipment failure for any reason, you won't lose more than 10 minutes (or whatever time you specified) of work.

❺ Click OK.

❻ When the power is restored after a failure, restart your computer.

❼ All presentations that were open when the power failed will automatically reopen. You need to do a Save As (giving them their original names back) for each one.

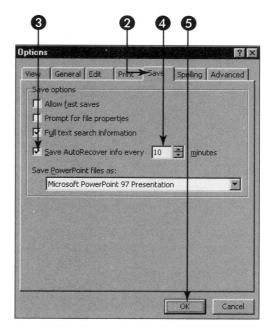

NOTE

This is critically important. If you fail to save a recovered document using the Save As feature, then it will disappear forever when you exit PowerPoint.

7

Odds & Ends — An Eclectic Collection of Tips and Tricks

Using AutoRecover

The following table lists the standard default settings on each tab in the Options dialog box.

STANDARD DEFAULT SETTINGS

Tab	Option	Default Setting
View	Show: Startup dialing	Selected
	Show: New slide dialog	Selected
	Show: Status bar	Selected
	Show: Vertical ruler	Selected
	Slide Show: Pop-up menu on right mouse click	Selected
	Slide Show: Show pop-up menu button	Selected
	Slide Show: End with black slide	*Not* selected
General	General Options: Provide feedback with sound to screen elements	*Not* selected
	General Options: Recently used file list	Selected — 4 entries
	General Options: Macro virus protected	Selected
	General Options: Link sounds with file size greater than . . .	100K
	User information	Your name in the "Name" field (or the name of the licensee)
		Your initials in the "Initials" field (or the initials of the licensee)
Edit	Text: Replace straight quotes with smart quotes	Selected
	Text: Automatic word selection	Selected

Tab	Option	Default Setting
	Text: Use smart cut and paste	Selected
	Text: Drag-and-drop text editing	Selected
	Inserting: New charts take on PowerPoint font	Selected
	Undo: Maximum number of undos	Selected — 20
Print	Printing Options: Background printing	Selected
	Printing Options: Print TrueType fonts as graphics	*Not* selected
	Printing Options: Print inserted objects at printer resolution	*Not* selected
	Options for current document only	Entire section *not* selected
Save	Save Options: Allow fast saves	Selected
	Save Options: Prompt for file properties	*Not* selected
	Save Options: Full-text search information	Selected
	Save Options: Save AutoRecover info every . . .	Selected — 10 minutes
	Save PowerPoint files as:	Microsoft PowerPoint 97 presentation
Spelling	Check spelling as you type: Spelling	Selected
	Check spelling as you type: Hide spelling errors	*Not* selected
	Suggest: Always	Selected

continued

Odds & Ends — An Eclectic Collection of Tips and Tricks

7

Skills Challenge

Tab	Option	Default Setting
	Ignore: Words in UPPERCASE	Selected
	Ignore: Words with numbers	Selected
Advanced	Picture: Render 24–bit bitmaps at highest quality	Selected
	Picture: Export pictures–best for printing	Selected
	Picture: Export pictures–best for on–screen viewing	*Not* selected
	File Locations: Default file location	Shows path for your default file location

SKILLS CHALLENGE

Are you beginning to feel more powerful? More masterful? Well, you should. In this Skills Challenge, you'll make some changes to the Setup Options, create the banner for the meeting, restore the blue and gold template (yes, your boss saw what Huey, Dewey, and Louie made you do; their ducks are cooked), and add some things to the Microsoft Clip Gallery.

 Do you remember how to change the number of files shown at the bottom of the File drop–down menu?

❶ Turn the Allow Fast Saves back on (you don't even have to open a presentation to do this).

 Do you remember how to define a custom page layout?

❷ Turn Render 24–Bit Bitmaps at Highest Quality back on.

 Do you remember how to view your presentation in black and white?

Troubleshooting

3 Restore the Blue and Gold Template to the Annual Employee Meeting presentation.

4 Change all bullets in the Annual Employee Meeting presentation to smiley faces. Remember to set their color to Automatic.

TIP

When you get to the Where We Are slide, apply the smiley face bullets only to the main bullets, not the subbullets.

  Do you remember how to Show Formatting in Outline view?

5 Delete Slides #8, #9, and #10.

6 Save and close the presentation.

TROUBLESHOOTING

This lesson covered a lot of ground, most of which is not shaky, but you still might have a few questions. Use this troubleshooting table to see if you can find the answers.

Problem	Solution
I tried and tried and tried, but I cannot select a bullet.	And you never will! Individual bullets cannot be selected, but when you select the text associated with the bullet, you achieve the same goal.
All of a sudden, my bullets are all clock faces.	This will probably never happen to you, but if it does, here's what's going on. PowerPoint uses the Symbol font as the basis for its default bullet. If that file becomes corrupted or damaged, PowerPoint switches to WingDings clock face. You need to reinstall the Symbol font files (or cop out entirely and just choose a different bullet).

Wrap up

Problem	Solution
I tried to insert a bullet, but they are so teeny tiny on the Bullets dialog box that I gave up.	Click what you *think* might be the one you want. When you single-click, it gets much larger. Then, if it is one you want, click Insert.
I had AutoRecover turned on, but after power was restored following a power failure, I couldn't save the recovered presentation.	No problem. Stop sweating. Navigate to the Temp folder for the active drive (it's usually in the Windows folder). Select "All Files" in the Files of Type box and then look for the file(s) you need. They should all be named *AutoRecover Save of xxx*, with "xxx" representing the original filename. Open the file you want and then save it normally. Remember that all unsaved recovered files will be permanently sent to the Big Byte Bucket in the Sky when you turn PowerPoint off.

WRAP UP

A busy lesson, eh? But you learned a lot and fine-tuned the presentations. Specifically, you learned how to

- Set custom options
- Customize the Page Setup
- Change bullet styles
- View slides in black and white
- Expand and collapse individual slides as well as all at once
- Turn formatting on and off in Outline view
- Save your presentation as a template
- Apply templates to presentations
- Use the AutoClipArt feature to suggest clip art possibilities

- Insert clip art, sound, video, and picture files into the ClipArt Gallery

- Undo more than one action at a time

- Recover from a power failure

In the next lesson, you'll learn how to use PowerPoint with other Microsoft Office components.

7

Odds & Ends — An Eclectic Collection of Tips and Tricks

Working with Other Office 97 Components

30 MINUTES

GOALS

In Lesson 8 you'll learn how to use PowerPoint 97 with two other Microsoft products: Microsoft Word and Microsoft Excel. You'll learn about:

- Exporting PowerPoint outlines to Microsoft Word
- Importing outline text from Microsoft Word
- Linking files to Microsoft Excel

Linking versus embedding

Whether your copy of PowerPoint 97 came as a stand–alone product or as part of the Office suite of programs, you'll learn in this lesson how to use other Microsoft programs to enhance your presentation. In addition to having PowerPoint up and running, you should copy the following files from the Lesson 8 folder on the CD–ROM to your hard disk: Career Day Outline.rtf, The Money.xls, and Inventory.xls. In order to be able to successfully work through this lesson, you must also have Microsoft Word and Microsoft Excel installed and available. When you're through with this lesson, your files should look like the following ones: AEM–EOL8.ppt, AEMoutline.rtf, CareerDay97–EOL8.ppt, Diabetes97–EOL8.ppt, and Diabetes97Outline.rtf.

LINKING VERSUS EMBEDDING

Before you plunge into the lesson's exercises, you need to have at least a smattering of understanding about what it means for PowerPoint 97 to "work with" other Microsoft products. Basically, it means that text, data, or objects in one program may be used in any of the others.

There are two ways to achieve that cooperation: linking files or embedding objects. When you link files, there is an invisible connection running between them. For example, in the Annual Employee Meeting presentation, the Balance Sheet could have been linked to Microsoft Excel, but instead you inserted it as an object. What's the difference? While a linked file may be visible in a presentation, all its data remains in the source file. For example, if the Balance Sheet had been linked and changes to the numbers were made in the Excel file, they would automatically and instantly be reflected in the slide. Since the Balance Sheet is not linked, however, it would have to be deleted and reinserted to reflect data changes. An embedded object is static; a linked object is dynamic.

WORKING WITH MICROSOFT WORD

Whether you were aware of it at the time or not, you've already worked with Microsoft Word in the course of completing the exercises in this book! Remember creating tables? That was Word's Table function. In the next few exercises, you'll learn more about how PowerPoint 97 and Word 97 cooperate.

Sending files to Word

Now that you've pretty much finished the Annual Employee Meeting (yes, you're almost done!), your boss asks if you can produce the entire presentation outline in report form. Of course, you agree it'll be no problem. Well, guess what. You're right. No problem! (Unless you don't have Word installed on your computer—then there could be a teensy, weensy problem—like, you can't do any of the stuff in this exercise—none of the really important stuff, anyway.)

1 Open the Annual Employee Meeting in Outline view.

2 Select File ➢ Send To.

3 Choose Microsoft Word. The Write-Up dialog box appears.

4 Click Outline Only.

5 Click OK. The outline in Word should look something like the illustration to the right.

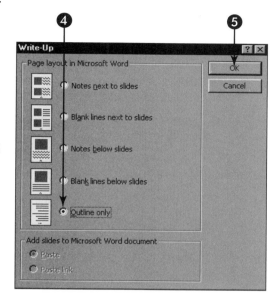

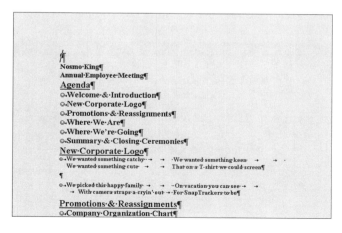

Importing files from Word

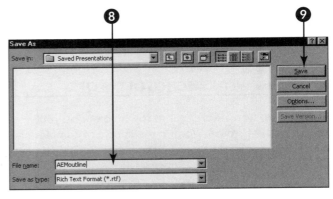

NOTE *PowerPoint automatically opens Word. Then it starts a new, blank file and copies your outline, complete with some formatting and bullets, into the new file. Depending on your machine and the size of your outline, this could take several seconds.*

6 Maximize Word, if necessary.

7 Select File ➤ Save As. The Save As dialog box appears.

8 In the File Name box, replace the default filename with the following: **AEMoutline**.

9 Click Save. (Word automatically adds the .rtf ending, but just to be safe, make sure "Rich Text Format *.rtf" is visible in the Save As Type box.)

10 Select File ➤ Exit.

Importing files from Word

Did you know that you don't have to create your presentation entirely in PowerPoint? You can create a full outline in Word and then import it into PowerPoint. I was recently invited to speak to fourth, fifth, and sixth graders at a local elementary school about the life and career of a writer. In this exercise, you'll import the Career Day outline I created into a PowerPoint presentation.

CREATING YOUR OWN OUTLINE IN WORD

When you create your own outline in Word, keep in mind a couple of important things.

First, in order for the transition from Word to PowerPoint to work properly, you should use Headings 1, 2, 3, and so on for your slide title and bullets.

Second, if you need to make global changes, you can do that in PowerPoint's Outline view. For example, the bullets in Career Day.ppt were originally standard bullets, but I selected all text in Outline view, clicked Format ➤ Bullets, and selected the pencil. It still needed a bit of tweaking, though. Finally, when you save the file, save it using rich text format (.rtf) in the Save As Type box on the Save As dialog box.

Importing files from Word

① Select File ➢ New. The New Presentation dialog box opens.

② Select the Presentation Designs tab.

③ Double-click Portrait Notebook.pot. The New Slide dialog box appears.

④ Double-click the blank AutoLayout. The first slide of the presentation appears (blank of course) with a spiral notebook background.

⑤ Select Insert ➢ Slides from Outline. The Insert Outline dialog box appears.

⑥ Double-click Career Day Outline.rtf. The outline is transferred to the Portrait Notebook style presentation, complete with indented bullets. The first slide is left blank so that you can create a title.

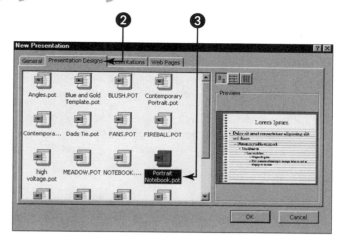

 NOTE

Remember, you're importing a Word outline, not a presentation, so you're looking for a file with the .rtf extension.

⑦ Switch to the first (blank) slide.

⑧ Select Edit ➢ Delete Slide. The blank first slide disappears.

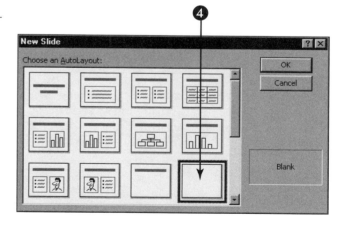

8

Working with Other Office 97 Components

Importing files from Word

9 Click anywhere in the title text of what is now the first slide.

10 Position the cursor over the text box's frame until the cursor turns into a four-way arrow.

11 Drag the text box into the middle of the slide, as shown on the illustration to the right.

12 Now you can edit this presentation the way you would any other presentation, adding slide transitions, clip art, audio or video clips, charts, graphs, or whatever. You can also rearrange it and reformat it.

13 Select File ➤ Save.

14 Navigate to where you stored the files that came with this book.

15 In the File Name box, type **Career Day SlideShow**, as shown on the illustration to the right.

16 Click Save.

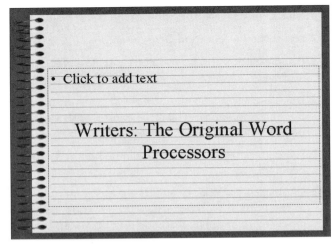

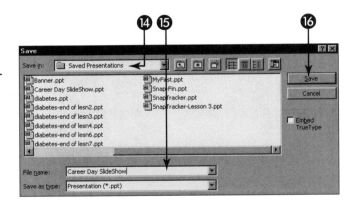

WORKING WITH MICROSOFT EXCEL

You've also already used Microsoft Excel, but you probably didn't realize it. The Balance Sheet you inserted was actually an Excel file. You can move information back and forth between Excel and PowerPoint just as you can with Word.

Linking files from PowerPoint to Excel

Linking files from PowerPoint to Excel

When you inserted the Balance Sheet into the Annual Employee Meeting presentation, you inserted it as an embedded object. That means that if it needs to reflect changed information, someone has to go in and change the data manually. In this exercise, you'll learn how to insert a linked file object. That means that when the data is changed in the source application (in this case, Excel), the table or chart in PowerPoint immediately and instantly reflects those changes the next time the presentation is opened.

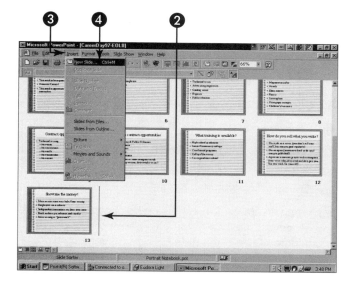

❶ Open the Career Day SlideShow presentation in Slide Sorter view.

❷ Position the cursor to the right of the last slide, as shown to the right.

❸ Select the Insert menu.

❹ Select New Slide. The New Slide dialog box appears.

❺ Double-click the Blank AutoLayout.

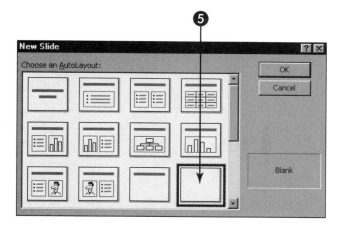

6 Double-click the new, blank slide to switch to Slide view.

7 Select Insert ➢ Object. The Insert Object dialog box opens.

8 Click Create From File. The Insert Object dialog box changes, as shown.

9 Click Link. This puts a check mark in the Link box.

10 Click Browse.

11 Navigate to where you installed the files that came with this book.

12 Double-click The Money.xls.

13 When the Insert Object dialog box comes back, click OK. The Money.xls file is an Excel spreadsheet that drops down in the middle of the blank slide.

14 Use the handles to resize and reposition the object as shown below.

15 Save, but do not close, the presentation.

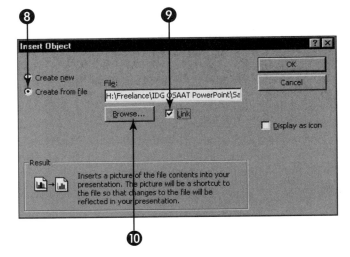

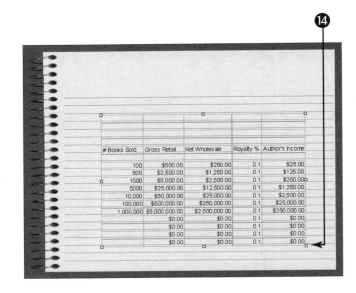

SKILLS CHALLENGE

In this Skills Challenge, you will send the Diabetes presentation to Word in outline form; make some cosmetic changes to the new Writing Careers presentation; and make changes to the money slide on the Writing Careers presentation.

 Do you remember the difference between embedded objects and linked objects?

1 Add a title to the Writing Career's new last slide by typing the following so that it looks like the illustration to the right: **Money? What Money?**

TIP

You may have to resize the spreadsheet object in order for everything to fit. When you create the title in a new text box, use Times New Roman, 44, Centered.

2 Add the following text to the Writing Careers new last slide also: **Let's pretend you wrote a book and a publisher published it. Let's also pretend it'll sell for $5. The publisher gives a 50% discount to the book's distributors and you, the author, get 10% of the other 50% (sometimes more, sometimes less). Here's what your earnings would look like. Remember that VERY FEW books make it to the Best Seller list. You're doing OK if you sell 5000–25,000 copies as a newcomer— over a period of several years!**

 Do you remember what, besides creating tables, you can do in Word for PowerPoint?

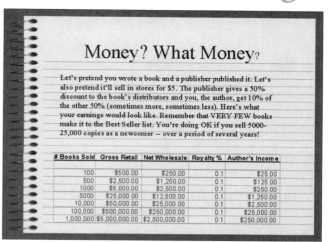

Money? What Money?

Let's pretend you wrote a book and a publisher published it. Let's also pretend it'll sell in stores for $5. The publisher gives a 50% discount to the book's distributors and you, the author, get 10% of the other 50% (sometimes more, sometimes less). Here's what your earnings would look like. Remember that VERY FEW books make it to the Best Seller list. You're doing OK if you sell 5000-25,000 copies as a newcomer -- over a period of several years!

# Books Sold	Gross Retail	Net Wholesale	Royalty %	Author's Income
100	$500.00	$250.00	0.1	$25.00
500	$2,500.00	$1,250.00	0.1	$125.00
1000	$5,000.00	$2,500.00	0.1	$250.00
5000	$25,000.00	$12,500.00	0.1	$1,250.00
10,000	$50,000.00	$25,000.00	0.1	$2,500.00
100,000	$500,000.00	$250,000.00	0.1	$25,000.00
1,000,000	$5,000,000.00	$2,500,000.00	0.1	$250,000.00

Skills Challenge

3 On the Show Me The Money slide insert one half line between bullets.

 Do you remember what extension to assign to a file you create in Word in order to successfully import it into PowerPoint?

4 Send the Diabetes presentation to Word in outline form. Save it under the name Diabetes97 Outline.rtf.

5 Close the Diabetes presentation.

 Do you remember how to import and link an Excel file into PowerPoint?

6 In the Annual Employee Meeting presentation, insert a new, Title Only slide between the Projected European Sales slide and the Pricing slide.

7 Title the slide **Inventory** and import the Excel program: INVENTORY.XLS. Do not link the file.

8 Reposition and resize it so that it looks like the slide in the illustration.

9 Change the font color in the table to dark blue, if necessary.

10 Save and close the presentation file.

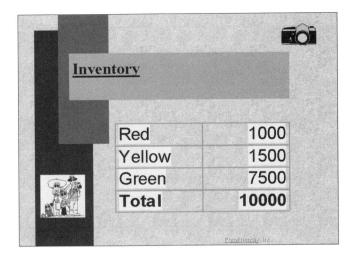

Inventory	
Red	1000
Yellow	1500
Green	7500
Total	**10000**

TROUBLESHOOTING

This chapter has provided you with the tools necessary to exchange files and information between PowerPoint and other Microsoft programs. If you have questions about those other Microsoft programs, consult their user manuals. However, if you thought up any questions about PowerPoint with respect to those programs, maybe this troubleshooting table will help.

Problem	Solution
I keep getting a message that the program can't be found.	There could be a couple of reasons for this. First, is the program installed? If not, you'll get an error message. Second, it may be installed but not properly registered. To remedy this, you need your Office 97 disc handy. Click Start ➢ Run and in the Open dialog box type the path to the Setup program followed by "/y/r" (without the quotation marks). Press Enter.
My Word file isn't coming into PowerPoint properly.	Make sure you save it in .rtf format.

WRAP UP

This lesson has helped you figure out how to share data between Microsoft programs and, if you use Office 97, it should have helped you figure out how to use the suite of programs together. Among other things, you've learned how to

- Tell the difference between linked and embedded objects

- Send files to Word

- Import files from Word

- Link files from PowerPoint to Excel

    In the next lesson, you'll learn how to polish the presentation.

Polishing the Presentation

GOALS

In this lesson, you're going to make a last ditch effort to really perk up the Annual Employee Meeting presentation. Here's a list of just some of the things you'll be doing:

- Adding action buttons
- Changing tabs
- Adding comments
- Adding narration
- Playing music from a CD
- Timing the presentation
- Viewing the presentation on two computers
- Rehearsing slide timings
- Using the Style Checker
- Previewing the finished product

Adding action buttons

To complete this lesson, you'll need the CareerDay97–EOL8.ppt and Diabetes97–EOL8ppt files in the Lesson 9 folder. You may also want to look at CareerDay97–EOL9.ppt and Diabetes97–EOL9.ppt when you've finished. In addition, you'll need some special tools to complete this lesson: a microphone; a CD drive that will also play audio CDs, and a sound recording capability in your computer. You'll also need access to a second, connected computer. Don't worry if you don't have all these items. Just skip the exercises you're not outfitted to do.

SPIFFING UP THE SLIDES

There's not much you can add to the slides at this point without making them too busy, but in this lesson, you'll learn how to add action buttons and change tabs.

Adding action buttons

Action buttons are embossed objects, usually located at the bottom of a slide, that allow you to complete some action during the slide show without having to use the Standard (or any other) toolbar. In this exercise, you'll add Action buttons to all the slides in the Career Day SlideShow presentation and format the buttons' appearance and performance.

❶ Open the Career Day SlideShow presentation in any view.

❷ Switch to the Slide Master.

❸ Open the Slide Show menu.

❹ Select Action Buttons.

❺ Choose the Forward or Next button. The cursor changes to a big plus sign.

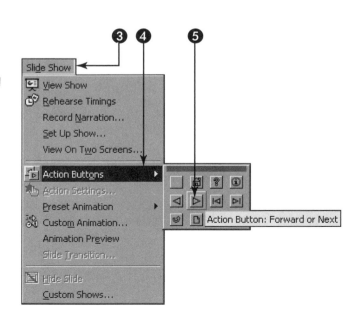

6 Click in the lower right–hand corner of the Slide Master. The Next Slide action button appears and the Action Settings dialog box opens.

7 Click OK.

NOTE

When you accept the default settings, you set up the button to move the presentation to the next slide whenever you click the button. Notice on the Action Settings dialog box that the Hyperlink To button is selected, showing the "Next Slide" as the hyperlink destination.

8 Grab one of the button's handles and resize it so it's much smaller.

9 Select the button again.

10 Click the down arrow of the Fill Color button on the Drawing toolbar, as shown on the illustration to the right.

11 Select light brown (third from the left) to change the color of the action button from green to brown.

12 With the action button still selected, click Slide Show.

13 Select Action Settings from the Slide Show menu. The Action Settings dialog box reappears.

14 Click Play Sound to put a check mark in the box.

15 Click the down arrow of the Sound box.

16 Select Laser.

17 Click OK.

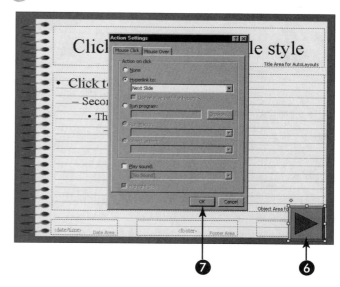

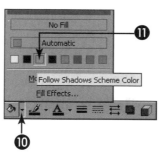

9

Polishing the Presentation

Adjusting tabs

Now, when you click the Next Slide button to advance slides in this presentation, you'll hear the laser sound. Go ahead! Try it! Try clicking anywhere else in the slide. You'll still advance to the next slide, but there won't be any sound.

18 Save, but do not close, the presentation.

Adjusting tabs

As with any typewritten document there will be times when you want to adjust the tab settings. If you're familiar with Word, then you already know how to do this. This lesson will give you a chance to see just what you do know, but don't worry, if you don't know how to do it, you will by lesson's end!

1 With the Slide Master still onscreen, select View ➤ Ruler if it's not already selected. A ruler appears at the top of the slide work area.

2 Click anywhere in the text in the Object Area for AutoLayouts. The ruler at the top shows where all the current tab stops are.

3 Grab the last tab on top (it should start out just above the 2 on the ruler) and move it to the right until it's directly over the number 3 on the ruler, as shown.

If you're not sure exactly what happened, keep your eyes on the slide and click Edit ➤ Undo. The "Fifth level" tabbed text skootches over to the right just a bit.

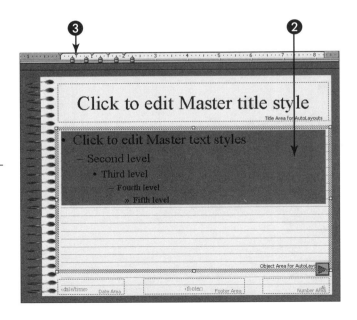

Click to edit Master title style

Title Area for AutoLayouts

- Click to edit Master text styles
  - Second level
    - Third level
      - Fourth level
        » Fifth level

Object Area for AutoLayouts

date/time   Date Area   footer   Footer Area   Number Area

④ Save, but do not close, the presentation.

COMMENTING ON THE SLIDES

In these exercises, you're going to pretend a colleague has given you the Career Day presentation to evaluate. You'll communicate your comments about each slide by using the Comments feature.

Adding comments

❶ Switch to Slide #2 in Slide view.

❷ Open the View menu.

❸ Select Toolbars.

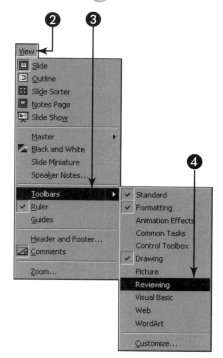

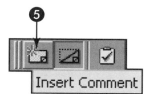

9

Polishing the Presentation

Hiding comments

4 Choose Reviewing. The Reviewing toolbar opens.

5 Click Insert Comment. A yellow text box opens with your name in it and the cursor anxiously awaiting your input.

6 Type the following in the Comment box: **Shouldn't there be a question mark after "Writer or Author"?**

6

Marilyn Kyd:

Shouldn't there be a question mark after "Writer or Author"

TIP *You can resize the comment box, or you can just type in it. It will expand as necessary to accommodate what you type, keeping the same right and left margins. If you'd rather have a wider comment box, then drag the right–middle handle (left will work, too, but there's less room to maneuver).*

7 Drag the whole comment so that its right edge rests just off the left edge of the slide.

NOTE *If you leave the comment anywhere within the boundaries of the slide and then switch to Slide Show view, you will see the comment. By placing it off to the side, you can read the comment and the full slide at the same time.*

8 Save, but do not close, the presentation.

Hiding comments

No matter how wonderfully creative or constructive, sometimes the show must go on before you have a chance to respond to the comments. You don't want to run the presentation with the comments showing, yet you don't want to get rid of them. PowerPoint includes a Hide Comments feature that lets you literally hide the comments. Later, when no one is looking, you can unhide them and do your editing. In this exercise, you learn how to hide and then unhide a comment.

1 With Slide #2 still open in Slide view, click Show/Hide Comments on the Reviewing toolbar.

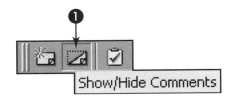

1

Show/Hide Comments

You can actually perform this exercise with the slide displayed in any view except Slide Show or Slide Sorter. When you click Hide/Unhide Comment, all comments within the presentation immediately disappear — from view — not from the presentation. This ensures that no comments will be visible during the showing of a presentation.

② To unhide comments, click Show/Hide Comments again.

③ Save and close the presentation.

ADDING NARRATION

You can add narration to a slide show in a variety of ways and for a variety of reasons. For example, if you give your presentation to a bunch of people, but some key people are unable to make it, you can give them a copy of the presentation, complete with your narration, to look at and listen to at their leisure. You can even record comments made *during* the slide show and then keep the presentation file as a record of what was said. By the way, no narration has been added to the files on the CD-ROM.

Adding narration to a presentation

In this exercise, you'll add narration to the entire Diabetes presentation. If your system does not include sound and recording capabilities, however, you'll be stopped cold at step 2. The Record Narration option will not be available to you (it will appear grayed out).

① Open the Diabetes97–EOL8.ppt presentation in any view.

Adding narration to a presentation

If you've been working straight through the lessons, then the ruler is probably still visible at the top of your screen. If you find this annoying, it's easy to get rid of. Click View ➤ Ruler to deselect it, and it will go away.

2 Select Slide Show ➤ Record Narration. The Record Narration dialog box appears. In the Current Recording Quality portion of the Record Narration dialog box, you see a description of the quality of recording about to take place (the options are Untitled, CD, Radio, and Telephone). The recording type dictates the access speed. This portion of the Record Narration dialog box also shows you the amount of free space available on your hard drive and how many minutes of recorded narration that translates to. Keep in mind that the longer the narration, the more disk space will be required.

3 Click Settings. The Sound Selection dialog box appears superimposed over the Record Narration dialog box as shown in the illustration to the right.

4 Click the down arrow of the Name box.

5 Choose CD Quality.

6 Click OK on the Sound Selection dialog box.

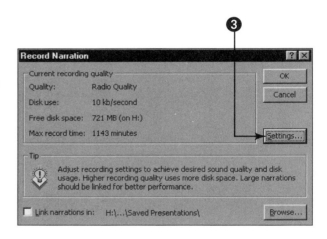

NOTE

Notice the change in Max Record Time. Recording in CD Quality requires massive hard disk space.

7 Click OK on the Record Narration dialog box.

8 As soon as the first slide appears, say this: **Welcome Ladies and Gentlemen**.

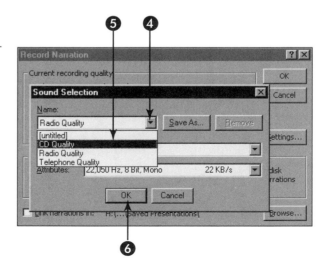

9 Click to move to the next slide.

10 Say this: **Millions of people in the United States and all over the world have diabetes. Thousands more have it and don't know it. How do you know if you're likely to have or develop diabetes?**

11 Click to move to the next slide. Say **This is Slide number** (whatever the slide number is).

12 Repeat step 11 throughout the presentation.

13 When you click the last slide to signal that you're done with it, your screen will go black except for the following message: "The narrations have been saved with each slide. Do you want to save the slide timings also?" as shown to the right. Click Yes.

13

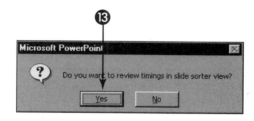

14 A new message appears: "Do you want to review timings in slide sorter view?" You would normally say yes to this, but right now, just say no. You'll be returned to the view you were in when you started the narration.

14

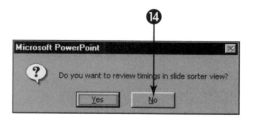

15 Save, but do not close, the presentation.

Adding narration to a single slide

There may be a time when you only want narration associated with one or two slides. In this exercise, you'll learn how to do that.

1 Switch to Slide #4 in Slide view.

2 Open the Insert menu.

3 Select Movies and Sounds.

9

Polishing the Presentation

Deleting narration

4 Choose Record Sound. The Record Sound dialog box appears.

5 In the Name box, type **SMBG**. This tells PowerPoint that you're about to record narration for the SMBG slide.

6 Click the big red Record button and begin the following narration: **SMBG, or Self-Monitoring Blood Glucose, is critically important to a person with diabetes. By monitoring your own blood glucose level, any time or anywhere, you can respond immediately to highs (which may require insulin) or lows (which require food) and avoid trips to the local ER.**

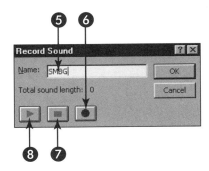

 NOTE *As you talk, the Total Sound Length line on the Record Sound dialog box shows you the total elapsed time for the narration.*

7 Click the black square (Stop) to stop recording.

8 Click the right-pointing triangle (Play) to listen to your recording. If it sounds hunky-dory, click OK. A little sound icon appears on the slide to remind you there is narration. It will probably drop into an inappropriate place.

9 Drag the speaker icon to the lower right-hand corner.

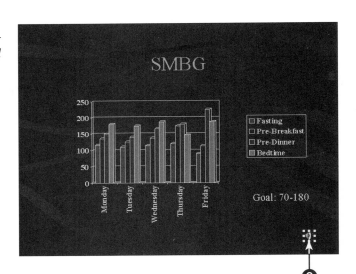

Deleting narration

A person can only listen to the recorded sound of his or her own voice so many times before going legally berserk. Fortunately, PowerPoint makes it easy to delete narration. Really, really easy!

1 With the SMBG slide still displayed in Slide view, click the little sound icon.

2 Press Delete. The narration is gone.

3 Save, but do not close, the presentation.

ADDING MUSIC

While the LAcool music clip that you inserted into the Annual
Employee Meeting was fun, it ran for just under one minute. In
PowerPoint you can actually play music from a CD during your
presentation.

▶ ## Inserting music from a CD

Grab one of your favorite sound CDs and, in this exercise, learn how
to make it play during your presentation.

1 Switch to the first slide in Slide view, if necessary.

2 Insert a music CD in your computer's CD player.

3 Open the Insert menu.

4 Select Movies and Sounds.

5 Choose Play CD Audio Track. The Play Options dialog box
appears.

*Notice that this dialog box automatically shows you
the total playing time for the CD.*

6 Click Loop Until Stopped. This causes the audio CD to play over
and over and over again until your ears bleed.

*When you choose Loop, you also need to select a start
and stop point for the loop. The CD in my CD player
has 20 tracks. Check yours. If you want to play the
entire CD over and over again, just click OK. If you
want to restrict the repetitive play to the first track or a set of tracks,
specify that preference in the Start Track and End Track boxes.*

7 Click OK. A little CD appears, probably in the center of your
slide, as shown in the illustration to the right.

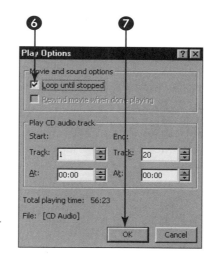

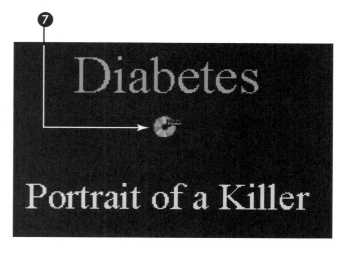

9

Polishing the Presentation

Rehearsing time settings

8 Drag the CD icon to the lower-left corner of the slide.

9 Double-click the CD icon to play the CD.

10 Double-click it again to stop the music (this works even when the music was set to loop).

11 Save, but do not close, the presentation.

REHEARSED TIME SETTINGS

You're getting closer and closer to show time! Before you give the presentation, though, you need to have a pretty good idea of how long it will take. How long should each slide be on screen? On the Annual Employee Meeting presentation, you arbitrarily set each slide to five seconds. In the Diabetes presentation, though, you're going to set more realistic times. First, review the text in Appendix C. You'll use it in the following exercises.

Rehearsing time settings

1 Switch to the first slide in Slide Sorter view.

2 Select Slide Show ➤ Rehearse Timings. After a few seconds, the slide show will begin and a Rehearsal dialog box appears in the lower right-hand corner.

3 Read aloud the appropriate text for each slide (refer to Appendix C for that text) as you would deliver it in a real presentation situation.

4 When you finish the text for a slide, click the right-pointing triangle (Forward) button on the Rehearsal dialog box. The next slide appears, and you can read the text for that slide.

⑤ Continue reading text and advancing slides until you finish.

⑥ When you finish the last slide, PowerPoint tells you how long it took to go all the way through the presentation and then asks if you want to record those timings and use them when you view the slide show. If you answer Yes, these rehearsed timings take precedence over any automatic slide advancement settings you may have assigned previously. Click No for now.

TIP

If you botch up a slide (like those TV bloopers), just click Repeat on the Rehearsal dialog box. You'll get a second chance without messing up anything else.

⑦ Save, but do not close, the presentation.

VIEWING A PRESENTATION ON TWO COMPUTERS

What do you do if your computer won't run a presentation? You use the View on Two Computers feature and control the presentation from one computer while displaying it on another computer. Probably the most common situation where you would use this feature would be if you were controlling the presentation from your own computer, but your audience was watching a different one—say, a really big one. Naturally, the two computers must be linked.

Viewing one presentation on two computers

In this exercise, you'll learn how to control the presentation from one computer and view it on another.

9

Polishing the Presentation

Viewing on two computers

① Select Slide Show ➢ View on Two Screens. The View on Two Screens dialog box appears.

② Click Presenter. This will be the controlling computer.

③ Click the down arrow of the Select the Port You Want to Use box to view the port choices.

④ Select the port appropriate to your equipment setup.

⑤ Make sure the two computers are, in fact, connected to one another.

⑥ Go to the other computer.

⑦ Open PowerPoint.

⑧ Select Slide Show ➢ View on Two Screens.

⑨ On the View on Two Screens dialog box, click Audience.

⑩ Click the down arrow of the Select the Port You Want to Use box to view the port choices.

⑪ Select the port appropriate for the equipment setup.

⑫ Click OK.

⑬ Return to the original computer.

⑭ Click OK and run the presentation normally.

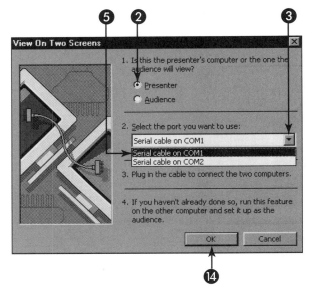

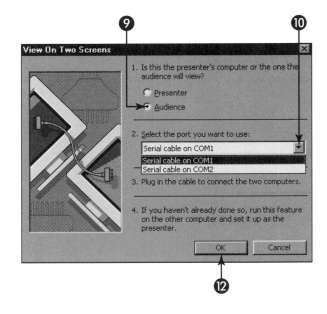

Checking with the Style Checker

CHECKING STYLES

You're getting really close to being ready to present this slide show. First, you need to make sure you haven't made any embarrassing gaffes. The Style Checker works like a human editor. It looks for errors that would cause distractions from your presentation: too many different fonts, too many words, screwy punctuation, and so on.

Checking the presentation with the Style Checker

In this exercise, you'll run the Diabetes presentation through the Style Checker to see how it fares.

① With the Diabetes presentation still open to any slide, select Tools ➢ Style Checker. The Style Checker dialog box appears.

② Make sure there is a check mark in each of the three boxes (Spelling, Visual Clarity, and Case and End Punctuation).

③ Click Options. The Style Checker Options dialog box appears with the Case and End Punctuation tab visible.

④ If your settings are different from the illustration, change them so that they match the illustration.

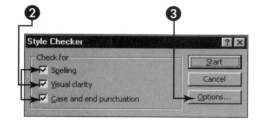

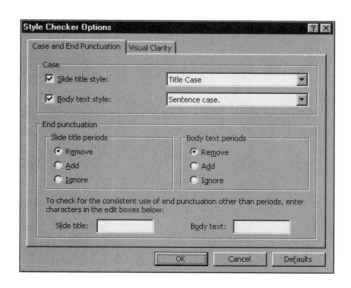

Skills challenge

⑤ Switch to the Visual Clarity tab, as shown on the illustration to the right.

⑥ If your settings are different from the illustration, change them so that they match the illustration.

⑦ Click OK. The Style Checker dialog box reappears.

⑧ Click Start. The Style Checker begins with the spelling check and finds *Humalog*, as shown.

⑨ Click Ignore All to ignore future instances of *Humalog*.

⑩ Next it warns you that the text on Slide #3 is too small. Ignore it for now by clicking OK.

⑪ Save, but do not close, the presentation.

SKILLS CHALLENGE

❶ Insert the Home action button on the last slide of the Diabetes presentation.

❷ Change the color of the Home action button on the last Diabetes slide to Follow Accent Scheme Color (hint: it's the third from the right under Automatic).

✴ *Do you remember how to activate an Action button?*

❸ Add one 2-Column Text slide at the end of the Diabetes presentation and title it **Why Diabetes Is A Silent Killer**.

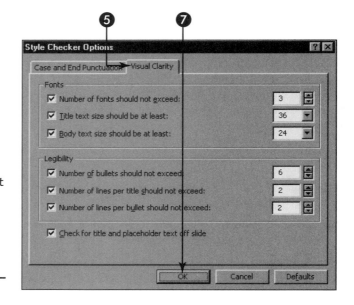

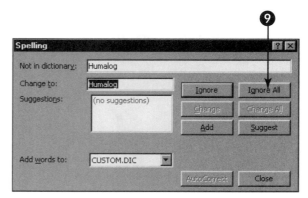

Make the new slide look like the one in the illustration to the right (hint: you'll have to use Format ➤ Line Spacing).

2 *Do you remember how to play a CD during your presentation?*

5 Read the following text for this new slide and retime your presentation:

Diabetes is a silent killer. Untreated or improperly controlled it works silently destroying your body's systems. Vision becomes a problem, complicated by focus difficulties, cataracts and a condition known almost exclusively to diabetes, retinopathy.

Diabetics are also more susceptible to many forms of heart disease ranging from high blood pressure to strokes and heart attacks.

Kidney failure is quite common with diabetes. Most of the patients on dialysis today are diabetic patients.

Neuropathy is a common nervous system ailment that causes a loss of sensation, pain or tingling in hands and/or feet and loss of normal reflexes.

Because people with diabetic neuropathy lose sensation in their feet, they can develop numerous problems ranging from heat, pressure, cold, infections and so on. It's not uncommon for later-stage diabetics to require several amputations, usually beginning with toes.

3 *Do you remember how to hide comments?*

6 Save and close the presentation.

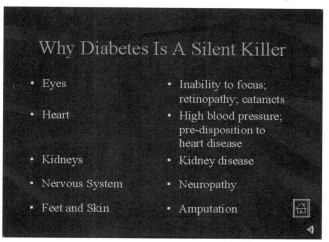

9

Polishing the Presentation

Troubleshooting

7 Add the following comment to the last Career Day slide (hint: you may have to "unhide" comments before you can record a new one): This whole presentation needs to be adjusted so text rests on lines.

 Do you remember how to record narration for a presentation?

8 Check the styles in the Career Day presentation, but first set the following parameters: On the Case and End Punctuation tab, have the Style Checker add periods to just the text, not the slide titles. On the Visual Clarity tab, don't allow more than seven bullets on a slide.

 Do you remember how to link the narration to a different file?

9 Fix the errors found by the Style Checker.

TROUBLESHOOTING

As usual, you probably still have questions and may even have encountered messages or unexpected performance. I hope this troubleshooting table helps.

Problem	Solution
I need to send my PowerPoint 97 file to someone with an older version of PowerPoint.	Open the presentation in PowerPoint 97 then click File ➢ Save As. In the Files of Type list, choose the appropriate PowerPoint version (PowerPoint 95 = .ppt; PowerPoint 95 & 97 = .ppt; PowerPoint 4.0 = .ppt; or PowerPoint 3.0 = .ppt). Assign it a name different from the original.

Problem	Solution
I keep trying to open a PowerPoint 4.0 (or 2.0 or 3.0) in Slide Sorter view (or Outline view or Notes Page view), but it always comes up in Slide view.	Yup. And it always will. That's because when you open it, it's automatically converted to PowerPoint for Windows 95 format, which always changes it to Slide view.
When I try to open a file using Microsoft Quick View for Windows 95, I cannot see the presentation.	That's because the Microsoft Quick View for Windows 95 can't preview files created in any of the Office 97 programs. But, there is a way around the problem. . . .

Open the file in PowerPoint 97, then click File ➢ Save As, and save it as a PowerPoint 4.0 file. |
| Even though I hid the comments, I still see comment outlines. | Microsoft knows this is a problem. As of April 1997, they are working on it. In the meantime, here's what's going on. You probably included it in a grouping and then tried to move the group. If a comment is hidden all by itself, then you don't see the outline, but if it's included in a grouping, you do. |

WRAP UP

Another busy chapter. You learned how to

- Add action buttons
- Adjust tabs
- Add comments

Wrap up

- Hide comments
- Add narration to an entire presentation
- Add narration to a single slide
- Delete narration
- Link narration to another file
- Insert music from a CD
- Rehearse time settings
- View a presentation on one computer and control it from another
- Check styles

In the next lesson, you'll learn how to actually present a presentation!

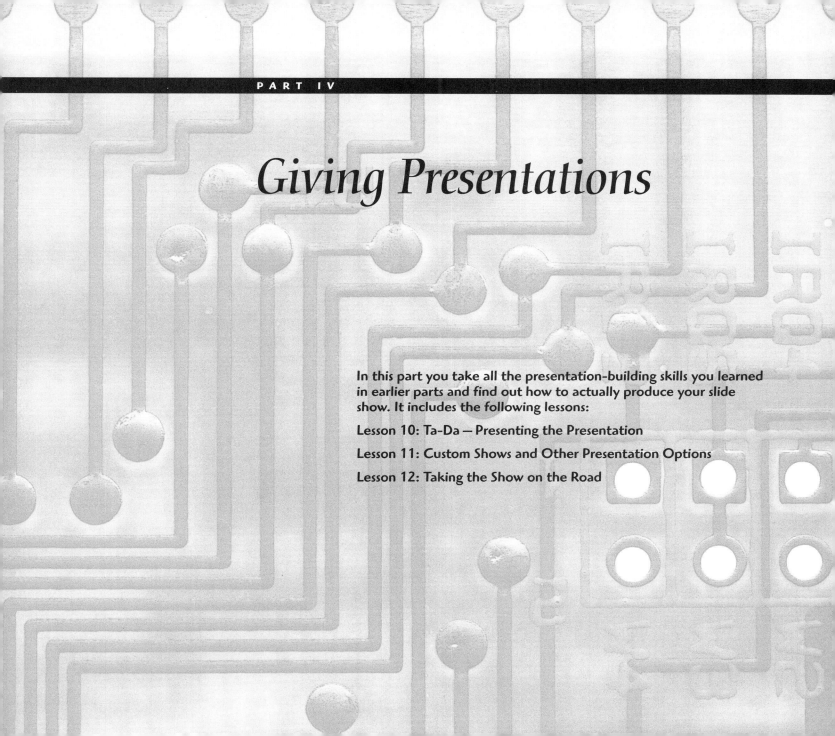

PART IV

Giving Presentations

In this part you take all the presentation-building skills you learned in earlier parts and find out how to actually produce your slide show. It includes the following lessons:

Ta Da — Presenting the Presentation

30 MINUTES

GOALS

Are you ready? In this lesson you get to give the presentation! Along the way, you'll pick up the following skills:

- Setting up the slide show

- Doing various things *while the presentation is running*

- Printing or distributing the presentation in many different ways:

    - Working with color slides

    - Working with overhead projector slides

    - Producing audience handouts

    - Creating speaker notes

    - Printing in black and white

    - Printing outlines

Doing a speaker-controlled presentation

GET READY

To get through this lesson, you'll need your continued and unflagging enthusiasm plus PowerPoint. You'll also need CareerDay97–EOL9.ppt and Diabetes97–EOL9.ppt from the Lesson 10 folder on the CD–ROM to complete the exercises. You may want to look at CareerDay97–EOL10.ppt and Diabetes97–EOL10.ppt at the conclusion of the lesson to see how they compare to your own work. You'll also need a standard noncolor printer (though a color printer would be OK, too).

SETTING UP THE PRESENTATION

The popcorn's popping and the coffee's perking. Your audience is about to arrive, so you need to get set up. The Set Up option on the Slide Show menu lets you choose how you're going to run the presentation. Are you going to run it yourself? Are you going to let it run over and over and over and over so that you can leave it going, as you might at a trade show? Are you going to advance the slides with a mouse click or let the presentation automatically advance according to settings defined earlier? During the setup phase, you answer all these questions and more.

Doing a speaker-controlled presentation

In this exercise you'll set up the Set Up Show parameters so that you can be the one giving the presentation.

❶ Open the CareerDay97–EOL9ppt presentation in any view.

❷ Open the Slide Show menu.

❸ Select Set Up Show. The Set Up Show dialog box appears.

④ In the Show Type box, click Presented by a Speaker (Full Screen), if it is not already selected.

⑤ In the Slides portion of the dialog box, click All to put a check mark in the box (if one is not there already).

NOTE

Selecting "All" means that the entire presentation, from the first slide to the last slide, will run when you start the show. If you only wanted a range of slides, say excluding the first and last, you would type, for instance, a 2 in the From box and a 13 (or whatever is the next-to-last slide in your presentation) in the To box.

⑥ Because you didn't define any slide transitions or automatic advances for this presentation, click Advance Slides Manually in the Advance Slides portion of the dialog box.

⑦ Click OK; the view you started out in returns.

⑧ Click Slide Show.

⑨ Select View Show to see the results of your settings. Remember you will have to click the mouse to advance the slides. This is basically the same kind of slide show you've been viewing throughout this book.

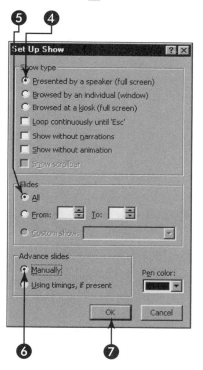

Doing a browsed presentation

In this exercise, you'll set up a presentation to run for an individual viewer. You won't even have to be around. The presentation will run in a window on the screen with the scroll bar visible so that the viewer can advance the slides.

Doing a browsed presentation

① Select Slide Show ➢ Set Up Show to reopen its dialog box.

② Click to put a check mark in the Browsed by an Individual (Window) box.

③ Click Show Scrollbar, if necessary, to select the option.

> **TIP** *When you choose this run option, you must make sure a mouse is available for the viewer (if you're not using automatic slide timings) so that he/she/it can click Next Slide or Previous Slide to advance the*

presentation.

④ Click Loop Continuously Until Esc box to keep the presentation running continuously (or until someone dashes it to the floor or calmly presses Esc).

⑤ The Set Up Show dialog box should still reflect the All Slides and Advance Slides Manually settings from the previous exercise. Click OK.

> **NOTE** *Remember that you can select a range of slides instead of running all of them, and, if you have defined automatic slide timings, you should probably choose to advance slides automatically now. If you do*

use the automatic slide advance option, then you should probably not click the Show Scrollbar option in the Show Type area.

⑥ Select Slide Show ➢ View Show.

⑦ Click to advance the slides and scroll through the presentation. Notice that when you come to the last slide and click, you return to the first slide and start the whole presentation over again.

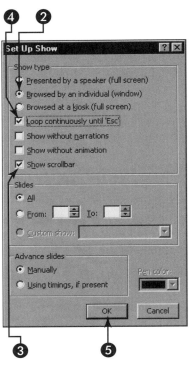

Doing a nonnarrated presentation

Doing a kiosk presentation

What is a kiosk presentation? It's a full-screen, unattended display. You might use such a presentation at a trade show, for example, providing general information about your products or company and leaving the booth personnel free to answer questions and qualify customers. When the presentation is set up for Browsed at a Kiosk, it automatically restarts after five minutes of keyboard inactivity. You can also choose to loop the presentation so that it runs continuously. Another benefit of this option is that while the viewer can advance slides and activate hyperlinks, he/she/it cannot modify the presentation.

1 Select Slide Show ➤ Set Up Show. The Set Up Show dialog box opens.

2 Click to put a check mark in the Browsed at a Kiosk (Full Screen) box. The Loop Continuously Until 'Esc' box is automatically checked and grayed (so you can't turn it off). The Show Scrollbar box is automatically off and unavailable.

3 The Set Up Show dialog box should still reflect the Slides and Advance Slides settings from earlier exercises. Click OK.

4 Select Slide Show ➤ View Show and click your way through it. Notice that the difference between this setup and the one for individual browsing is that this one devotes the full screen to each slide.

5 Press Esc to get out of the kiosk presentation, then save your changes and close the presentation.

Doing a nonnarrated presentation

No matter what other settings you select, if you have recorded a narration, you can opt to turn it off, which you will do in this exercise. The narration is not deleted. It is merely disabled (turned off) until you turn it back on.

1 Open the Diabetes presentation in any view.

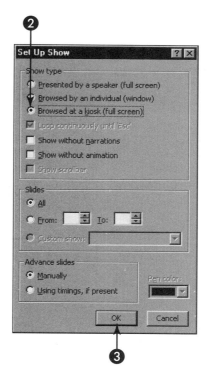

② Select Slide Show ➤ Set Up Show. The Set Up Show dialog box opens.

③ In the Show Type area, click Show without Narrations. The show will still run normally, but if there is a recorded narration, it will not play. This works for all Show Types.

Doing a nonanimated presentation

Sometimes you just want to see the slides and their content without a lot of foofaraw. Whereas you might include all the animation in a more formal setting, once in a while you just want to run it and get out of it. But you don't want to permanently disable the animation.

① With the Set Up Show dialog box still open change the show type to Presented by a Speaker.

② Click Show without Animation. The show will still run normally, but if there are animations on any slides, they will not be active. This works for all Show Types.

TIP *This means that for slides that do have animation, the text will simply appear. It will not fly in from the left or dissolve on or scroll up from the bottom or whatever. As soon as a slide comes up, it will be in a finished, ready-to-view condition.*

③ Click OK.

④ Select Slide Show ➤ View Show and click through the presentation.

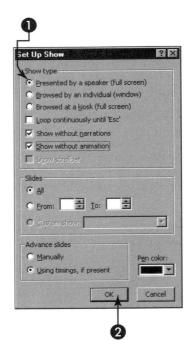

RUNNING THE PRESENTATION

Once you've defined the environment for running the presentation, as covered in the previous exercises, you're ready to actually let the show begin. In these exercises, you'll learn several things you can do while the show is running!

▶ *Marking on a slide during a presentation*

While you're giving your presentation and showing the slides, you might want to draw the audience's attention to a particular item on the slide. You do not need a 10-foot pole to do this. You do not need a newfangled, high-tech, GPS-oriented Star Wars laser pointer to do this (though, admittedly, that might be more fun). In this exercise, you'll learn how to point to things and/or draw on a slide while the presentation is running. One word of warning: When you use the pen (especially if you use it a lot), your slide begins to look like a football play because the lines you draw are usually jaggy.

1 With the Set Up Show dialog box set up for Presented by Speaker, Show without Narrations, Show without Animation, All Slides, and Advance Slide Manually, switch to Slide Show view.

NOTE *Because you selected "Show without Animation," the flying disk that usually cruises across the top of the slides in this presentation is inactive.*

2 Move the mouse on the slide until the standard arrow cursor appears.

3 Right-click anywhere in the slide to open a drop-down menu.

4 Click Pointer Options. The next submenu automatically opens.

5 Choose Pen Color. The submenu further expands.

6 Pick Green. The cursor turns into a little pencil, and now you can actually mark on the slide in the middle of your presentation. The marks will be green.

7 Underline the word "killer" as shown in the illustration.

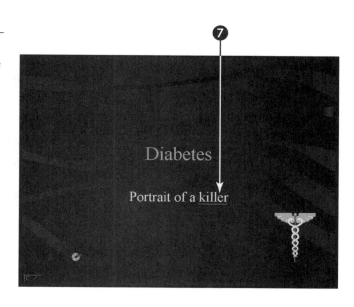

10

Ta Da – Presenting the Presentation

Navigating

TIP

The pointer is active only on the current slide. As soon as you move to another slide, the pointer disappears. If you want to use it again, you must repeat previous steps 2–4. Also, any marks that you make on a slide during a presentation are temporary. When you rerun the presentation, it will be "clean."

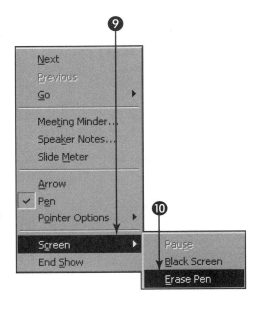

8 Right-click anywhere in the slide.

9 On the drop-down menu, click Screen, as shown on the illustration to the right.

10 Select Erase Pen, and all your pen-made markings disappear. The slide itself will remain unchanged.

11 Press Esc twice to stop the presentation.

Navigating

There are several ways to navigate in Slide Show view. You've already learned how to advance on a mouse click and how to set up automatic advances. In this exercise you'll learn how to use the Slide Navigator to skip around in the presentation.

1 Select Slide Show ➢ View Show.

2 While the first slide is still onscreen, right-click anywhere in it to open a drop-down menu.

3 Select Next; the slide show will advance to the next slide.

4 While the second slide is still onscreen, right-click anywhere in it to open the drop-down menu again.

5 Select Previous to return to the first slide.

TIP

If you don't want to open the pop-up menu during a slide show, you can press N on the keyboard for Next and P on the keyboard for Previous.

6 With the first slide still displayed in Slide Show view, right-click to reopen the drop-down menu.

7 Select Go.

8 Select Slide Navigator. The Slide Navigator dialog box appears.

NOTE

At the bottom of the Slide Navigator dialog box is a statement telling you what slide was last viewed. You can move to any slide in the presentation by clicking its title in the Slide Titles box.

9 Select Slide #6.

10 Click Go To; the presentation jumps ahead to the sixth slide (the one with the syringe on it).

11 With Slide #6 displayed in Slide Show view, right-click anywhere to open the drop-down menu again.

12 Select Go ➢ By Title. A list of all the slides in this presentation, by slide title, opens.

13 Select Insulin Types (Slide #5). The presentation hops straight to the fifth slide.

14 Press Esc to exit the slide show.

15 Save, but do not close, the presentation.

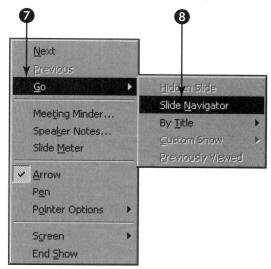

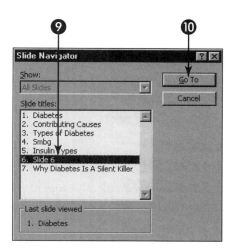

10

Ta Da – Presenting the Presentation

Printing slides in pure black and white

PRINTING THE PRESENTATION

There are several ways and reasons to print a presentation. You can print individual slides or the whole presentation in Slide view; you can print audience handouts from either Notes Pages or Handouts; you can print the presentation in Outline view; you can print the presentation in a way that will create 35mm slides or transparencies for use on an overhead projector; and you can print slides in black and white or in color.

Printing individual slides

Printing individual slides is one of the easiest print jobs associated with presentations.

1 With the Diabetes presentation open in any view, select File ➤ Print. The Print dialog box appears.

2 In the Printer area of the Print dialog box, verify that the designated printer information is correct.

3 Click Current Slide in the Print Range area.

4 Click the down arrow of the Print What box to see a list of printing options.

5 Select Slide (Without Animation), if it's not already selected.

6 Click OK and the selected slide prints.

Printing slides in pure black and white

Printing in pure black and white eliminates all shades of gray. PowerPoint automatically changes every color in the presentation to either black or white.

1 With the Diabetes presentation open in any view, select File ➤ Print. The Print dialog box opens.

2 In the Print What portion of the Print dialog box, click Pure Black & White to put a check mark in its box.

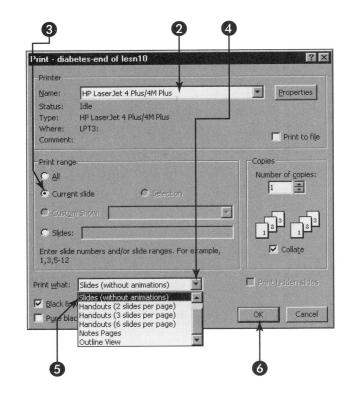

3 Click OK and the slide(s) will print in pure black and white format. Compare this to the output in the next exercise.

▶ Printing slides in black and white

Standard black and white actually prints in many shades of gray. Wherever there is color, it takes on a shade of gray.

1 With the Diabetes presentation open in any view, select File ➤ Print. The Print dialog box opens.

2 In the Print What portion of the Print dialog box, make sure Black & White is checked. (If Black & White is grayed out, first uncheck Pure Black & White.)

3 Click OK and the slide(s) will print in black and white (or, more accurately, grayscale). Compare this output with that from the previous exercise.

▶ Printing the entire presentation

There are actually three ways to print the entire presentation in standard grayscale format.

- With the Diabetes presentation open in any view, click the Print button on the Standard toolbar.

- Select File ➤ Print, select the All print range, and click OK to print one copy of the entire presentation.

- Press Ctrl+P on the keyboard.

▶ Printing audience handouts

There are several ways to print audience handouts. Handouts can be the Outline, Notes Pages, or Handouts printed two, three, or six slides per page. You can also print full-page copies of the slides.

1 With the Diabetes presentation open in any view, select File ➤ Print.

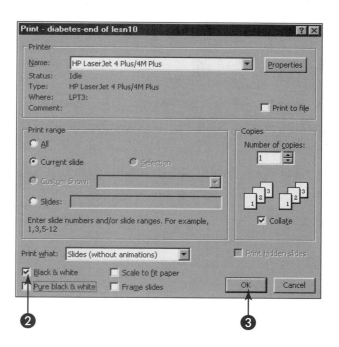

Printing for an overhead projector

2 In the Print dialog box, click the down arrow of the Print What box.

3 Select Handouts (3 Slides Per Page).

 NOTE *When you select any Handouts option, the Frame Slides box automatically is checked so that the slides will be lightly outlined (that is, "framed") on the printout.*

4 Click OK. The Handouts will print in a three-slides-per-page format.

5 Select File ➢ Print. The Print dialog box opens again.

6 This time, click Notes Pages in the Print What box.

7 Click OK. The Notes Pages will print out.

8 Select File ➢ Print to open the Print dialog box one more time.

9 Select Outline View in the Print What box.

10 Click OK. The presentation will print in Outline view.

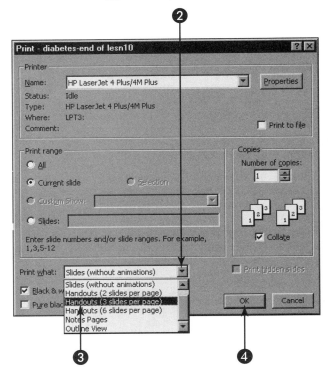

Printing for an overhead projector

In spite of the fact that you're using state-of-the-art technology to create the spiffiest slide show in town, you're going to have to use an overhead projector at the actual presentation (or so you're told by your boss). That means you have to figure out a way to get those gorgeous slides out of your computer and onto transparencies. Unfortunately, of course, you also lose all animation.

Printing 35mm slides and color copies ◀

1. With the presentation open in any view, select File ➢ Page Setup. The Page Setup dialog box opens.

2. Click the down arrow of the Slides Sized For box.

3. Select Overhead.

4. Click OK.

5. Scroll through the presentation before printing it to make sure that changing the Page Layout didn't cause any problems.

6. Select File ➢ Print and select the print options you want.

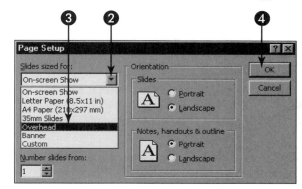

▶ Printing 35mm slides and color copies

You can't actually produce slides from your desk, but there are several companies that can convert your PowerPoint presentation into color slides or color transparencies, 35mm slides, overheads (including color overheads), and posters, as well as provide other services. You should contact each company to find out about pricing and transmittal requirements and select the one best suited to your needs. PowerPoint includes a link to one of those companies: Genigraphics in Memphis, Tennessee.

1. Select File ➢ Send To.

2. Choose Genigraphics. The Genigraphics Wizard opens to the introductory page.

NOTE *Read the information about Genigraphics on page 1 of the Wizard and click Genigraphics on the Web for even more information.*

3. If this is the first time you've ever used Genigraphic's services, click New Customer to put a check mark in the box.

4. Click Next. Page 2 of the Genigraphics Wizard opens.

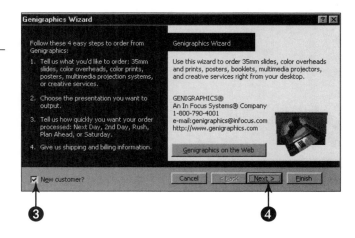

5 Click 35mm slides.

6 Click Display Pricing Information.

NOTE *Be aware that all prices are subject to change without notification. Use this information as a guide, but be sure to contact the company directly to confirm prices.*

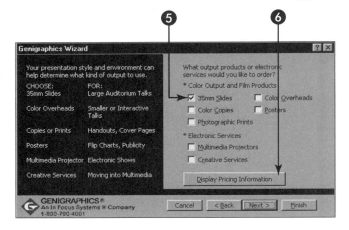

7 Scroll through the pricing information so that you're familiar with their pricing.

8 Click OK to close the Pricing Information box.

9 Click Next to open Page 3 of the Wizard.

NOTE *Becaue you started this whole Genigraphics process with the Diabetes.ppt file open, that's what should be displayed on the left side of the page. If it is not, click the Previously Saved Presentation button, and then Browse till you find it.*

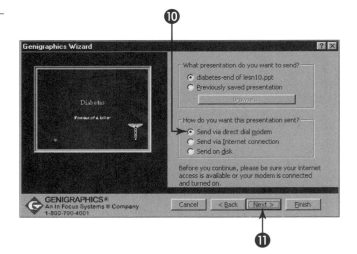

10 Click Send via Direct Dial Modem. This is the fastest way to communicate your presentation file to Genigraphics.

11 Click Next. The fourth page of the Wizard opens.

Printing 35mm slides and color copies

⑫ Click Plastic Mounts.

⑬ Click the up arrow of the Sets box.

⑭ Select 2. This means Genigraphics will make up two sets of plastic-mounted slides for you.

⑮ Click Next to open the fifth page of the Wizard. If the Wizard found any problems, it tells you about them on this page.

⑯ Click Next to open the sixth page of the Wizard. If there are hidden slides in your presentation, you can click Include Hidden Slides to ensure that they're prepared, too. If you leave it blank, those slides will be excluded. In the example, the option is unavailable (grayed out) because this presentation includes no hidden slides.

⑰ Click Image Each Build Step as a Separate Slide to remove the default check mark.

TIP *When Image Each Build Step as a Separate Slide is turned on, then Genigraphics will create a slide for each animation associated with a slide. If a slide has multiple animations (for instance, title flies on; bullets shoot on one at a time), each one will result in an individual slide. When you turn this feature off, then Genigraphics will create only one slide — after all animation effects are finished.*

⑱ Click the down arrow of the Turnaround box to see a list of possible delivery options.

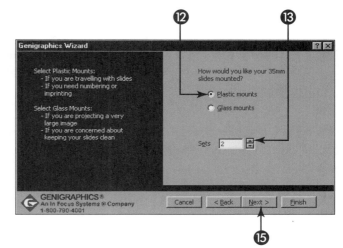

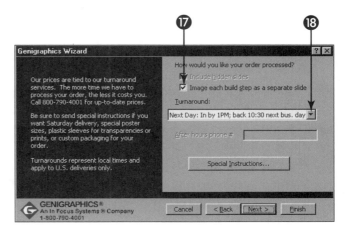

10

Ta Da – Presenting the Presentation

19 Select Plan Ahead: In by 5PM; Back in 3–7 Bus. Days. This is by far the least expensive way to get your presentation prepared.

20 If you have any special concerns or instructions to communicate, click Special Instructions. A window opens into which you can type your comments.

21 Click Next to open the seventh page of the Wizard.

22 Fill in the shipping information (for instance, your name, company name, address, phone).

23 Click to select Bill Delivery on Invoice.

24 Click Next to open the eighth page of the Wizard.

25 Click the down arrow of the Card box to see a list of acceptable credit cards.

26 Select MasterCard.

27 In the Account # box, type in the phony (I hope) account number shown in the illustration to the right.

28 In the PO# box, type a PO for your company (for the exercise, use 98057).

29 If you have an Internet address, type it into the Internet Addr box.

30 Fill out the other billing information so that Genigraphics can send their bill to you.

31 If you do not want Genigraphics to maintain credit information on you or your company, click to deselect the Delete Credit Information from System box.

32 Click Next. The Genigraphics Wizard Confirmation Page appears so that you can review all the information you're about to send them.

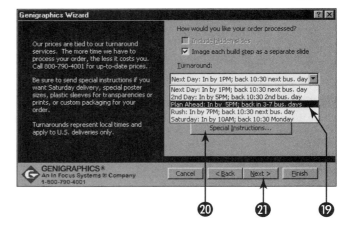

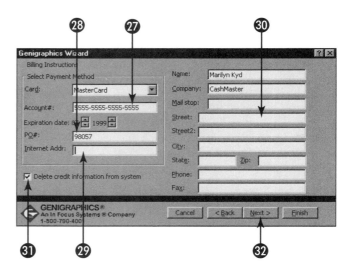

㉝ Verify that all the information is correct. If it's not, click Back to return to the page where you can make a correction.

㉞ At this point you would normally click Finish. Your computer would attempt to make a modem connection and transmit both your order and your presentation file(s). However, as this is just for practice and no one wants to incur charges to transfer this presentation into overheads, click Cancel.

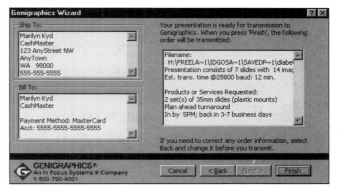

SKILLS CHALLENGE

In this Skills Challenge, you'll move the CD icon in the Diabetes presentation so that it's not hidden by the default Advance buttons, set up Diabetes as a self-running kiosk presentation, restore animation and narration to it, and circle an object on a slide with the pen. In addition, you'll print the entire Diabetes presentation to a regular black and white printer and print audience handouts.

❶ In the CareerDay97 presentation, hide the note on the last slide.

❷ In the Diabetes presentation, relocate the narration icon on the first slide so that it's about 1/2 inch higher.

❸ Set up the Diabetes slide show as a kiosk presentation.

 Do you remember how to set up the standard you're-in-full-charge-all-the-time slide show?

❹ Restore animation and narration to the Diabetes presentation.

Do you remember how to erase markings you made on a slide while the slide was running?

❺ On the SMBG slide, hand-draw a yellow circle around Goal: 70–180.

Troubleshooting

3 *Do you remember how to advance slides from the keyboard during a presentation?*

6 Print the entire Diabetes presentation to a regular black and white printer (do *not* use pure black and white).

4 *Do you remember how to get 35mm slides?*

7 Print audience handouts, three per page.

5 *Do you remember how to print the presentation in Outline view?*

8 Save and close the presentation.

TROUBLESHOOTING

Wipe the sweat from your brow and take a deep breath. You've done it. You've created a presentation from scratch and delivered a presentation. And lived to tell about it! Along the way, you've probably thought of some questions. See if they match any of the answers in this troubleshooting table.

Problem	Solution
When I try to print my presentation, my computer apparently takes a nap and nothing happens.	You are probably trying to print a graphics- and color-rich presentation to a standard color printer. What's happening is the computer is sending too much information to the printer too fast. It's overwhelmed. If it could talk, it would be weeping.

Problem	**Solution**
	In the meantime, Windows is still trying to send information to the printer, but the printer is not responding. If Windows could talk, it would probably say something like "Yo! You there with the flying phalanges! Whatsa'matta with your printer?" When it sends you a message that offers Retry as an option, click it. You may have to do that several times before the presentation is finished printing.
Yikes! My slides are all black!	You could be trying to print a color presentation to a black and white printer. Make sure you make the right selections on the Print dialog box. If you're printing to a black and white printer, make sure you choose the black and white printing option (*not* the pure black and white) so that you get grays as well as black and white.
Ack! I started to print the wrong presentation. It takes a long time and I'm in a hurry to print the right presentation so I can't wait!	Click Start ➢ Settings ➢ Printers. Click the printer you want to stop. Click the name of the file you want to delete from the print list, and then on the printing dialog box, click Document ➢ Cancel Printing. Whatever information has already been sent to and received by your printer will finish printing, unless you reset the printer *at* the printer, but no more information will be sent.

Wrap up

Problem	Solution
My slides just don't look right.	Make sure when you print the slides that the printing configuration matches the Page Setup configuration. In other words, if you defined the presentation for 35mm in Page Setup but then try to print it for overheads, it'll print fine but it might look funny.
When I'm in Slide Show view and click to advance to the next slide, nothing happens.	In order to advance the slide show, you must make sure nothing else is open. Then you can use the keyboard (N for Next or P for Previous) or the mouse to advance slides.

WRAP UP

This has been another busy lesson, bringing you closer still to your goal of entering the Master PowerPointer's Hall of Fame. It's review time. In this lesson you learned how to

- Set up a presentation with you as the presenter
- Set up a presentation with the viewer calling the shots
- Set up a presentation that runs itself
- Turn the narration on and off in a presentation
- Turn the animation on and off in a presentation
- Write or mark on slides *during* a presentation (and erase those markings)
- Navigate through a presentation using the keyboard or pop-up menus
- Print individual slides or the whole presentation

- Print slide in black and white or *pure* black and white

- Print audience handouts

- Prepare the presentation for a service bureau to create 35mm slides, overhead transparencies, or other forms

In the next lesson you'll learn how to create a custom show, send presentations across the Internet, and work with the Meeting Minder.

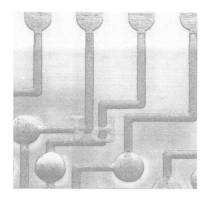

Custom Shows and Other Presentation Options

GOALS

You've made it! You've created and delivered presentations. In this lesson, you'll create a custom presentation and an agenda slide, among other things. Here's a list of what you have to look forward to in this lesson:

- Creating a custom slide show
- Editing and running the custom slide show
- Creating an agenda (or summary) slide
- Using Meeting Minder to take notes during the presentation
- Using Meeting Minder to take notes before or after a presentation

Creating a custom slide show

To successfully complete this lesson, you'll need the ever-present PowerPoint 97 installed and running on your computer. In addition, you should copy the following files from the Lesson 11 folder on the CD-ROM (if you haven't already): Logo.bmp, SnapTracker Sample.bmp, Nosmo King.bmp, CareerDay97–EOL10.ppt, Diabetes97–EOL10.ppt, and AEM–EOL8.ppt. When you're done, you can compare your work with that in the following files, also stored in the Lesson 11 folder: CareerDay97–EOL11.ppt, Diabetes97–EOL11.ppt, Snap–Web97.ppt, and AEM–EOL11.ppt.

CUSTOM SHOWS

What is a custom show? A custom show is one drawn from the elements of another show but geared for a specific audience. For example, you may have a presentation consisting of 100 slides, but you'd probably never bore any one audience with all 100 slides (unless they were of your family's vacation to the Grand Canyon or something equally compelling).

On the other hand, you could pick and choose slides from within that pool of 100 to put together dozens of audience–targeted presentations. For example, if you were presenting a show to a bunch of prospective buyers, you'd select the slides that point out your product's features, benefits, specifications, and pricing; if you were pitching the bank for more money, you'd select mostly charts and graphs showing your company's current financial status and order backlogs and so on.

Custom Shows permit you to tailor each presentation for a specific audience, which, of course, enhances the impact of the show and helps you reach your objective, whatever it may be.

Creating a custom slide show

In this exercise, you'll use the Annual Employee Meeting presentation to create a smaller, custom show.

1 Open the AEM–EOL8.ppt presentation in Slide Sorter view.

② Select Slideshow ➢ Custom Shows. The Custom Shows dialog box appears.

③ Click New. The Define Custom Show dialog box appears.

④ In the Slide Show Name box, type **AEM-Finances**.

⑤ In the Slides in Presentation box on the left, click Slide 1. The Add button becomes active.

⑥ Click Add to copy Slide #1 to the Slides in Custom Show box on the right.

⑦ Click the eighth slide (Balance Sheet 1998) in the Slides in Presentation box.

⑧ Click Add to copy it to the box on the right.

⑨ Click the ninth slide (Monthly Sales: December . . .) in the Slides in Presentation box.

⑩ Click Add to copy it.

⑪ Click OK to return to the Custom Shows dialog box, as shown at the bottom.

⑫ Click Show to see how the custom presentation looks in Slide Show view. (Click on the slide to fast-forward through the presentation.)

⑬ Click Close.

⑭ Save, but do not close, the presentation.

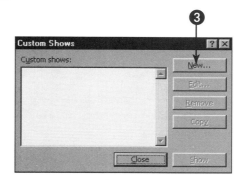

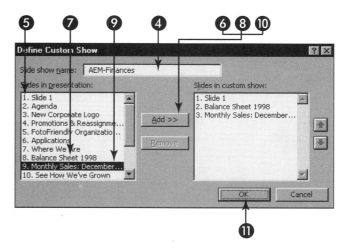

Editing a custom show

Just creating a custom show isn't always enough. You may want to rearrange the slides. In this exercise, you'll rearrange the Current Inventory slide and the Pricing slide.

① Select Slide Show ➢ Custom Shows. The Custom Shows dialog box reopens.

② On the Custom Shows dialog box, select AEM-Finances in the Custom Shows box.

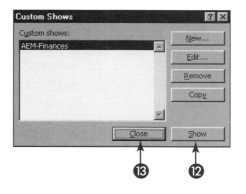

Custom Shows and Other Presentation Options

11

Editing a custom show

NOTE *Of course, if no one has ever created any custom shows, then the Custom Shows box will come up automatically selected.*

3 Click Edit. The Define Custom Show dialog box appears with the three slides you selected in the first exercise already in the Slides in Custom Show box.

4 Click the Inventory slide (you'll probably have to scroll down to see it). The Add button immediately becomes active.

5 Click Add to copy the Inventory slide into the Slides in Custom Show box.

6 Click the Pricing slide.

7 Click Add to copy the Pricing slide into the Slides in Custom Show box.

TIP *There's a faster way to select multiple slides. Hold the Shift key down while simultaneously clicking the slides you want to move. When they're all selected, click Add; all marked slides will be copied to the custom show. Slide order is dictated by selection order.*

8 In the Slides in Custom Show box, click Slide 1.

9 Click Remove. This takes Slide #1 out of the custom show but does not affect its position in the main presentation.

10 In the Slides in Custom Show box, click Inventory.

11 With the Inventory slide selected, click the down arrow of the Slides in Custom Show box to move the Inventory slide to the last place and the Pricing slide up one, as shown.

12 Click OK in the Define Custom Show dialog box.

13 Click Close in the Custom Show dialog box.

14 Select Slide Show ➤ Set Up Show.

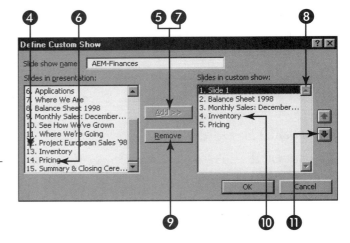

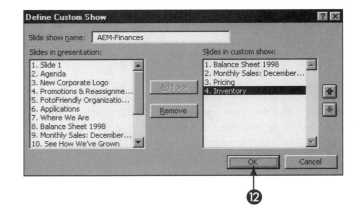

15 Click Custom Show and make sure the AEM-Finances is the listed custom show (if it's not, click the down arrow and find it).

16 Click OK.

17 Save and close the presentation.

Creating an agenda slide

An Agenda slide is another term for a Summary slide. You can create a slide listing the titles of other slides as bulleted text and then use that as an Agenda slide.

1 Open the CareerDay97-EOL10.ppt presentation in Slide Sorter view. (If you are asked about links, click Cancel.)

2 Select Slide #2.

3 Simultaneously press Shift and click each of the following slides: 3, 6, 11, 12, and 13. Six slides should be selected.

4 Click the Summary Slide button on the Slide Sorter toolbar.

 NOTE

PowerPoint automatically creates a Summary slide using the titles of the selected slides as a text for bullets. It inserts this slide right after the title slide, as shown in the illustration to the right. You have an agenda. Now, if you want to, you can even create hyperlinks.

5 Save and close the presentation.

MINDING MEETINGS WITH THE MEETING MINDER

The Meeting Minder provides you with a set of tools you can use while a presentation is going on. You can record minutes and export them to Word for future formatting; you can record notes to yourself about how to make the next presentation more effective; you can record action items along with whose action it is and when it's due; and you can control how the slide show gets shown.

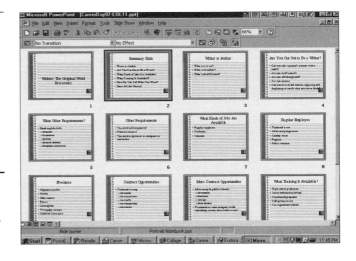

Using the Meeting Minder

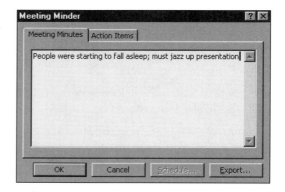

Using the Meeting Minder

The Meeting Minder is a dandy little tool that lets you keep track of meeting notes and minutes and simultaneously schedule tasks and assign action items. You can use it in any view of PowerPoint, including Slide Show view. This exercise assumes that you are using one computer to control the output of the presentation that is being displayed on another monitor (not another computer).

❶ Open the Diabetes presentation to Slide #2 in Slide view.

TIP *You can actually do this exercise from any slide in any view (except Slide Show).*

❷ Select Tools ➢ Meeting Minder. The Meeting Minder dialog box appears as shown in the illustration to the right.

❸ On the Meeting Minutes tab type this: **People were starting to fall asleep; must jazz up presentation.**

❹ Switch to the Action Items tab, as shown in the illustration to the right.

❺ Type the following into the Description box: **Contact American Diabetes Association for more information.**

❻ Press Tab to move to the Assigned To field.

❼ Type the name of the person assigned to follow up on the comment. For this exercise, type **Mike**.

❽ Press Tab to move to the Due Date field.

❾ Type in **10/17/98** (the default is today's date, but you can just overtype it). This is the date by which Mike should have completed the task.

❿ Press Tab to move to the Add button.

⓫ Click Add. This moves the action item details into the big box and allows you to enter another action item.

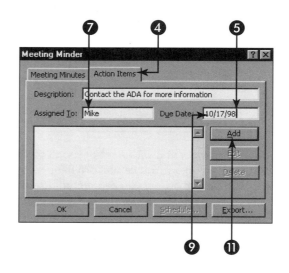

12 If your system setup includes Microsoft Outlook, you can click Schedule to post this action item in your Outlook files. If you do not have Outlook installed, this button will be inactive (grayed out).

13 If your system setup includes Microsoft Word, you can click Export and send the information either to Outlook or to Word. If you took minutes of the meeting using the Meeting Minder, exporting them to Word gives you a chance to spruce them up before publishing and distributing them.

14 Click OK.

Using the Meeting Minder during a presentation

If you're actually in the same room with your audience, you're probably too busy sweating and trying to avoid stammering to worry about who said what when and to whom, yet some of those comments could be vitally important to your business (or even your *job*). You can use the Meeting Minder to keep track of things while you're giving the presentation. (Make sure the Set Up Show dialog box is set for "presented by a speaker.")

If you're giving the presentation online or remotely, then the Meeting Minder screens appear only on your computer. If you're using your computer to actually run the show in a room with only one monitor, this might not be your best choice; however, if you can round up a second monitor, then you can keep the Meeting Minder screen to yourself.

A word of warning. If you have assigned automatic slide advance timings to these slides and then get caught up in typing notes or comments, the slide show will progress without you! If you plan to use the Presentation Conference feature, you probably ought to forget about automatic timings and set them all for manual advance.

1 With the Diabetes presentation still open, go to Slide #1 so you can begin the presentation.

2 Click the slide to progress to the next slide. When Slide #2 appears, right-click anywhere on the slide to open the Slide Show utilities menu.

Skills challenge

3 Select Meeting Minder. The Meeting Minder dialog box opens.

4 Switch to the Action Items tab.

5 Type the following in the Description field: **Research liver's role in diabetes**.

6 Press Tab to move to the Assigned To field.

7 Type the following in the Assigned To field: **Dr. Dan**.

8 Press Tab to move to the Due Date field.

9 Type the following in the Due Date field: **10/28/98**.

10 Click Add. The information moves to the big box so that you can add more action items.

11 Click OK.

12 Finish the show (or press Esc to get out of it) when you're ready.

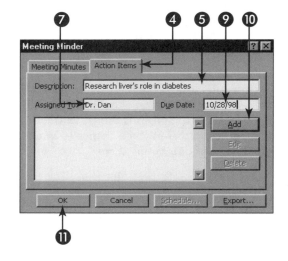

 NOTE

If you create action items during a presentation, PowerPoint automatically creates a new slide, which appears at the end of the presentation. The new slide contains all the action items along with the names of the people responsible for them and due dates, as shown in the illustration to the right.

SKILLS CHALLENGE

In this Skills Challenge, you'll add a logo to a Web presentation; add a picture to a Web presentation; create a custom slide show from the Annual Employee Meeting presentation; create an Agenda slide for the Diabetes presentation; use the Meeting Minder to add a note in the Career Day presentation; add an action item to the Career Day presentation; and save the Career Day presentation for the Internet.

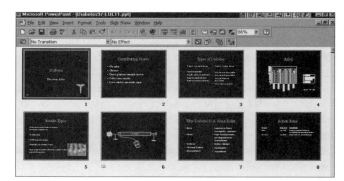

① Create a custom show called Writing Careers from the Career Day presentation. Use the following slides, in this order: 1, 12, 7, and 13.

 Do you remember how to run a custom show?

② Create an Agenda slide for the Diabetes presentation.

 Do you know how to rearrange slides in a custom show?

③ Delete the nonbulleted text on Slide #1 of Snap-Web.ppt (you see "Click to Add Text" when you're done — don't worry about it).

④ Adjust the bullet spacing on Slide #1 of Snap-Web.ppt (this includes deleting two bullets and moving the remaining bullets), as shown to the right.

⑤ Insert Logo.bmp into the appropriate spot on the third slide of the Snap-Web presentation, as shown (hint: the logo will resize itself automatically, to fit the space!).

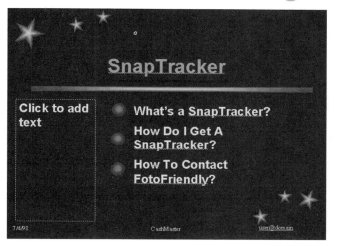

Troubleshooting

6 Crop Nosmo King's picture to get rid of all the white on the right and insert it in the appropriate place on Slide #4 of the Snap–Web presentation. Add his name as the caption (Arial 14), as shown.

7 Save and close the presentation.

8 Use Comments to create the following note on Slide #13 in the Career Day presentation, and then position the comment so that it's outside the slide (but touching it) on the left. The comment should read: **Tell them about the many trade magazines and organizations.**

9 Add the following action item to the last slide of the Career Day presentation (Money? What Money?) and assign it to you and today's date: **Call my agent NOW.**

10 Save the Career Day presentation for the Internet (call it Writing Careers.html and store it in the PPT HTML Stuff folder.

11 Save and close the presentation.

TROUBLESHOOTING

You are so close to being a Master PowerPointer! Here are a few answers. With any luck, they'll match up to your questions.

Problem	Solution
In Slide Show view my slides don't advance — not even when I click the mouse.	Check Slide Show ➤ Set Up. Make sure the presentation is set up to run as Presented by a Speaker.

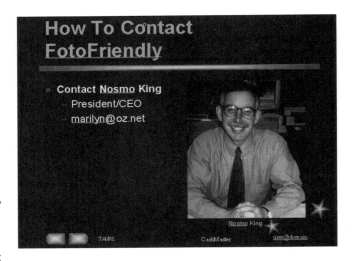

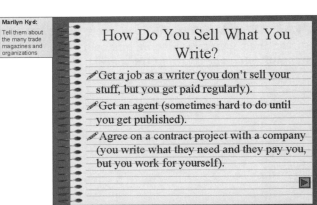

WRAP UP

In this lesson, you learned how to focus your presentation for a specific target audience. In addition, you learned how to make notes during a presentation and export those notes to Word. Specifically, in this lesson you learned how to

- Create a custom slide show
- Edit a custom slide show
- Create an Agenda slide
- Use the Meeting Minder when you are *not* running a presentation
- Use the Meeting Minder when you *are* running a presentation

In the next and final lesson, you'll learn how to take the show on the road.

Taking the Show on the Road

GOALS

Okay. You've dazzled your peers, impressed the honchos, and gone hoarse from practicing presentations in front of the mirror, your dinner companions, every member of your family, and a few strangers you dragged in off the street. You are now ready for the Big Time — the Road Show. Here's what you'll learn in this lesson to prepare for the road:

- Saving the slide show to present on another computer

- Using the Pack-and-Go Wizard

- Unpacking your presentation

- Using the PowerPoint Viewer

Saving the slide show for someone else

GET READY

To successfully complete this lesson, you'll need the ever-popular PowerPoint, of course, plus Microsoft Notepad, the Microsoft PowerPoint viewer, a computer with a floppy disk drive, and a floppy disk. You'll also need to access the CareerDay97.-EOL11.ppt and Diabetes97-EOL11.ppt files on the CD-ROM.

PACK 'EM UP AND MOVE 'EM OUT

Before you drag your presentation with you on the road, you need to make sure you have all the elements you'll need. The rule of thumb here is if you're not sure whether you'll need it or not, take it anyway, just to be safe. Remember, the only thing worse than waking up in the morning and finding no chocolate in the house is smiling at a large audience that is giving you their undivided attention and adoration, only to give them screen after screen of unreadable fonts, black holes where charts and graphs should be, or other too-horrible-to-mention (or even imagine) glitches in your presentation.

So first you need to pack your presentation. Once you've reached your destination, you can unpack your presentation and get ready to roll. At least you don't have to worry about wrinkles.

Saving the slide show for someone else

When you take your show on the road, you need to be prepared to run it on someone else's computer — a computer that may or may not have PowerPoint available. The Pack and Go Wizard compresses everything you need to make your show run successfully and dumps it onto a floppy disk, including (if you want them) files, fonts, drawings, and the PowerPoint Viewer. (More on the Viewer later.)

You can include linked files and TrueType fonts, with no problem. If you make changes to the presentation after saving it with the Pack and Go Wizard, all you have to do is repack it.

In this exercise, you're preparing for a trip from sea to shining sea during which you'll visit numerous schools and try to convince at least one student somewhere to consider a career as a writer.

Saving the slide show for someone else

1 Open the CareerDay97–EOL11.ppt presentation in any view.

2 Select File ➢ Pack and Go. The Pack and Go Wizard Start page appears.

3 Click Next. The Pick Files to Pack Wizard page appears.

4 Make sure Active Presentation is already selected (if it's not, click to select it).

NOTE

If you want to pack a file other than the one that's displayed, click Other Presentation(s), browse till you find it, and then follow the rest of these instructions.

5 Click Next. The Choose Destination Wizard page appears.

6 The most common destination for a packed file is the floppy drive, which is usually A:\. However, you may identify any drive as the destination drive. For the purposes of this exercise, use the default (A:\). Don't forget to insert a floppy disk in the drive!

7 Click Next. The Links Wizard page appears.

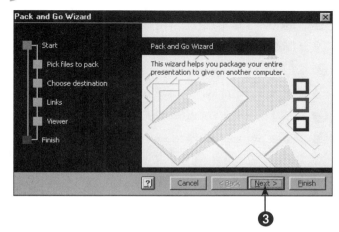

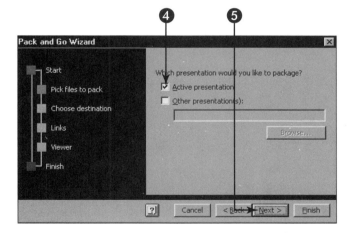

8 If Include Linked Files is checked, click to deselect it.

9 If Embed True Type Fonts is not checked, click to select it.

10 Click Next. The Viewer Wizard page appears.

11 Click Viewer for Windows 95 or NT.

12 Click Next. The Finish Wizard page appears.

13 Read it. It explains that when you click Finish (as you'll be doing very soon), PowerPoint compresses all relevant files (among them the presentation, graphics, scanned images, photographs, clip art, charts, graphs) and tries to cram them onto the disk you've inserted into Drive A (or wherever). If there's too much stuff to fit on one disk, you'll be instructed to insert a second one.

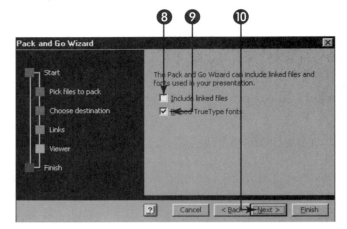

> *Remember, if you make any changes to the presentation, no matter how small or seemingly insignificant, you must run the Pack and Go process again before you take it on the road.*

14 Click Finish. The Pack and Go utility will start packing, giving you occasional progress or status reports onscreen, such as these:

- Packaging presentation files (into a single .ppz file)

- Adding files (it adds several files to your Windows/Temp directory, wherever that is)

- Copying presentation package

- Pack and Go has successfully packed your presentation(s)

15 Click OK at the "successfully packed" dialog box.

16 Carefully and clearly label each packed disk. Now go pack your suitcase. (Don't forget to close PowerPoint, either.)

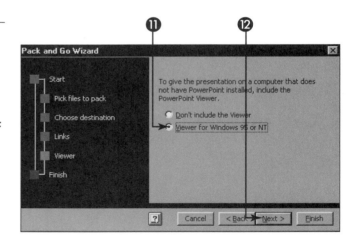

The show must go on

So you've packed up your presentation, and you're now ready to see how successful a packing job you did.

1 Whip out the disk (or disks) you created using Pack and Go.

2 Stick the first (or only) disk into the appropriate drive (probably the A drive) on the new host computer.

3 On the Windows taskbar, click Start.

4 Select Run. The Run dialog box appears.

5 In the Open box, type **A:\Pngsetup.exe** (unless, of course, you put the disk in some drive other than A, in which case, change the A to whatever is more appropriate).

6 Click OK. The Pack and Go Setup dialog box appears.

7 Assign a destination for the PowerPoint files. Remember, you're a guest on someone else's computer. Choose something that will be easy to remember so that you can clear your stuff off when you're done. (Try **C:\Show**.)

8 Click OK. If you specified a directory that does not exist, you'll see a message box asking if you want to create the directory. Since you're probably creating a special directory just for the purpose of running your presentation, you'll probably want to click Yes. If, on the other hand, the Head Audience Honcho has already prepared a place for you, then you should click No and find out where that special place is.

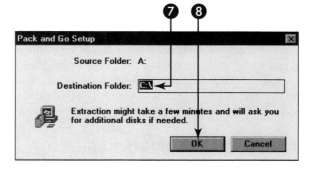

TIP

If you acquired PowerPoint 97 before June 1997, you may encounter the following message: "The viewer you have packed will not run on Windows 3.1."
Just click OK. Microsoft released a free upgrade in mid-May 1997. See the Troubleshooting section at the end of this lesson for more information.

12

Taking the Show on the Road

Running an unpacked presentation

⑨ When Pack and Go is through unpacking your presentation, you'll see the following message: "The presentation was successfully installed in *[whatever destination you specified]*. Would you like to run slide show now?" Click Yes. Enjoy.

THE POWERPOINT VIEWER

The PowerPoint Viewer is a handy little program that allows you to run your PowerPoint 97 presentation on a computer that *has no PowerPoint!* Once you've packed and gone, you can use the PowerPoint Viewer to view one presentation or a series of presentations, depending on what you packed.

The PowerPoint Viewer is located on the CD-ROM containing your PowerPoint program (either a stand-alone PowerPoint product or as part of the Office suite of programs). If your PowerPoint didn't come on a CD-ROM, then you will have to download the Viewer from the World Wide Web (in PowerPoint select Help ➤ Microsoft on the Web ➤ Free Stuff). The Viewer is also in the same directory as the unpacked presentation from the previous exercise, thanks to the Pack and Go Wizard.

You can use this PowerPoint Viewer on both PCs and the Macintosh.

Running an unpacked presentation

Once you've unpacked everything, you're ready to show the presentation to your audience. Here's how:

❶ Open Windows Explorer and navigate to wherever you unpacked the presentation.

❷ Double-click Ppview32exe. The Microsoft PowerPoint Viewer dialog box appears. (If you installed the Viewer from the Web, you launch it by selecting Start ➤ Programs ➤ Microsoft PowerPoint Viewer 97.)

Creating a presentation jukebox

3 Click the Options button.

4 In the Options dialog box, click Popup Menu on Right Mouse Click.

5 Select Show Popup Menu Button.

NOTE *It's usually a good idea to also choose End With Black Slide because you avoid the possible embarrassment of going from the last slide in your show to whatever was onscreen before you started the show (probably Windows Explorer).*

6 Click OK in the Options dialog box.

7 Select Career~1.ppt. A preview appears at the bottom.

8 Click Show (you'll see the message "Reading Presentation" as everything loads properly). Your slide show begins.

TIP *If you double-click Career~1.ppt, your slide show instantly starts. Regardless of how you start it, when your slide show is finished, it will stop on the black screen.*

9 If you added a black screen at the end, click anywhere in it to end the presentation. The Microsoft PowerPoint Viewer will be waiting for you. You can run another presentation (if you packed more than one) or close the Viewer.

10 Click Exit to close the Microsoft PowerPoint Viewer.

Creating a presentation jukebox

The PowerPoint Viewer allows you to set up a playlist of one or more presentations so that you can run them continuously and independently.

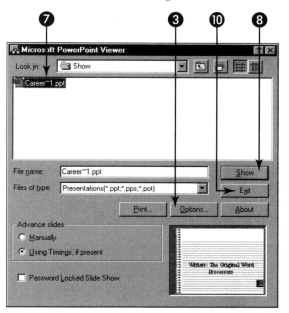

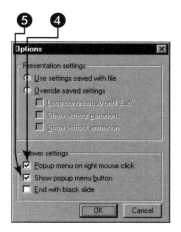

Skills challenge

1 Make sure PowerPoint Viewer is installed on your computer.

2 Select Start ➢ Programs ➢ Accessories ➢ Notepad to open Microsoft Notepad.

3 In the new, blank document, type whatever is the full path for the unpacked Career Day presentation (for example, **C:\Show\Career~1.ppt**). If you want to include more than one unpacked presentation in your playlist, type each presentation's full path name on a separate line, in the order that they will be shown.

4 Save the file as **Roadshow** in the same directory where the unpacked Career~1.ppt file is located.

5 Close Microsoft Notepad.

6 Open Windows Explorer.

7 Navigate to the Roadshow file you just saved.

8 Select the file and then choose File ➢ Rename.

9 Change the extension (which is .txt) to .lst *(that's the letters LST, not one-s-t).*

10 Press Enter to accept the change. (If prompted by a warning box, click Yes.)

11 Open PowerPoint Viewer.

12 Click open the Files of Type list box and choose Playlists.

13 Double-click the Roadshow.lst file (or select it and click Show) to enjoy the show.

Now if you go on the road and want to show several presentations in a particular order, all you need is one directory containing the unpacked presentation files and the playlist file.

SKILLS CHALLENGE

In this Skills Challenge you'll save the Diabetes presentation for someone else's computer, pack it up, unpack and run it, and create a playlist.

1 *Do you remember how to include linked files in your packed presentation?*

1 Pack the Diabetes presentation using the Pack and Go utility. Assume the destination computer is set up exactly like yours.

2 *Do you remember how to pack a presentation when you know you won't need the Microsoft PowerPoint Viewer?*

2 Run the Diabetes presentation unpacked.

3 Create a playlist consisting of the Diabetes presentation and then the Career Day presentation.

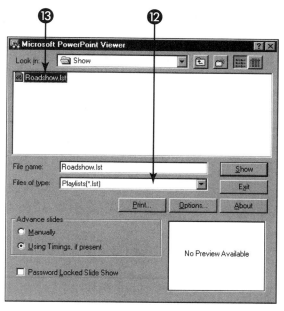

TROUBLESHOOTING

You Got Questions? I Got Answers. . . .

Problem	Solution
When I try to use the Microsoft PowerPoint Viewer, I get the following message: "The viewer you have packed will not run on Windows 3.1."	If you acquired PowerPoint 97 before June 1997, you are almost guaranteed to get this message. It simply means that the version of Microsoft PowerPoint Viewer that shipped with the product does not fully support it (the new version became available May 1997).
	You can still run your presentation, but if you use graphics, special effects, animation, or other special features, they will not work. This means that if your presentation relies on or uses any feature included in PowerPoint 97 that was not also in PowerPoint 95, you will lose that feature.

12

Taking the Show on the Road

Wrap up

Problem	Solution
	The good news is that the upgrade is free. You can download it from the Microsoft Web site. You can also call the Customer Service line (800-426-9400) or the direct PowerPoint line (425-635-7145) to order your free upgrade.
My WordArt objects don't look right in an unpacked presentation.	See the preceding item.
I can't find ppview32.exe.	Open Explorer (if it's not already open) and click Tools ➢ Find ➢ Files or Folders. In the Named box, type **ppview32** and in the Look In box, type the name of the drive where it's most likely to be. If you have no idea where it might be, start with the C drive and work your way down the list.

WRAP UP

In this presentation you learned how to take your show on the road — without dragging along all the roadies. For example, you learned how to

- Save a presentation for showing on another computer
- Pack up a presentation using the Pack and Go Wizard
- Unpack a presentation and then show it
- Create a playlist for more than one presentation

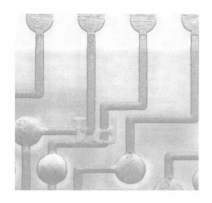

Answers to Bonus Questions

LESSON 1

 Do you remember how to start the AutoContent Wizard when PowerPoint is already open and the opening dialog box is gone?

Select File ➤ New, and on the New Presentation dialog box, select the Presentations tab. Then click the first option, AutoContent Wizard.prz.

 Do you remember how to indent a bullet on a slide and then return to the original indentation?

Click Demote to indent. Each time you click Demote, you indent the text one more level. Click Promote to return one level at a time.

 Do you remember how to insert a slide into a presentation?

In Slide Sorter view or Outline view, click where you want the new slide inserted and press Enter. From the insertion point forward all slides advance one position, and a new blank slide appears.

Lesson 2

 4 *Do you remember how to insert a name on all regular (not title) slides?*

In the Slide Master type the name in whatever box and position you want it to consistently appear (for example, Header or Footer areas, Title Area for AutoLayouts, Object Area for AutoLayouts).

 5 *Do you remember how to insert a logo on a slide?*

In the Slide Master select Insert ➤ Picture ➤ From File. When you find your logo file, click Insert then position and size it as you want.

 6 *Do you remember how to insert a slide from another presentation?*

In Outline view, position the cursor where you want the new slide inserted. Click Insert ➤ Slides from Files. In the Slide Finder dialog box click Browse to find the presentation file containing the slide you want to insert into this presentation. When you return to the Slide Finder dialog box with the filename pasted in the File text box, click Display to see the presentation three slides at a time. Scroll to the desired slide and double-click to insert it into the current presentation *or* change the display so that it lists all slides in the presentation, scroll to the one you want to insert, and double-click it.

LESSON 2

 1 *Do you remember how to add a new slide to a presentation in Slide view?*

Select Insert ➤ Slide.

 2 *Do you remember how to change text case?*

Select Format ➤ Change Case and make your choice.

Do you remember how to change font sizes?

There are four ways to change font size:

- Double-click the current font size as it is displayed in the font size box in the Standard toolbar and type over it with the desired font size.

- Click the down arrow of the font size box on the Standard toolbar and scroll to or type the desired font size.

- Select Format ➢ Font and choose the desired size from the Font Size box.

- Double-click inside the text you want to change, click Font, and then choose the desired font size (this only works when you're changing a single word).

 Do you remember how to delete text from a slide?

There are several ways to do this, too:

- Select the text and press Delete.

- Position the cursor at the right edge of the text and press Backspace until it is erased.

- Position the cursor at the extreme left edge of the text and press Delete until it is erased.

- Select Edit ➢ Undo Typing (assuming you are deleting just-typed text).

 Do you remember how to adjust line spacing?

Select Format ➢ Line Spacing. Decide whether you want to adjust line spacing within (Line spacing), above (Above paragraph), or below (Below paragraph). Then choose how you want to measure the spacing (lines or points). Finally, choose the distance.

A

Answers to Bonus Questions

Lesson 2

 6 *Do you remember how to move a slide from one position in the presentation to another?*

In Outline view, position the cursor to the immediate left of the slide you want to move, and then click either the Move Up button or the Move Down button until the slide is where you want it. You can do the same thing with bullets within a slide, by the way. In fact, you can even use this technique to move a bullet from one slide to another.

 7 *Do you remember how to move a text box on a slide?*

In Slide view, select the text or object box you want to move and then click the down arrow of the Draw button on the Drawing toolbar. Click Align or Distribute and then click the appropriate directional option. If the only option available is Relative to Slide, then click it first and repeat the process. The second time you click Align or Distribute, all the choices should be active.

 8 *Do you remember how to find and replace text globally?*

Select Edit ➢ Replace. In the Find What box, type the word or phrase you're looking for *exactly as it appears in text*. In the Replace With box, type the word or phrase you want to replace it with. If you want to replace all instances of the Find What word or phrase, click Replace All. If you only want to change some of them, click Find Next and when you find one you want to change, click Change.

 9 *Do you remember how to automatically correct what you type as you type it?*

Select Tools ➢ AutoCorrect. If you want AutoCorrect to be turned on, make sure there is a check mark in the Correct Text As You Type box. If you do not want text automatically corrected, make sure there is no check mark in that box. Click to toggle back and forth.

10 *Do you remember how to add a word to the AutoCorrect list?*

Select Tools ➤ AutoCorrect. In the Replace box, type the word as you might type it accidentally (for instance, **teh** for *the* — that's already there, of course). In the With box, type the word as you mean it to be (*the*). From now on (unless you turn AutoCorrect off), every time you type *teh*, PowerPoint 97 will automatically correct it to *the*.

11 *Do you remember how to check the spelling in your presentation?*

Remember that no matter what method you use to spell-check your presentation, you should also proofread it carefully. The spell-checker is not a mind reader. If you mistype a word but the wrong word is still a real word, the spell-checker will not identify it as a possible error. Want proof? Remember "cut" on the New Corporate Logo slide? That was supposed to be "cute," but since "cut" is a real word, the spell-checker didn't find it.

- Click the Spelling button on the Standard toolbar. This starts the spell-checker, which automatically shows you each word not found in the PowerPoint dictionary. You can either add the word to the dictionary, ignore it just this once, ignore it forever, or change it to either a suggested alternative or one you type.

- You can also start the spell-checker by selecting Tools ➤ Spelling.

- Finally, you can start the spell-checker by clicking the ABC button on the Standard toolbar.

 12 *Do you remember how to change the color of an object?*

Select the object, and then click the down arrow of the Fill Color button on the Drawing toolbar. Click Fill Effect and then you can change gradient, texture, pattern, and color.

A

Answers to Bonus Questions

Lesson 3

 13 *Do you remember how to connect two objects?*

Click the down arrow on the AutoShapes button and select Connectors. Click the connector you want to use and then position it in the first object. Drag it to the object you want to connect it to and let go of the left button on your mouse. Remember, when you're working with a single-arrow line, you want to drag away from the handle.

 14 *Do you remember how to rotate an object?*

Click the Rotate button on the Drawing toolbar, position the rotate cursor over the circle handle of the object you want to rotate, and then drag it into position. When you release the mouse, the Rotate feature turns off.

 15 *Do you remember how to flip objects?*

Click the down arrow of the Draw button on the Drawing toolbar. Click Rotate or Flip and then click the manner in which you wish to rotate or flip the object.

 16 *Do you remember how to group and ungroup objects?*

Select Edit ➢ Select All to group objects on a slide and click anywhere not included in the selection to ungroup.

LESSON 3

 1 *Do you remember what a color scheme is?*

A color scheme is a collection or set of eight coordinated colors that work well together and are available to use in a slide presentation. You can modify a default color scheme or even create your own from scratch.

Do you remember how to choose a different color scheme for your presentation?

With your presentation open (I prefer it open in Slide Sorter view), select Format ➢ Slide Color Scheme. On the Standard tab, double-click the format you want to use. This will apply the selected color scheme to all slides in the presentation.

 Do you remember how to apply a different color scheme to just one or two slides?

With your presentation open in Slide view (or with the slide to be changed selected in Slide Sorter view), click Format ➢ Slide Color Scheme. On the Standard tab, click the format you want and then click Apply. This will apply the format to the selected slide only. Repeat as necessary.

 Do you remember how to create your own color scheme?

Select Format ➢ Slide Color Scheme and on the Custom tab, select the part of the presentation you want to define (for instance, background, text and lines, shadow, title text, fills, accent, accent and hyperlink, or accent and followed hyperlink). Then define the color(s) and apply them to either a single slide or to all slides.

 Do you remember how to save a custom color scheme?

After you've defined a unique, custom color scheme, click Add As Standard Scheme and Apply to All. From now on your custom color scheme will be included in the choices on the Standard tab.

 Do you remember how to apply one presentation's color scheme to another presentation's slides?

Open both presentations and select any slide in the presentation from which you are "borrowing" the color scheme. Then click on the Format Painter button on the Standard toolbar, switch to the other

Lesson 3

presentation, and select Edit ➢ Select All. Click on any slide to transfer the format. The original presentation remains unchanged and its color scheme is applied to the second presentation.

 Do you remember how to choose a preset gradient background?

Select Format ➢ Background, then the down arrow, and Fill Effects. On the Gradient tab, click Preset. Click the down arrow under Preset Colors and select the background you like. Select the shading and variant styles you prefer, too.

 Do you remember how to create a one-color background?

Select Format ➢ Background, then the down arrow, and Fill Effects. On the Gradient tab, click One Color. Click the down arrow under Color 1 and select the color you like and use the slide control to adjust its lightness/darkness. Select the shading and variant styles you prefer, too.

 Do you remember how to create a two-color background?

Select Format ➢ Background, then the down arrow, and Fill Effects. On the Gradient tab, click Two Colors. Click the down arrow on each of the two colors to select the color you want. Then choose the shading and variant options you want.

 Do you remember how to select a pattern background?

Select Format ➢ Background, then the down arrow, and Fill Effects. On the Pattern tab, click the desired pattern and adjust the Foreground and Background as you wish. Then click OK and either Apply or Apply to All. If you know that you're not going to be making any changes to the Foreground or Background and want to go with the pattern as it looks, you can double-click the pattern and bypass the other stuff.

Do you remember how to use a picture for a background?

Select Format ➢ Background, then the down arrow, and Fill Effects. On the Picture tab, navigate to where you stored the picture you want to use and double-click it. Then click either Apply or Apply to All.

 Do you remember how to add WordArt to a slide?

Click the WordArt button on the Drawing toolbar and select a style from the WordArt Gallery. Click OK and type the desired text in the Edit WordArt Text area. You can also select a font style and size. Click OK and position the WordArt where you want it to appear on the slide.

 Do you remember how to give an object 3-D characteristics?

Select the object to which you want to apply 3-D characteristics and click the 3D button on the Drawing toolbar. Choose a 3-D style. If you want to further enhance the 3-D effect, click the 3D button on the Drawing toolbar again (with the object still selected) and click 3-D Settings to open the 3D toolbar. Make whatever enhancements you wish.

LESSON 4

 Do you remember where to find the Slide Transition button on the toolbar?

The Slide Transition button is on the Slide Sorter toolbar on the far left.

 Do you remember how to activate a hyperlink?

To activate a hyperlink (which you can only do during a slide show, remember), move the cursor over the appropriate text until it turns into a pointing finger and then click.

Lesson 5

 Do you remember how to stop (or escape from) a slide show in progress?

To stop a slide show in progress, press Esc.

 Do you remember the difference between Slide Show ➤ View Show and the Slide Show View button?

When you start a slide show using Slide Show ➤ View Show, you see the show beginning with Slide #1. When you click on the Slide Show View button, you see the slide show beginning with whatever slide was selected in whatever view you were in before you clicked the Slide Show View button.

 Do you remember how to show a hidden slide during a presentation?

To show a hidden slide during a presentation, press P as soon as the slide after the hidden slide is displayed. This returns you to the slide immediately before the hidden slide. On the slide before the hidden slide, right-click to open a drop-down menu. On the drop-down menu, select Go ➤ Hidden Slide and the presentation will progress from there, displaying the hidden slide. Future presentations, however, will still hide the designated slide.

LESSON 5

 Do you remember how to insert an organization chart slide?

Select Insert ➤ New Slide and on the New Slide dialog box, double-click the Organization Chart AutoLayout.

 Do you remember how to change box styles in an organization chart?

Select the box whose style you want to change, then click Styles, and click the desired style from the Groups options.

Do you remember how to add a table to a slide?

Select Insert ➢ New Slide and, on the New Slide dialog box, double-click the Table AutoLayout.

 Do you remember how to change the width of a column in a spreadsheet or a slide?

Position the cursor in the column header until it turns into a plus sign with left-right arrows, and then drag the border to the right (to make it wider) or the left (to make it narrower).

 Do you remember how to format the two axes or the legend on a chart?

Click the axis or legend that you want to modify, and then click Format Axis (or Format Legend) on the Chart toolbar.

 Do you remember how to insert a graph?

On a blank slide, select Insert ➢ Chart.

 Do you remember how to change the background of a graph legend?

Right-click anywhere in the Legend and then click Format Legend. In the Area portion of the Patterns tab, click whatever color you want or click Fill Effects to choose an effect. Click OK when you're done to apply it.

LESSON 6

 Do you remember how to adjust the contrast and brightness of a photograph?

Select the picture and click More Brightness, Less Brightness, More Contrast, and/or Less Contrast on the Picture toolbar to fine-tune the picture's appearance.

A

Answers to Bonus Questions

Lesson 6

 Do you remember how to adjust the line spacing on a slide that holds a picture?

Select the text, then select Format ➤ Line Spacing, and adjust any or all of the three line spacing options (line, before paragraph, and after paragraph).

 Do you remember how to turn the Picture toolbar on and off?

There are several ways to turn off the Picture toolbar:

- Click the Picture toolbar's *X* box.
- Click in any open toolbar and on the toolbar menu, click to deselect the Picture toolbar.
- Select View ➤ Toolbars and deselect the Picture toolbar.
- Double-click in the picture and click Hide Picture toolbar.

 Do you remember how to create a border around a picture or a photograph?

With the picture selected, click Line Style on the Picture toolbar and choose the thickness you want.

 Do you remember how to play a tune when the little speaker is on a slide?

Double-click inside the little speaker icon to play the sound.

 Do you remember how to "play" a movie clip?

Double-click inside the movie clip icon to turn it on (that is, to make it "play").

LESSON 7

 Do you remember how to change the number of files shown at the bottom of the File drop-down menu?

Select Tools ➢ Options and on the General tab, change the number in the Recently Used File List.

 Do you remember how to define a custom page layout?

Select File ➢ Page Setup. In the Slides Sized For box, select Custom and then type in the desired Height and Width.

 Do you remember how to view your presentation in black and white?

There are a couple of ways. First, you could click the Black and White View button on the Standard toolbar. Or you could select View ➢ Black and White. Or you could turn on the Slide Miniature.

 Do you remember how to Show Formatting in Outline view?

In Slide Sorter view, click Apply Design on the Standard toolbar. Click Blue And Gold Template.pot. Be patient.

LESSON 8

 Do you remember the difference between embedded objects and linked objects?

In a nutshell, linked objects reflect "real-time" data, whereas embedded objects are like pictures pasted in an album; what you see is what you get.

Lesson 9

 Do you remember what, besides creating tables, you can do in Word for PowerPoint?

You can create a basic presentation entirely in Word using Word's outline view.

 Do you remember what extension to assign to a file you create in Word in order to successfully import it into PowerPoint?

When you save a file created in Word with the intention of using it in PowerPoint, you need to assign the .rtf extension (rtf = Rich Text Format).

 Do you remember how to import and link an Excel file into PowerPoint?

Open the PowerPoint presentation to the slide to which you want to import the Excel file. Then select Insert ➤ Object ➤ Create from File. Use Browse to find the Excel file you want to import and when you find it, double-click it. Click Link and then OK on the Insert Object dialog box. Reposition and/or resize to your heart's content.

LESSON 9

 Do you remember how to activate an Action button?

To activate an action button, select Slide Show ➤ Action Buttons and choose the button appearance/function you want to use. The cursor turns into a big plus sign, so position it about where you want the button located and click. The Action Settings dialog box opens, and you can set the button to function on your mouse click or you can set it to function when you simply pass the cursor over the button. This is also where you indicate where you want to go in the presentation when you click this button.

Do you remember how to play a CD during your presentation?

If you want to include music from a CD during your presentation, select the slide to which you want to add music, select Insert ➤ Movies and Sounds ➤ Play CD Audio Track. On the Play Options dialog box, select how you want the music to play (that is, loop the whole thing; loop a segment; just play a segment).

 Do you remember how to hide comments?

You can hide comments so that they're not visible during a slide presentation simply by clicking the Hide Slide button on the Drawing toolbar.

 Do you remember how to record narration for a presentation?

Record narration for a presentation by clicking Slide Show ➤ Record Narration. On the Record Narration dialog box, set the desired quality, click OK, and begin your narration.

 Do you remember how to link the narration to a different file?

Linking a narration file to a presentation file, which saves tons of space, is done by selecting Slide Show ➤ Record Narration. On the Record Narration dialog box, make sure the Link Narrations In box is checked and then name the appropriate file.

LESSON 10

 Do you remember how to set up the standard you're-in-full-charge-all-the-time slide show?

Set yourself up as the supreme commander of the slide show by making sure that Presented by a Speaker (Full Screen) is clicked on the Show Type portion of the Set Up Show dialog box. If you want

Lesson 10

the show to include all slides, make sure All is checked. Also pay attention to the Advance Slides options. If you really want to be in control 100 percent of the time, you should click Advance Slides Manually.

 Do you remember how to erase markings you made on a slide while the slide show was running?

You can erase marks made on a slide during a presentation by right-clicking anywhere on the slide during the presentation. This opens a pop-up menu. Select Screen ➤ Erase Pen and all your pen-made markings disappear. The slide itself remains unchanged from its original condition.

 Do you remember how to advance slides from the keyboard during a presentation?

To move to the next slide, press N; to move to the previous slide, press P.

 Do you remember how to get 35mm slides?

You will probably have to go to an outside service to get 35mm slides, though you can set up the slides for 35mm by selecting Files ➤ Page Setup and clicking the down arrow of the Slides Sized For box. Scroll down to 35mm and you're ready. If your company has the ability to produce those slides, great. Otherwise, contact Genigraphics or some other company specializing in producing slides from PowerPoint files.

 Do you remember how to print the presentation in Outline view?

Select File ➤ Print and then click the down arrow of the Print What box. Choose the Outline style and click OK.

LESSON 11

 Do you remember how to run a custom show?

Select Slide Show ➤ Custom Shows. Click New on the Custom Shows dialog box to create a new custom show or click the title of the previously created show and then Close.

 Do you know how to rearrange slides in a custom show?

On the Define Custom Shows box, highlight the slide whose position you wish to change, and then click the up or down arrow to move it. Do this as many times as necessary until the slide is in the desired position.

LESSON 12

 Do you remember how to include linked files in your packed presentation?

Select File ➤ Pack and Go. On the Links page of the Pack and Go Wizard, be sure to click Include Linked Files. It's a good idea to click Embed TrueType Fonts, too, to ensure that your design work isn't trashed if you wind up on a computer with different fonts.

 Do you remember how to pack a presentation when you know you won't need the Microsoft PowerPoint Viewer?

Select File ➤ Pack and Go. On the Viewer page of the Pack and Go Wizard, be sure to click Don't Include the Viewer.

Practice Projects

You made it. You are now the official resident Master PowerPointer. But no one knows better than you that a skill unused is a skill soon forgotten. To avoid that dreadful fate, here are a few practice presentations you can throw together in your spare time just to make sure you don't lose your touch.

With any luck, one or two of these will even relate to your real-life presentation needs. Remember that with any presentation you'll want to include certain basic elements such as your company name and logo, a "cover" slide, and a summary slide. Remember, too, that if you start with a theme in your presentation, maintain it carefully.

PROJECT 1: CORPORATE FINANCIAL OVERVIEW

This project will give you a chance to create numerous graphs and charts to illustrate the company's financial position. In addition to a title slide including the company name, the presentation name, and the company logo, your presentation should include slides showing information for revenue, income, earnings, investments, assets, liabilities, and other financial data.

PROJECT 2: COMPANY ORGANIZATION

When you're creating a company organization presentation, you'll probably want to take advantage of the Organization Chart feature. In addition to creating an organization chart, you may want to include one or more slides addressing the functions or key personnel in various departments, such as upper management, finance, sales & marketing, legal, management information services, personnel, operations, R&D, and so on. Insert a photo of the company president.

PROJECT 3: KIOSK PRESENTATION

Create a presentation that you could set up at a trade show to run continuously while you meet and greet booth visitors. Focus the presentation on a specific product (or family of products) or service you are trying to promote. Use music and animation to make your presentation more lively and have it run without viewer input. If photographs are available, use them, too.

PROJECT 4: PACK-AND-GO PRESENTATIONS

Take any of the preceding presentations and pack them for use on a computer that does not have PowerPoint installed.

PROJECT 5: HYPERLINKED PRESENTATIONS

Create a presentation that addresses your company's goals and products and then hyperlink it to another presentation containing information about company finances and growth.

PROJECT 6: PRINTED PRESENTATIONS

For any of the preceding presentations, or even one you've created in "real life," produce a printed working copy with three slides per page, leaving room for audience notes.

A FEW FINAL THOUGHTS

Remember when you put together your presentations to concentrate on the message. If you get carried away with fonts, colors, graphics, animation, music or sounds, or other special effects, you may lose your audience. The slides are tools you use to enhance the audience's understanding of your presentation. Keep your text brief and to the point. Make all fonts readable under any lighting conditions and from any distance. Feel free to throw in a humorous graphic or animation to help hold your audience's attention. Put yourself in the audience's seat and fine-tune the presentation until it keeps you awake!

B

Practice Projects

Narration for Diabetes Presentation

Record the following text in the Diabetes presentation as discussed in Lesson 9.

TIME OUT FOR DIABETES: PORTRAIT OF A KILLER

Slide 1: Welcome, Ladies and Gentlemen, to today's presentation. Diabetes has been called the Silent Killer for a long time and today you'll learn why.

Slide 2: Millions of people have diabetes and thousands more have it and don't know it. When faced with a diabetes diagnosis, most people ask Why? What about *me* made me "catch" diabetes?

- First, you don't "catch" diabetes, though you may inherit a predisposition for it.

- There are many contributing causes, but these are the most common. Why these things happens, nobody knows — yet.

Slide 3: There are two main types of diabetes. Juvenile diabetes, which is also known as Insulin Dependent diabetes, usually strikes children and young people, which is how it got its name. People who have Type I diabetes (another name for Juvenile diabetes) are insulin dependent. That means that they must have regular, closely controlled dosages of insulin throughout the day or they will die.

Time out for diabetes

- Type II diabetes, also known as Adult Onset Diabetes, generally strikes adults (often those who are over 40 and overweight). In fact, the longer you live, the more likely you are to develop diabetes. Type II diabetics may require insulin injections, but often people are able to control their blood sugar levels with diet and exercise or oral medications.

- There is also a temporary form of diabetes known as gestational diabetes. While it is like Type II in that the woman is not insulin-dependent, many women with this form of diabetes must use insulin because most of the oral medications used to treat diabetes have dangerous side effects for unborn babies. It is important for a pregnant woman to seek medical care during her pregnancy because left untreated, gestational diabetes can cause serious problems for both the mother and the baby. In addition, women who develop gestational diabetes are more likely to develop full-blown Type II diabetes later in life (and for some, the gestational form progresses into Type II without delay).

Slide 4: What is SMBG? Self-Monitored Blood Glucose. That means that if you have diabetes, no matter what kind, you need to purchase a glucose monitor and test your blood sugar level about 4 times a day (or whatever your doctor suggests). There are several brands available, each offering a variety of features, but the most important task they perform is measuring the sugar level (glucose) in your blood at the moment you take the test. You can read the results, know your target ranges, and take immediate action to correct any problems. For example, if your blood sugar is too low, then you need to eat something or drink juice right away. When blood sugar falls to low, you can pass out or even go into a coma.

- Similarly, when blood sugar gets too high, you can also go into a coma. Both extremes should be avoided, of course. If you notice your blood sugar is too high, you should administer more insulin (or follow whatever regimen your doctor prescribed).

Slide 5: Until insulin was introduced in 1922, there was no treatment for diabetes. Patients had no way of knowing how high or low their blood sugar was and eventually went into a coma and died. Now there are several kinds of insulin and a variety of ways to inject it. The three most popular and most common forms of insulin are Regular (fast acting), NPH (long lasting) and a new one introduced late in 1996, Humalog (super fast acting).

Slide 6: If you have insulin–dependent or insulin–using diabetes, then you are probably already familiar with the syringe. Most diabetics inject their own insulin during the day and find that while they may have had a life-long fear of needles, when you're doing it to yourself and it's do or die, it's not so hard after all.

- The typical syringe consists of 3 basic elements. The *needle,* which pierces the skin and allows the insulin to enter the body through a small hole in the tip; the *body* of the syringe, which stores the insulin until you deliver it to the body; and the *plunger,* which serves two purposes. When you draw back on it (with the needle properly inserted into an insulin bottle) you load the syringe with the desired amount (or dosage) of insulin. When you press down on it (with the needle inserted into your skin), you deliver that insulin into your body.

What's on the CD-ROM

The CD-ROM includes the interactive *One Step at a Time On-Demand* software. This software coaches you through the exercises in the book while you work on a computer at your own pace.

INSTALLING THE ONE STEP AT A TIME ON-DEMAND INTERACTIVE SOFTWARE

The *One Step at a Time On-Demand* interactive software can be installed on Windows 95, Windows 98 and Windows NT 4.0. To install the interactive software on your computer, follow these steps:

1 Launch Windows (if you haven't already).

2 Place the *Microsoft PowerPoint 97 One Step at a Time* CD-ROM in your CD-ROM drive.

3 Click the Start menu open.

4 Select Run. The Run dialog box appears.

Installing the software

⑤ Type **D:\setup.exe** (where D is your CD-ROM drive) in the Run dialog box.

⑥ Click OK to run the setup procedure. The On-Demand Installation dialog box appears.

⑦ Click Continue. The On-Demand Installation Options dialog box appears.

⑧ Click the Full/Network radio button (if this option is not already selected).

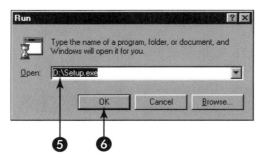

NOTE *Full/Network installation requires approximately 200MB of hard disk space. If you don't have enough hard disk space, click the Standard radio button to choose Standard installation. If you choose standard installation, you should always insert the CD-ROM before starting the software.*

⑨ Click Next. The Determine Installation Drive and Directory dialog box appears.

⑩ Choose the default drive and directory that appears, or click Change to choose a different drive and directory.

NOTE *If you would prefer to install the On-Demand software to a drive other than C, be sure to check the latest instructions in the file ONESTEPFAQ.TXT on the book's CD-ROM.*

⑪ Click Next. The Product Selection dialog box appears, enabling you to verify the software you want to install.

⑫ Click Finish to complete the installation. The On-Demand Installation dialog box displays the progress of the installation. After the installation, the Multiuser Pack Registration dialog box appears.

⑬ Enter information in the Multiuser Pack Registration dialog box.

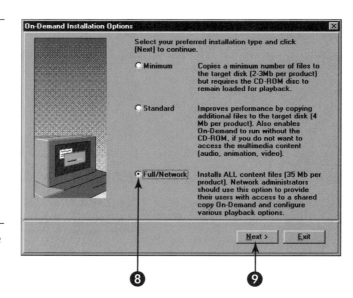

⑭ Click OK. The On-Demand Installation dialog box appears.

⑮ Click OK to confirm that the installation has been successfully completed.

RUNNING THE ONE STEP AT A TIME ON-DEMAND INTERACTIVE SOFTWARE

The *One Step at a Time On-Demand* interactive software includes the exercises in the book so that you can search for information about how to perform a function or complete a task. You can run the software alone or in combination with the book. The software consists of three modes: Demo, Teacher, and Concurrent. In addition, the Concept option provides an overview of each exercise.

- **Demo** mode provides a movie-style demonstration of the same steps that are presented in the book's exercises, and works with the sample exercise files that are included on the CD-ROM in the One Step folder.

- **Teacher** mode simulates the software environment and permits you to interactively follow the exercises in the book's lessons.

- **Concurrent** mode enables you to use the *One Step at a Time On-Demand* features while you work within the actual PowerPoint 97 environment. This unique interactive mode provides audio instructions and directs you to take the correct actions as you work through the exercises. (Concurrent mode may not be available to all exercises.)

■ Running Demo, Teacher, or Concurrent mode

If you run the *One Step at a Time On-Demand* software in Windows 98, we recommend that you don't work in Teacher or Concurrent modes unless you turn off the Active Desktop feature.

Once you've installed the software, you can view the text of the book and follow interactively the steps in each exercise. To run Demo mode, Teacher mode, or Concurrent mode follow these steps:

Running the software

1 Click open the Start menu on the Windows desktop.

2 Select Programs ➤ IDG Books ➤ PowerPoint 97 One Step at a Time. A small On-Demand toolbar appears in the upper-right corner of your screen.

3 Launch PowerPoint 97.

4 The On-Demand Reminder dialog box appears, telling you that the On-Demand software is active. If you don't want to display the dialog box, deselect the Show Reminder check box and then click OK.

5 Click the icon of the professor. The Interactive Training — Lesson Selection dialog box appears.

6 Select the Contents tab, if it isn't already selected. The contents appear, divided into parts. Please select the Module option, and follow the software using that option (rather than All Topics).

7 Click the plus icon (+) next to the part you want to explore. Lessons appear. The list of lessons corresponds to the lessons in the book.

8 Click the plus icon next to the lesson you want to explore. Topics appear. If you wish to work in Concurrent mode, start with the first available topic of the lesson, because the software will direct you to open a specific file which you will use to complete the steps in that lesson.

9 Double-click a topic of your choice. A menu appears.

10 Select Concept, Demo, Concurrent (if available), or Teacher.

11 Follow the onscreen prompts to use the interactive software and work through the steps.

In Demo mode, you only need to perform actions that appear in red. Otherwise, the software automatically demonstrates the actions for you. All you need to do is read the information that appears onscreen. (Holding down the Shift key pauses the program; releasing the Shift key activates the program.) In Teacher mode, you need to follow the directions and perform the actions that appear onscreen.

■ **Stopping the program**

To stop running the program at any time, press Esc to return to the Interactive Training — Lesson Selection dialog box. (To restart the software, double-click a topic of your choice and select a mode.)

■ **Exiting the program**

Press Esc when the Interactive Training — Lesson Selection dialog box appears to exit the program. The On-Demand toolbar appears in the upper-right corner of your screen. Click the icon that displays the lightning bolt image. A menu appears. Choose Exit. The On-Demand — Exit dialog box appears. Click Yes to exit On-Demand.

INSTALLING THE EXERCISE FILES

It's easy to install the exercise files used in the lessons of this book onto your computer. Follow these steps:

❶ Place the *Microsoft PowerPoint 97 One Step at a Time* CD-ROM in your CD-ROM drive.

❷ Click the Start menu open.

❸ Select Run. The Run dialog box appears.

❹ Type **D:\exercises.exe** (where D is your CD-ROM drive) in the Run dialog box and click OK. You will see a dialog box confirming that you want to install the files to the specified directory on your hard drive.

❺ Click Unzip to run the installation procedure.

❻ Click OK in the WinZip Self-Extractor dialog box to confirm that the procedure went smoothly.

❼ Click Close in the next dialog box to close it. Now you have installed the exercise files.

D

What's on the CD-ROM

Using individual exercise files

If you simply wish to use only the exercise files you need, when you need them, follow these steps instead:

1. Double-click the My Computer icon on your desktop.

2. In the My Computer window, double-click the hard drive (C).

3. Open the File menu and select New.

4. Choose Folder from the submenu. A new folder appears at the end of the list with the name New Folder.

5. Type **One Step** to name the folder and press Enter.

6. Double-click that folder to open it. Leave it open on the screen.

7. Place the *Microsoft PowerPoint 97 One Step at a Time* CD-ROM in the CD-ROM drive.

8. In the My Computer window, double-click the CD-ROM icon, usually labeled D:, to open the drive in which you placed the CD-ROM.

USING INDIVIDUAL EXERCISE FILES OFF THE CD-ROM

Whenever you copy individual exercise files directly off the CD-ROM, you must first remove the Read Only attribute from the file(s) you copied to your hard drive before you use those files. Otherwise, when you attempt to save your work, your screen will display an error message.

To remove the attribute, open the One Step folder on your hard drive. Select the files you copied by choosing Edit ➤ Select All from the menu bar. Select File ➤ Properties. The

Properties dialog box appears. In the Attributes area, click the Read Only check box to remove the checkmark. Click OK.

Following the first procedure (that is, running the Exercises.exe file) to copy all exercise files to your hard drive removes this Read Only attribute automatically, so you don't have to. We recommend taking that route.

9 In the CD-ROM (D:) window, display the contents of the Lesson folder you wish to copy to your hard drive and choose Edit ➤ Select All.

10 Select Edit ➤ Copy, then close the CD-ROM window and all other open windows.

11 Click inside the One Step folder on your screen and select Edit ➤ Paste to copy the exercise files you selected on the CD-ROM to the folder on your hard drive.

TROUBLESHOOTING

If the installation or operation of the *One Step at a Time On-Demand* software does not go quite as planned, there may be a simple answer to the problem. The CD-ROM contains a text file that answers almost every question you could have relating to installing and running the On-Demand software. To view the file, follow these steps:

1 Launch Windows (if you haven't already).

2 Place the *Microsoft PowerPoint 97 One Step at a Time* CD-ROM in your CD-ROM drive.

3 Click the Start menu open.

4 Select Run. The Run dialog box appears.

5 Type **D:\onestepfaq.txt** (where D is your CD-ROM drive) in the Run dialog box.

6 Click OK to open the text file. Notepad should launch automatically, with the ONESTEPFAQ.TXT file in the window.

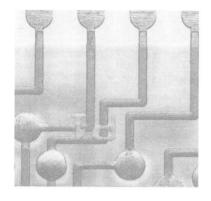

A–B

buttons, adding to slides, 224–226
By Column button, 144
By Row button, 144

C

canceling print jobs, 263
case, text, changing, 46–47
category axis, 144
Change Case dialog box, 46–47
changing views. *See* switching views
chart area, 144
chart boxes
    adding to organization charts, 132–135
    moving between, 132
    moving in organization charts, 137–138
chart objects, 144
Chart Options dialog box, 154–155
charts. *See* Excel charts; organization charts
Chart toolbar, 144

Chart Type button, 144
Choose Destination Wizard, 281
clip art. *See also* Microsoft Clip Gallery; pictures
    finding, 194, 197
    moving, 41
    sizing, 41
Clip Properties dialog box, 197, 198, 200
clock face bullets, 207
Close Window, 3
closing
    Office Assistant, 41
    presentations, 10
    toolbars, 4
Collapse All button, 18, 188, 189
Collapse button, 18, 189
collapsing slides, 188–189
color copies, printing, 257–261
Color dialog box, 139, 140–141
colors
    changing in objects, 59

one-color gradient backgrounds, 81
printing in gray, 187
two-color gradient backgrounds, 82
Color Scheme dialog box, 73, 74, 75, 76, 77
color schemes, 72–78
    adding to standard list, 76–77
    applying to presentations, 77–78
    copying, 92
    custom, creating, 73–76
    default, 72–73
    removing, 77, 92
    visual effectiveness of slides, 72
comments, 227–229
    adding to slides, 227–228
    hiding, 228–229
    outlines displayed in presentation, 241
Common Tasks toolbar, 3
    turning off, 41

Index

Index

O

objects
  adding text, 57–58
  animating, 115
  animating text within, 113–115
  changing color, 59
  connecting, 60–61
  definition, 57
  deselecting, 66
  embedding, 212–213
  flipping, 61
  grouping and ungrouping, 62
  multiple, selecting, 66
  rotating, 61
Office Assistant
  counting replacements, 54
  turning off, 41
one-slide presentations, 8–9

One Step at a Time On-Demand
    software
  installing, 315–317
  installing exercise files, 319–321
  problems, 321
  running, 317–319
Open button, 3
Open dialog box, 3, 44–45, 57
opening
  existing presentations, 2–3
  toolbars, 4
Options dialog box, 179, 203–206,
    285
  appearance, 40
  default settings, 204–206
ordering slides, 7
Organization Chart application, 130
  failure to open, 160
organization charts, 130–141
  adding chart boxes, 132–135

  appearance, 138–141
  changing format, 136–137
  editing, 135–136
  reassigning positions, 137–138
  starting, 130–132
outlines
  creating in Word, 214
  formatting, 189–190
Outline view, 6, 18
  adjusting spacing, 50–51
  collapsing slides, 188–189
  creating presentations, 19–21
  formatting outlines, 189–190
  handouts, 33
  inserting slides, 22
  moving slides, 65
  positioning text, 52–53
  removing slides, 41
  slide icons, 41

S

Index

Index

Now it's easy to remember what you just learned and more...

With *On-Demand*, you'll never rely on the help function again – or your money back.

Introducing *On-Demand Interactive Learning*™ — the remarkable software that actually makes corrections to your documents for you. Unlike the standard help function that merely provides "canned" responses to your requests for help or makes you write down a list of complicated instructions, *On-Demand* lets you learn while you work.

Concurrent Mode — makes the *changes for you* right in your document.

Teacher Mode — *guides you* step-by-step to make changes safely outside your document.

Demo Mode — *shows you* how the changes are made safely outside your document.

Let *On-Demand* take care of the software commands for you. Just follow the on-screen pointer and fill in the information, and you'll learn in the fastest and easiest way possible — without ever leaving your document.

In fact, *On-Demand* makes your work so easy, it's *guaranteed* to help you finish complicated documents neatly and on time. With over eleven years in software education and a development staff that's logged more than 5,000 hours of classroom teaching time, it's no wonder that Fortune 500 corporations around the world use *On-Demand* to make learning for their employees quicker and more effective.

"On-Demand Interactive Learning for Word 97. The best training title of this group..." —PC World

The Concurrent Mode Difference
Concurrent Mode guides you through learning new functions without having to stop for directions. Right before your eyes, a moving pointer clicks on the right buttons and icons for you and then lets you fill in the information.

"On-Demand lets me get my work done and learn without slowing me down." —Rosemarie Hasson, Quad Micro

---

TITLES AVAILABLE FOR: Windows® 3.1, 95, NT, Microsoft® Word, Microsoft Excel, Microsoft PowerPoint, Microsoft Access, Microsoft Internet Explorer, Lotus® SmartSuite, Lotus Notes, and more! Call for additional titles.

---

30 DAY GUARANTEE:
Try *On-Demand* at the introductory price of **$32**^{95} (U.S. dollars) for one title or pay **$29**^{95} (U.S. dollars) each for two titles. That's a savings of almost 10%. Use *On-Demand* for 30 days. If you don't learn more in a shorter period of time, simply return the software to PTS Learning Systems with your receipt for a full refund (this guarantee is good only for purchases made directly from PTS).

On **Demand**
Interactive Learning™

Call PTS at 800-387-8878 ext. 3053 or 610-337-8878 ext. 3053 outside the U.S.

© 1997 PTS Learning Systems

IDG103197

IDG BOOKS WORLDWIDE, INC.
END-USER LICENSE AGREEMENT

READ THIS. You should carefully read these terms and conditions before opening the software packet(s) included with this book ("Book"). This is a license agreement ("Agreement") between you and IDG Books Worldwide, Inc. ("IDGB"). By opening the accompanying software packet(s), you acknowledge that you have read and accept the following terms and conditions. If you do not agree and do not want to be bound by such terms and conditions, promptly return the Book and the unopened software packet(s) to the place you obtained them for a full refund.

1. **License Grant.** IDGB grants to you (either an individual or entity) a nonexclusive license to use one copy of the enclosed software program(s) (collectively, the "Software") solely for your own personal or business purposes on a single computer (whether a standard computer or a workstation component of a multi-user network). The Software is in use on a computer when it is loaded into temporary memory (RAM) or installed into permanent memory (hard disk, CD-ROM, or other storage device). IDGB reserves all rights not expressly granted herein.

2. **Ownership.** IDGB is the owner of all right, title, and interest, including copyright, in and to the compilation of the Software recorded on the disk(s) or CD-ROM ("Software Media"). Copyright to the individual programs recorded on the Software Media is owned by the author or other authorized copyright owner of each program. Ownership of the Software and all proprietary rights relating thereto remain with IDGB and its licensers.

3. **Restrictions on Use and Transfer.**

   (a) You may only (i) make one copy of the Software for backup or archival purposes, or (ii) transfer the Software to a single hard disk, provided that you keep the original for backup or archival purposes. You may not (i) rent or lease the Software, (ii) copy or reproduce the Software through a LAN or other network system or through any computer subscriber system or bulletin-board system, or (iii) modify, adapt, or create derivative works based on the Software.

   (b) You may not reverse engineer, decompile, or disassemble the Software. You may transfer the Software and user documentation on a permanent basis, provided that the transferee agrees to accept the terms and conditions of this Agreement and you retain no copies. If the Software is an update or has been updated, any transfer must include the most recent update and all prior versions.

4. **Restrictions On Use of Individual Programs.** You must follow the individual requirements and restrictions detailed for each individual program in Appendix D of this Book. These limitations are also contained in the individual license agreements recorded on the Software Media. These limitations may include a requirement that after using the program for a specified period of time, the user must pay a registration fee or discontinue use. By opening the Software packet(s), you will be agreeing to abide by the licenses and restrictions for these individual programs that are detailed in Appendix D and on the Software Media. None of the material on this Software Media or listed in this Book may ever be redistributed, in original or modified form, for commercial purposes.

my2cents.idgbooks.com

Register This Book — And Win!

Visit **http://my2cents.idgbooks.com** to register this book and we'll automatically enter you in our fantastic monthly prize giveaway. It's also your opportunity to give us feedback: let us know what you thought of this book and how you would like to see other topics covered.

Discover IDG Books Online!

The IDG Books Online Web site is your online resource for tackling technology — at home and at the office. Frequently updated, the IDG Books Online Web site features exclusive software, insider information, online books, and live events!

10 Productive & Career-Enhancing Things You Can Do at www.idgbooks.com

- Nab source code for your own programming projects.

- Download software.

- Read Web exclusives: special articles and book excerpts by IDG Books Worldwide authors.

- Take advantage of resources to help you advance your career as a Novell or Microsoft professional.

- Buy IDG Books Worldwide titles or find a convenient bookstore that carries them.

- Register your book and win a prize.

- Chat live online with authors.

- Sign up for regular e-mail updates about our latest books.

- Suggest a book you'd like to read or write.

- Give us your 2¢ about our books and about our Web site.

You say you're not on the Web yet? It's easy to get started with IDG Books' *Discover the Internet,* available at local retailers everywhere.

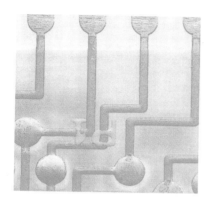

CD-ROM Installation Instructions

The CD-ROM at the back of this book includes all the exercise files and the exclusive, interactive *One Step at a Time On-Demand* software. This software coaches you through the exercises in the book while you work on a computer at your own pace.

The *One Step at a Time On-Demand* interactive software can be installed on Windows 95, Windows 98, and Windows NT 4.0. Full installation requires 200MB of hard disk space. To install the interactive software on your computer, follow these steps:

1 Launch Windows (if you haven't already).

2 Place the *Microsoft PowerPoint 97 One Step at a Time* CD-ROM in your CD-ROM drive.

3 Click the Start menu open.

4 Select Run. The Run dialog box appears.

5 Type **D:\setup.exe** (where D is your CD-ROM drive) in the Run dialog box.

6 Click OK to run the setup procedure. The On-Demand Installation dialog box appears.

7 Click Continue. The On-Demand Installation Options dialog box appears.

8 Click the Full/Network radio button (if this option is not already selected).

9 Click Next. The Determine Installation Drive and Directory dialog box appears.

10 Choose the default drive and directory that appears, or click Change to choose a different drive and directory.

11 Click Next. The Product Selection dialog box appears, enabling you to verify the software you want to install.

12 Click Finish to complete the installation. The On-Demand Installation dialog box displays the progress of the installation. After the installation, the Multiuser Pack Registration dialog box appears.

13 Enter information in the Multiuser Pack Registration dialog box.

14 Click OK. The On-Demand Installation dialog box appears.

15 Click OK to confirm that the installation has been successfully completed.

To install the exercise files for the lessons in this book, follow these steps:

1 Place the *Microsoft PowerPoint 97 One Step at a Time* CD-ROM in your CD-ROM drive.

2 Click the Start menu open.

3 Select Run. The Run dialog box appears.

4 Type **D:\exercises.exe** (where D is your CD-ROM drive) in the Run dialog box and click OK. You will see a dialog box confirming that you want to install the files to the specified directory on your hard drive.

5 Click Unzip to run the installation procedure.

6 Click OK in the WinZip Self-Extractor dialog box to confirm that the procedure went smoothly.

7 Click Close in the next dialog box to close it. Now you have installed the exercise files.

Refer to Appendix D for more information about running and troubleshooting the *One Step at a Time On-Demand* software, as well as using the exercise files.